METHODS OF TEACHING BIOLOGY

METHODS OF TEACHING BIOLOGY

By

Dr. Gadde Bhuvaneswara Lakshmi
M.Sc., M.Ed., Ph.D.
Principal, M.M. College of Education
Dean, Faculty of Education
Chairman, Board of Studies in Education
Nagarjuna University
Nagarjuna Nagar–522 510
Andhra Pradesh

Dr. K. Subba Rao
M.Sc., M.Ed., M.Phil., (Ph.D.),
Principal, A.S.R. College of Education
Kovvur–534 350
W.G. Dist., (A.P.)

General Editor
Dr. Digumarti Bhaskara Rao
M.Sc., M.A., M.A., M.Ed., Ph.D.
Reader
R.V.R. College of Education
Srinivasa Nagar Colony
Guntur–522 006
Andhra Pradesh
India

DISCOVERY PUBLISHING HOUSE
NEW DELHI-110002

Published by:

Tilak Wasan

DISCOVERY PUBLISHING HOUSE PVT. LTD.
4383/4B, Ansari Road, Darya Ganj
New Delhi-110 002 (India)
Phone : +91-11-23279245, 23253475, 43596065
E-mail : discoverypublishinghouse@gmail.com
sales@discoverypublishinggroup.com
web : www.discoverypublishinggroup.com

Edition: **2020**

ISBN: 978-81-7141-914-2

Methods of Teaching Biology

Printed at:
Infinity Imaging Systems
Delhi

CONTENTS

Foreword

Teacher education is quantitatively marching ahead towards quality education. The central and state governments through the NCTE and the Directorates of School/Higher Education are rendering their legitimate service in improving the quality of teacher education by formulating and implementing various academic policies and educational programmes. Along with these policies and programmes, the teacher educators and the prospective teachers teaching and studying in teacher education institutions need good curriculum and quality books.

The methods of teaching each subject play a pivotal role in enhancing the efficiency of their practitioners. Identifying the very importance of the methods of teaching and the quality of books, a series of books on the methods of teaching different subjects have been developed by experienced teacher educators for the benefit of teachers in making in teacher education institutions. Thanks to the authors.

Valuable suggestions for the improvement of these books are welcome from fellow teacher educators, prospective teachers and other academicians involved in the arena of teacher education.

The authors and the editor dedicate this series of books on the methodology of teaching to Mr. Tilak Raj Wasan, Proprietor, Discovery Publishing House, New Delhi, for taking up this commendable task of publication to meet the felt needs of teacher education faculty and clientele.

Dr. Digumarti Bhaskara Rao
Research Director in Education
Nagarjuna University
br_digumarti@rediffmail.com

PREFACE

The movement of modern education in India is almost two century old. It has come of age now. Over the decades, great educationists have contributed towards the development and evolution of education, as a discipline. Thus, education in India has been enriched a lot.

As a result, the Indian education system can be placed at par with any advanced education system in the modern world. In fact, education is a vast sea and Teachers' Training is a stream in it. So, it makes it essential that the responsibilities of the faculty members are focused on the task of providing better training to the future teachers, for their better learning and proper development. And this responsible exercise can only be undertaken, if the trainers are equipped with all the needed skill and knowledge of the subject, they are supposed to teach. Hence, it becomes essential for making adequate provisions, for each course to the teacher-trainees. Methods of Teaching are very important for the successful training of teachers and for their career in future.

In order to provide all related material in one cover, here is this book, on this important subject. Of course there are several books on the subject in the market, but, every book has its own style and way of presentation. Similarly, the present one, too has its own merits and advantages.

During the course of the preparation of this book, the undersigned has done his best for the accomplishment of the job. He would be pleased and feel contented, if this book is acknowledged, as a textbook and a reference tool for the teachers and students, alike.

Author

1

INTRODUCTION

Many reasons can be listed to ensure a secure and perhaps an increasingly large place for biology in education at school stage. The developments in this field are one of the man's major intellectual and creative achievements. Sciences unfold picture of the universe and allow man to extend his knowledge and to exercise control over his surroundings, whether it is concerned with the care of his family or of the society. These developments are only of value when the ordinary people can appreciate them and can help him to act responsibly in an increasingly technological world and permit him to appreciate the values and power, as well as the limitations of science. This aim of teaching biology can be attained only when this subject forms an adequate part of the curriculum of every student.

THE SIGNIFICANCE

Inclusion of biology in school curriculum is important and essential due to the following values of the subject :

(1) Importance of life sciences in mental discipline.

(2) Utility of life sciences in daily life.

(3) Cultural and moral importance of life sciences.

Keeping in view the above values that determine the place of education of life sciences in any school curriculum we can include suitable subject matter considering the standard of the class, economic factors and environment prevailing in the concerning school system under consideration. We can elaborate the above said values as follows:

Importance of life sciences in mental discipline. Learning in life sciences gives a stock of factual knowledge, some skills and a particular attitude towards the universe.

Knowledge : Study in life sciences gives us knowledge that helps to develop an adequate concept of the world around us. We come to know the structure and functions of organisms, organization of organism body, unity of life, chemical basis of structure and function, interrelations of plants and animals, place of man in the universe, evolution, heredity and ecological principles. We can also understand the applications of knowledge of life sciences in other fields like agriculture live stock management, medicine and horticulture. This knowledge also makes a basis for undertaking studies in more intricate fields.

Skills : Everybody studying life sciences develops certain skills consciously or unconsciously. These may be experimental constructional or drawing skills. Apart from this one also develops inquiry skills which help to develop scientific method of working in the students. "Scientific Method" helps the students solve problems of academic importance and of daily life.

Attitudes : Students studying life sciences develop a particular bent of mind that helps them in learning in this field as well facing and solving daily life problems. This attitude of mind (scientific attitude) involves maintaining mathematical accuracy in every type of recording desire for verification of claims, impartiality towards ideas and events, objectivity and a desire for undertaking experimental work to test the hypotheses. People with scientific method of working and having a scientific bent of mind are distinct in their way of working and behaviour.

They have an adequate concept about the physical and living world and have a specific power of reasoning and giving shape to their ideas.

The way, knowledge and methods of life sciences play role in our lives can be discussed as follows :

Fundamenlal Science : This discipline as fundamental science gives answers to many of our personal questions as :

(i) What determines sex?

(ii) How are twins born ?

(iii) Why do babies resemble their parents?

(iv) How do we acquire immunities against diseases?

(v) How do we become weak in old age?

(vi) How are we dependent on plants?

For Intelligent Citizenship : Knowledge of life sciences helps people live intelligently as it develops-in them the habits of sanitation, balanced diet and prevention of diseases. This also gives them the ways and means of solving food problem, over population, conservation of fauna and flora. The knowledge of agents of diseases avoids is them superstitions and witchcraft practices. Our economy is agriculture based and knowledge of scientific principles in farming, cattle management and poultry can add to the prosperity of our nation.

Life Sciences and Health : The field of medicine has contributed a lot towards the survival of human race. Man faces various diseases such as:

(i) infectious diseases caused by virus, bacteria, protozoa, fungi and worms,

(ii) .degenerative diseases like those of heart and nervous system,

(iii) deficiency diseases to deficiency of certain proteins, fats, vitamins and minerals in the diet.

(iv) Allergies due to substances not suiting to the body and

(v) cancers or uncontrolled growth of cells in the body.

Man has controlled almost all these diseases and this has been possible due to developments in life sciences. Today we have sulpha drugs, antiseptics, antibiotics, antiseptic surgery, heart, kidney and cornea transportations, injections and vaccines, X-rays and radio-therapy, blood transfusions, artificial limbs and principles of balanced diet in order to combat these diseases and disorders. Trials are going on to find some cure for cancers.

Vocational Importance : A student of life sciences can specialize in any branch of this discipline or he can choose a profession of *his taste* infuture. One can become a doctor, a nurse, an agriculturist, biochemist, microbiologist or a teacher. Some other fields in which one can specialize are : fisheries, soil sciences, plant breeding, forestry, cattle and poultry management, dairy sciences, canning and food preservation etc. When one is interested in pure sciences one can become an embryologist, physiologist, genetist or one can specialize in environmental sciences and can become a scientist of great fame.

CULTURAL AND MORAL IMPORTANCE

A student undertaking studies in life sciences is expected to acquire himself of the value inherent in the spirit of science. Studies in this field lead to the understanding of nature, flexibility and creativity. It demands interaction and co-operation with colleagues, exposing results of one finding to their scrutiny and seeking their criticism etc. Some aesthetic values like honesty, love and truth are also inherent in the study of this subject. Scientific method of working and scientific attitude play a great role in daily-life activities and behaviour and these are the ultimate results of studies in this subject.

Science and technology has played a great role in shaping the culture of nations and it is apparent in case of developed countries. Discoveries and adventures in sciences have influenced the writers and rulers of times.

The contributions of life sciences have greatly influenced modern life. Other than helping man in getting food, shelter and clothing, the basic necessities of life, developments in medicine are guarding happy survival of human race.

In India duration of secondary education differs from state to state and the schools are 5+3+2 (High Schools followed by one year Pre-University class), 5+3+2 followed by two years intermediate classes, 5+3+3 (Higher Secondary), 5+3+2 (High Schools) +2 (Higher Secondary stage also called 10+2 system).

Teaching of science subjects at these stages of secondary education, in different magnitudes, has been recommended from time to time. When there were only high schools the general sciences books had a few topics on life sciences. When Higher Secondary schools of eleven year duration came up general science was only upto 8th class and one could specialize in biology in 9th upto 11th class. Where high schools existed specialization was introduced in Pre-University class. Now under 10+2 system, life sciences are taught in integrated form (with increased volume) upto 10th class and one can specialize in this subject in 11th and 12 classes.

Questions

1. Why does the subject life-sciences find a larger space in present school curriculum?
2. Why should life sciences be taught at school stage? Discuss the reasons.
3. What is the importance of life sciences in school curriculum? Discuss with suitable examples.
4. Write short note on "Place of life-sciences in school curriculum".

2

Evolution and Development

Growth of biology education can be divided into four phases.

Phase I : This is the earliest phase and at this time education in the field of life sciences was meant for adults. This period started with the observations made by Greek philosopher *Aristotle* (384-322 B.C.). Education was observation based. Knowledge in life sciences started with man's curiosity about his surroundings. The early man wanted to know about his body, health and sickness. He also observed growth, death and decay in the living world. The earliest knowledge in this field includes observations made on plants, animals and man and events related to these organisms.

PhaseII : This phase starts with the work of *Darwin*. School courses in biology were introduced in U.S.A. and U.K. (1890-1929) but the course served the purpose of only preparing students for college and university education. In India courses in biology were introduced in 1940's but there were also meant for preparing students for college and education.

In U.S.A. and U. K. the subject remained in this state of affairs upto 1957 and in India upto 1967.

Phase III : This phase occurred in U.S.A. during 1929-1957. Due to the explosion of student population and democratization of educational facilities, courses for different community interests were prepared. Materials were also prepared for large scale training of teachers to meet the scarcity of properly trained teachers. A need for proper education in the field of life sciences was also felt in U.K and India. Secondary Education Commission in India (1952-53) recommended eleven years of secondary education in which general science was recommended to be taught upto middle or eighth standard and the subject of biology could be taken as optional subject by the science student and secondary stage.

Phase IV : The present phase of improvement in life sciences education started with the establishment of B.S.C.S. (Biological Sciences Curriculum Study 1959) in U.S.A. and Nuffield Foundation (1962) in U.K. Large scale preparation of material and student population testing has been undertaken by B.S.C.S. and it has developed a basic curriculum for secondary schools and a lot of audio-visual material and help books for the teachers. Similarly Nuffield Foundation has also prepared some general sciénce books with biology material integrated in them and various methods and teaching techniques have been developed.

In India, *Indian Education Commission* (1964-66) recommended teaching of life sciences as a part of general science education upto 10th standard and the students who offer science subjects and +2 stage can specialize in life sciences. N.C.E.R.T. (National Council of Educational Research and Training, New Delhi), which came into being in 1961, is trying its best to develop curriculum material, help books and aids for teaching the new material in order to meet the objectives lad down in the National Policy on Education.

FROM BIOLOGY TO LIFE SCIENCES

The developments in different fields of biology reached a point where the discipline demanded tools, techniques and skills of other disciplines. Physics, Geography, Chemistry, Mathematics,

Computer Sciences, Geology and graphic arts came in the field of biology. The net result was that from biology, which was once only one discipline, came out several twilight disciplines like biophysics, bio-chemistry, biometry, biomedicine, bio-statistics and bio-engineering etc. Application of findings of other disciplines also influenced studies in biology and it smutted from systematics, morphology and anatomy to functional aspects of the organisms. Recently the approach in studying biology has shifted to environmental aspects.

Application of the knowledge of biology in the ways and means of human comfort has given certain applied fields like agriculture, fisheries, dairy sciences, medicine and microbiology etc.

VARIOUS ASPECTS

Some other disciplines like Anthropology, Phycology and Sociology also study life regarding its various aspects. These disciplines also contribute to the understanding of various phenomena related to life.

So biology with its shifted approach to environmental aspects along with its earlier structural and functional aspects plus the twilight disciplines that emerged due to the Application of knowledge of other disciplines to biology, plus those disciplines which emerged by the application of knowledge of biology, plus those disciplines which also study life from various angles, are today included under a vast discipline called Biology.

Questions

1. What have been the developments in life-sciences education at school stage?
2. The word 'Biology' has been replaced by 'Life-Sciences' in modern school books. Why?

3

THE FUNDAMENTALS

Our learning products are either in the form of facts, concepts, generalizations or unifying themes. Facts are isolated bits of knowledge, that are perceived by direct observations as terminology dates, events etc. A concept is an abstraction used to classify words, ideas and objects etc. These are the mental constructs that the individuals possess about organisms, objects, phenomena etc. Concepts change, with experience, along dimensions and these are either adequately or inadequately developed. A generalization can be any statement of relationships, which is of broad applicability. Here we are treating unifying themes or major concepts to be of similar nature. Major concept is an organization of facts, concepts and generalizations that represents body of knowledge of the field to which it is related.

In structuring Its curriculum B.S.C.S. identified nine major concepts or themes in life sciences. These can be discussed as follows:

THE EVOLUTION

The characteristics of all living things are products of evolutionary process and the process of change continues in the present. The study of evolution permits biologists to establish a relationship of similarities and differences among the living things. Every where we see the action and consequences of natural selection regarding the variations in organisms and their populations.

DIVERSITY OF TYPE AND UNITY OF PATTERN

A unity of pattern at all levels of biological organization brings order to the diversity of life. We find different living forms, due to their adaptations to differing environmental condition and evolution. Among this diversity we find a definite pattern, as A.T.P. works as energy transferer in all organisms and D.N. and R.N.A. control heredity. Mitosis and meiosis, cell divisions are common to all and we find a similar pattern in the form of limbs of vertebrates.

GENETIC CONTINUITY OF LIFE

Life exists as a stream and its continuity is not broken with the death of an individual. It emphasizes that germ plasm is immortal potentially and it is passed from generation to generation. We sometimes also find errors in genetic replications that create variability and diversity in organisms.

COMPLEMENTARITY OF ORGANISM

The interaction between organisms and environment at all levels of organization modifies both organisms and environment. Chromosomes and Chloroplasts have their environments. Cell or group of cells interact and tissues and organs have their own environments within the organism further in the form of populations and communities act on or are acted upon by their surroundings. Abiotic factors as air water and temperature play their role in the biosphere. So there is a reciprocal relationship between the organisms and environment.

BIOLOGICAL ROOTS OF BEHAVIOUR

Behaviour not only arises from learning in the individual but from experience of its ancestors stored in the heredity material. Our genetic composition puts limit on us that we cannot live in water like fishes and fishes on land. Hydrophytes cannot withstand the xerophytic conditions as the structure of the plants is not suitable for these conditions. The determiner of the structure is the genetic composition of the organisms.

COMPLEMENTARITY OF STRUCTURE AND FUNCTION

The function of any part of a living organism depends upon its structure and from its structure its function can be inferred. Structure of our heart suits its function or the structures of mitochondria and chloroplasts are such that these can carry on the activities of respiration and photosynthesis. By studying the muscles and bones and their arrangement we can infer the functions of the limbs.

REGULATION AND HOMEOSTASIS

Changes in structure and function maintain organization of living organism in the face of changing environment. Homeostasis means maintenance of a stable internal environment such as maintenance of concentration of metal ions and *pH* or glucose level in the blood. Regular ion relates to the long term and large scale variations in the structure as well as in function. Variations in the organism body keep co-ordination with the internal and external environmental changes and maintain the stability in well functioning of the organism.

SCIENCE AS ENQUIRY

This theme relates to the organization of the subject matter to be presented to the students. Subject matter that will presented in conventional text-books gave the impression that science consists of unchangeable truths and could not induce critical thinking and a desire for enquiring about things. By adoption of this theme the B.S.C.S. had an entirely different approach and presented the matter in the form of series of investigations. It develops in the students the knowledge of facts, how such facts were derived and how the scientific process is valid.

HISTORY OF BIOLOGICAL CONCEPTS

Giving the students the knowledge of scientific concepts enables them to have a realistic understanding of how science progresses and avoids fantastic views about science. By this the students also come to know the nature of scientific process and its planning.

The first five major concepts or themes concern with the content of the B.S.C.S. text books and the last two concern with the logical structure of the texts, that is how the content is conveyed to the students. The themes 6 and 7 are intermediate and these concern with both structure and content.

RELATING TO SCHOOL BIOLOGY

The Biological Sciences Curriculum Study (B.S.C.S.) started it activities in January 1959. Financial support to this organization was given by National Science Foundation (N.S.F., U.S.A.)

Over 2000 biologists and specially competent persons had contributed to the development of various programmes of B.S.C.S., within ten years of its inception. The efforts of B.S.C.S. have been to:

(1) produce modern biology courses (text-books) for the spectrum of students who take biology in high school.

(2) develop special resource materials for the teaching of these courses as teacher help books, laboratory blocks, films-equipment and etc.

(3) formulate programmes and materials for in-service and pre service education of the teachers.

Regarding the development of text books and integration of conceptual schemes in the subject matter, to which we are concerned here, B.S.C.S. adopted the procedure given ahead.

First of all BSCS identified seven level of Biological Organization; these are Molecular, Cellular, Organ and Tissue, Individual Organism, Population, Community and Biosphere. At every level of biological organization student learn some common as well as diverse phenomena about living things. At molecular level they learn the structure and types of molecules in living systems and their role in metabolism. At cellular level they learn about the various constituents of cells, cell divisions and cell as unit of life. At organ-tissue level they study the organization of cells in the form of tissues and their special functions and further the various tissues in associations forming various organ systems as digestive, nervous and skeletal systems. At organism level the students learn about the functioning of organisms their diversity in nature, reproduction, energy utilization and their behaivioural interactions. While undertaking studies at population level they learn about growth maintenance, food requirements, competitions, population changes and population problems etc. At community level they come to know the structure of various communities, dominant species, community relationships, food chains and food webs, matter cycles, interaction of organisms with the physical environment etc. At the world Biome or Biosphere level they learn the biotic and abiotic relationships of ecosystems, relationship among various ecosystems of biosphere, changes along time and man's place in the biosphere.

The B.S.C.S. team was convinced that there should be considered nine themes in the preparation of reading materials for the students, out of that the seven should relate to the content and the two with the organization of the matter (as discussed above).

The next thing considered was the objectives of teaching biology at school level. There were considered six levels, along which the students can organize their learning products and these were Knowledge. Comprehension, Application, Analysis, Synthesis and Evaluation. In this way we find that the B.S.C.S team adopted a three dimensional model in developing and organizing the subject matter.

During the summer 1960 the B.S.C.S. assembled three writing teams of high school biology teachers and university research Biologists, about equal in numbers, to prepare preliminary trial materials in terms of the new conceptual schemes. During 1960-61 school year B.S.C.S. materials were taught in 100 schools. Based on feed back, courses were rewritten during 1962 and tried in 500 schools. In 1963 the material was again written and tried in 950 schools. On the whole the B.S.C.S. materials had been tried and tested on over 1000 teachers and 1,50,000 students before the first edition (1963) of the B.S.C.S. three books came out.

The basic curriculum programme of B.S.C.S. consists of three distinct biology text books (written by each team) and related material for the use of 10th grade American High School. Originally the three versions were classified in terms of their approach to biology. These are also known by the colour of their covers.

1. Molecules to Man *(Blue Version).*
2. High School Biology *(Green Version).*
3. Biological Science-An Inquiry into Life *(Yellow Version).*

As whole of the B.S.C.S. material is based on the same goals and conceptual schemes, so those books are more alike than different. There is—an altimated overlap of 70% in topics but the topics are not treated identically. The remaining 30% is particular to each teat book and in treatment. The B.S.C.S. texts are quite different from traditional biology.

From the curriculum point of view the B.S.C.S. Versions in content and organization, have served to break the traditional pattern of biology Courses in which organisms were treated according to their classes regarding their structures and functions. The course design sometimes called fern-frog organization was laid down around 1860. In general B.S.C.S. versions minimize organ-tissue concepts and concentrate more on molecular and cellular at one hand and community population and world biome at the other. The degree of emphasis upon these topic areas is different for each B.S.C.S text book. The blue version has its emphasis on molecular levels and physiological aspects, the Green Version relates more to community and population aspects while the Yellow Version has its emphasis on cellular classical and evolutionary aspects.

The 1968, 1973 and 1971 editions of the above mentioned versions contain upgraded information about new developments in life sciences but the emphasis is on the same major concepts. It appears that the revised versions have somewhat more topics in common than the 1963 versions although the treatment of these topics remains unique to particular versions.

After the inception of N.C.E.R.T. (India), A Text-Book for Higher Secondary Schools was developed by Biology Panel but in this the approach in treating the material was modernized traditional. The content was balanced regarding knowledge included but treatment is according to groups of organisms or branches of biology. Preparation and testing of material on biology teaching by N.C.E.R.T with the help of UNESCO and other agencies has been going on since 1968 and balanced curricula have been developed. There has not been identification of any type of concepts and their integration in the school life sciences subject matter.

Questions

1. Discuss the major concepts (themes) identified by Biological Sciences Curriculum Study (U.S.A.).
2. Discuss the model adopted by B.S.C.S. in developing a new curriculum of biology for schools.
3. Give an account of the curricular material developed by B.S.C.S. and the experimentation involved in the development of this material.

4

OBJECTIVES AND AIMS

There are certain philosophies that suggest how we should live our lives. We have adopted a democratic way of life and our education should prove to be an instrument to achieve our individual and social aims. Every subject, therefore, taught in the school has some aims and objectives of its teaching.

Teaching of life sciences has also certain aims and objectives for which this is taught in the schools. These can be discussed as follows:

1. Knowledge.
2. Skills.
3. Abilities
4. Scientific Method.
5. Scientific attitude.
6. Interests.
7. Appreciation.

8. Habit formation.
9. Career specialization.
10. Use of leisure.
11. Better living.

KNOWLEDGE

One of the major aims of teaching life sciences has been imparting knowledge to the students. Knowledge in the form of content may be of various plants and animal groups, structure and functions of organisms, interdependence of plants and animals, genetic principles, molecular basis of life, evolution, dates, events, terminology and formulae involved, and application of the knowledge in our daily life activities etc.

Nowadays more stress is laid on the organization of knowledge in the form of conceptual schemes so that the students can have real under standing of that subject matter rather than rote memorization. Knowledge in the form of facts, concepts and generalizations should be organized from simple to complex, teaching should be activity based and it should be investigatory rather than illustrative.

A concept is said to be a sort of generalization or mental construct an individual has about an object, organism, place, phenomena or event. A concept can also be defined as an abstraction used to classify words, ideas, objects, feelings or skills etc.

Concepts are generally of three types viz.

Classification : as all flowering plants are angiosperms

Correlational : When you enter a warm room you perspire sweating is related to rise in temperature.

Theoretical : An atom is made up of electrons, protons and neutrons.

Concepts are never right or wrong but these may be either adequately or inadequately developed in an individual. Concepts grow in dimensions with the experience.

Skills : Teaching of life sciences also aims at developing certain skills in the students. These may be experimental, constructional and drawing skills. In experimental skills we can include handling of apparatus that are used in life science practicals and setting of experiments. We can also make students learn collection, culturing and preservation of plant and animal organisms. In constructional skill we can teach the students making of some simple apparatus that can be used for experiments as light screens for photosynthesis experiments or some glass apparatus or preparation of certain stains or preservatives and molds etc. In developing drawing skills we can teach the methods of drawing of figures of plants and animals and their internal structures. They can be asked to prepare certain charts of organisms and systems. Along with this student skills in taking observations, solving problems and making inquiry can be developed.

Abilities : Teaching of life sciences should also aim at developing certain abilities in the students. These can be ability to sense problems, organization and interpretation of data, analysis and drawing of generalizations or conclusions. Students studying life sciences should be able to locate reliable source for data collection. They should also be able to argue, discuss and use the terminology in the subject. Students should also be able to apply their acquired knowledge in solving their daily life problems.

Scientific Attitude : Teaching of life sciences should aim at developing a particular bent of mind in the students towards ideas events of living world that is based on scientific explanations. This is scientific attitude. For this purpose this subject should be taught in a systematic way. Scientific attitude involves several things but some major are ;

(a) *Mathematical accuracy.* which means students should observe mathematical accuracy in every type of collection and analysis of data.

(b) *Observations.* Students studying life sciences should have a way of observing things critically. Their perceptions should have meanings and observations should be explained by applying the knowledge one has acquired.

(c) *Verification.* Students should try to verify the claims of other people and they should not accept those as such. One should not believe the tall claims of quacks about their medicines but should have a desire to test and verify those.

(d) *Impartiality*. Students should be impartial towards events and phenomena. Analysis and interpretation of data should be undertaken objectively. Data should not be manipulated and results of experiments should not be influenced by personal prejudice or bias.

(e) *Experimentation*. Students should have a desire to undertake experiments and should not draw conclusions based on anticipations. In order to get accurate results controlled experiments should also be set up.

SCIENTIFIC METHOD

Scientific method is a systematic way of solving problems or this is a method that scientists undertake in every type of working.

Scientific method involves :

(a) Defining the problem that is to be solved or it is specifying the problem.

(b) Making observations and collection of data, involves collection of information related to the solution of the problems from all sources that are available.

(c) Making hypothesis is listing the possible solution or solutions of the problem under consideration.

(d) Testing the hypothesis involves undertaking of experiments in order to test the hypothesis or hypotheses. A hypothesis may appear to be correct solution but it is not accepted till it is experimentally proved.

(e) Drawing of conclusion or generalization, the proposed hypothesis are tested experimentally and the one that holds good is retained and results are generalized If all the hyphtheses are disproved then another hypothesis is laid down and tested experimentally. If the generalization so drawn can be applied in the solution of other problems it becomes a principle or rule.

INTERESTS

Teaching of life sciences should arouse interests in students about scientific literature, science club activities, nature study, science fairs, exhibitions, excursions, field, trips, projects, collection, culturing and presentation of plant and animal materials. Interests should also be developed in undertaking discussions and debates. Interests can be aroused by motivation, punishment, praise, criticism and rivalry etc.

APPRECIATION

Students studying life sciences should be able to appreciate the discoveries of scientists, the ways discoveries were made, adventures undertaken by the scientists, beauty of nature, organization of organism body, the ladder of life (arrangement of organisms from the point of view of evolution), diversity in organisms, inter-relationship of plants and animals etc. Only those students can appreciate these things and phenomena who really understand them.

HABIT FORMATION

Teaching of life sciences should also aim at developing certain socially desirable habits in the students. Some of these habits may be truth, honesty, self dependence, giving regard to other's point of view thinking scientifically and undertaking solution of problems in a scientific way. Most of the above said values are inherent in the development of scientific attitude and scientific method which are the ultimate result of understanding the subject matter adquately.

CAREER SPECIALISATION

One of the aims of teaching life sciences should be giving the students knowledge and training so that they can enter some profession or they come continue their studies in some pure or applied field. Some professions that life science students can aim at choosing are : doctor, nurse, agriculturist, genetist, microbiologist, teacher or one may specialize in horticulture, fisheries, live stock management or in some pure fields as physiologist, embryologist etc.

USE OF LEISURE

Students should use their leisure time in some economic and socially desirable activities and some of these can be, making and maintenance of aquarium, gardening, collection of seeds, flowers special type of organisms as insectivorous plants and insects or some economic plant and animal products. All these activities can be taught while teaching life sciences, involving activities.

BETTER LIVING

The ultimate aim of life sciences teaching should be to make the future citizens able to adjust in their social and economic environment. They should be taught about balanced diet, sanitary habits, prevention and eradication of diseases, avoiding superstitions, population problem, better ways of farming and dairying etc. Students should also adequately understand the inter-dependence of plants and animals and ecological balances in nature.

OBJECTIVES ACHIEVED BY FORMAL EDUCATION

Our educational programme is an attempt to bring out some behavioural changes in the students. Every subject taught in the schools or institutions aims at bringing out some behavioural changes in the students (learning). Bloom divides these behavioural changes in three categories, which are the terms descriptive of the type behaviour. These are also known as three domains.

Cognitive : These behavioural changes or objectives are concerned with thinking, knowing and problem solving.

Affective : These objectives deal with attitudes, values, interests and appreciation.

Psychomotor : These objectives are concerned with manual and motor skills. Much of our teaching-learning process in the schools is concerned with bringing out behavioural changes in the cognitive domain and these are tested through our examinations because we hardly include any item in our tests that measure values, interests, appreciation, manual or motor skills.

Cognitive structure is a term used to describe the particular store of concepts and generalizations of an individual at any given time and his ability to use them in total thinking process. A person's cognitive structure is a product of his intellectual and physical abilities, his environment and his past experience and training. It develops at different rates, in children and the differential tends to increase with age.

Bloom's taxonomy of cognitive domain suggests that there is a hierarchy of cognitive skills possessed by each individual. Learning takes place at a different level in each individual, depending upon his cognitive structure. The different levels are levels of maturity of concepts and generalizations. These will determine at what level new information will be learned as it is presented to him. The levels are arranged in the following hierarchy.

Knowledge : The learner recalls specific facts or simply brings to mind the appropriate matter (not the type of knowledge or its organization but how it is retained, recalled or reproduced-relates with mental operations).

Comprehension : The learner can translate, re-order, re-arrange learned material and to some extent extrapolate.

Application : The learner can apply concepts and generalizations he has learned to new, practical and unfamiliar situations.

Analysis : The learner, when presented with an organized whole or structured situations, can break it down and identify its elements, as for instance when presented with experimental situation, he can identify variables, controls, assumptions etc.

Synthesis : The learner puts elements or parts together form a whole, a new structure or pattern. For instance the student is able to design an experiment or propose ways of testing hypothesis.

Evaluation : The learner makes judgements about value and accuracy of presented materials against established criteria. For instance he evaluates proposals or hypotheses, probable outcomes etc.

The cognitive skill of knowledge and application are the foundations which are necessary for the assimilation of skills like analysis, synthesis and evaluation.

First Asian Regional Conference on School Biology held in Manila from Dec. 4 to 10, 1966, recommended the following aims and objectives of School Biology Teaching in Asia:

(i) To develop and instil in students the scientific attitude of inquiry and experimentation.

(ii) To provide sufficient understanding of the concepts of biology to enable students to become worthy citizens of the world.

(iii) To provide the opportunities for a practical understanding of the method of biologists which give them the confidence to attempt the solution of problems which they have to face in their individual and social lives.

(iv) To give the students the incentive to pursue the study at higher levels of biology and related fields.

(v) To encourage respect and feeling for living things.

NCERT VIEW

NCERT (India) considers the following objectives of teaching life sciences at school level:

Knowledge : Students should acquire the knowledge of biological terms, facts, concepts, principles and formulae. They should be able to recall and recognize biological terms, facts, concepts, principles, processes, specimens and apparatus etc.

Understanding : As a result of teaching life sciences, students should be able to understand biological terms, facts, concepts, principles and processes. This means that they should be able to translate tables, floral diagrams, floral formulae from one form to another, interpret charts, graphs, data, illustrate biological phenomena, detect errors in faulty statements, concepts, processes, identify relationship between various facts, concepts, processes, compare biological facts, concepts, processes, discriminate between closely related concepts, principles, processes, explain biological concept, principles, and processes etc.

Application : The students should be able to apply knowledge of life sciences in new situations. They should be able to judge adequacy of the data, utilize data, make hypothesis based on observations, select required methods and material, establish relationship between cause and effect, give reasons for biological phenomena, draw conclusions from observed facts and predict biological phenomena from the given data.

Skills : As a result of studying the subject of life sciences students should develop certain skills inherent in the study of this subject. They hould develop skills in manipulation, dissections, observations, drawing, collection, culturing, mounting, preservation and locating biological information.

In manipulative skills they should be able to arrange apparatus, handle instruments, maintain apparatus and instruments, improvise apparatus and models and manipulate apparatus and instrument at a reasonable speed. In dissectional skills we can include selection of appropriate organism for the purpose, killing the organisms by appropriate methods, placing and fixing the organisms in right petspective, proper handling of the dissecting instruments, exposing and displaying required parts.

Observational skills include noting relevant details of the specimens, reading the instruments carefully, discriminating between closely related structures, parts, phenomena, and specimens accurately, locating desired parts correctly and detecting errors in experimental setups and procedures.

The students should be able to make drawings that represent parts, and structures in their proper proportions. They should be able to draw sketches and diagrams at a reasonable speed and should label them neatly. Collection, culturing, mounting and preservation skills include locating the organisms in their habitats, selection of proper instrument and time for collection and culturing of the organisms, adopting proper procedures, mounting the specimens, utilizing correct procedures, selecting, proper preservatives and methods for preservation of organisms and arranging the material in systematic order.

Skills in locating biological information constitute tapping of different sources for collection of biological information, using of index cards and library facilities properly, referring the content table, shifting the material according to need and referring to the relevant bibliography.

Interests : Learning in life science should arouse interest of students in different plants, animals and their environments. The students should develop interests in collecting; mounting and preserving plants and animals, observing plant and animal behaviour, participating in activities of biological club, contributing biological material to the school, reading extra books and journals, visiting botanical gardens, zones, museums, fields and forests and improvising biological apparatus and models etc.

Attitudes : Students should be able to develop scientific attitude as a result of studying life sciences. This includes students' curiosity for biological phenomena willingness to consider new interpretations of biological data development of intellectual honesty in expressing and recording biological data, belief in the relationship of cause and effect of biological phenomena, rejection of views and conclusions which are without valid reasons, suspension of judgement in absence of proper evidence, showing perseverance in accomplishing various biological tasks.

Applications : As an outcome of studies in life sciences students be able to appreciate biological phenomena in nature and role of life sciences in our lives. This objective is achieved when students realize the significance of interdependence of plants and animals, wonders of nature inherent in plants and animals, role of micro-organisms in our lives, role of life sciences in developing aesthetic sense, struggle for existence in life, contribution of biologists in human welfare, balance of life in nature and unity of structure in diverse plants and animals.

Questions

1. What should be the general aims of teaching life-science at the school stage?
2. What objectives should be kept in mind while framing a life sciences programme for school stage. Discuss.
3. What objectives have been identified by N.C.E.R.T. (India) for teaching life-sciences at school level?
4. What do you understand by scientific attitude? Discuss how and when man needs scientific attitude.
5. Enumerate the specific objectives of teaching life-sciences at higher secondary stage. How should the teacher proceed in the class for effective attainment of these objectives?
6. What are the objectives of teaching life sciences at school stage? Discuss any three in detail.

5

OBJECTIVES OF BEHAVIOUR

In Biology the plants and animals are categorised into phylum, class, order, family, genus, species and variety. This is done with the following two objectives in view :

(i) To ensure accuracy of communication.

(ii) To understand the organisation and inter relation of the various parts of the animal and the plant world.

In the same way it was desired to classify the goals or objectives of the educational system. But the difficulty is that there is no consensus about the different objectives because

(i) Some teachers say that the students should understand knowledge.

(ii) Other teachers say that the student should understand the essence or core.

(iii) Still other teachers say that they should comprehend. Different people interpret the same objective in different ways.

THE ADVANTAGES

1. To define and translate the objectives in the same way. The knowledge of taxonomy should enable the teacher to define and translate the objectives in the same way.
2. To faciliate the exchange of information curriculum development and evaluation devices.
3. To help in modifying the educational outcomes.

HISTORICAL RETROSPECT

The idea for the classification of educational objectives first of all came up at an informal meeting of college examiners attending the 1948 American Psychological Association convention in Boston. The examiners at this meeting felt the same theoretical frame work which could be utilized to exchange ideas and materials, among test worker to facilitate communication among examiners.

The examiners agreed that educational objectives be classified under the following three domains :

(i) Cognitive
(ii) Affective
(iii) Psychomotor.

The group was of the view that the objective should be stated in behaviour form which can be observed and described. The group discussed the principles by which the taxonomy was developed. The group agreed that taxonomy should have educational logical and psychological basis.

The work done by the Taxonomy group started in 1949. This group for the first time systematically and comprehensively classified the educational objectives into three cotegories or domains mentioned above. It deliberately used the easily and readily available term 'Taxonomy' in place of 'classification'. According to H. N. Tripathi, "The essential difference between classification and taxonomy has not been realized by many educationists. Different schemes of classification have been called taxonomies. This is wrong. There can be only one taxonomy though there can be several schemes of classification. If some one used a new taxonomy either he is wrong or Bloom is wrong. Simplified schemes of classification have been used by teachers and educationists because they are more convenient to use than the elaborate taxonomy prepared by Bloom and his co-workers. These schemes are rightly to be called classifications and not taxonomies.

The taxonomy group consisting of Benjamin E. Bloom, May Engel hard, Edward First, Walker Hill and David R. Krathwohl made a comprehensive attack on the problem of educational objectives.

PURPOSES OF BLOOM'S TAXONOMY

Bloom's taxonomy can be use for the following purposes:

(1) To facilitate communication among teachers, examiners and others educational workers.

(2) To set up a comprehensive, systematic list of the types of behaviour at which educational procedures may aim.

(3) To provide a source of hypotheses and questions for methods of developing curricula, teaching methods and testing techniques.

(4) To arrange educational behaviours or objectives, from simple or complex.

(5) In general, to lay bare many of the hitherto concealed assumptions underlying the statements of objectives that educators have developed in the past.

THE DOMAINS

The educational objectives were divided into three major parts the cognitive, the affective and the psychomotor domains they are described ahead in detail.

COGNITIVE DOMAIN

It has been till now very well investigated and may include those objectives which deal with the recall and recognition of knowledge and development of intellectual abilities and skills.

Knowledge : Knowledge, as defined here, involves the recall of methods and processes, or the recall of a pattern, structure or setting. For measurement purposes, the recall situation involves little more than bringing to mind the appropriate material. Although some alteration of the material may be required, this is a relatively minor part of the task. The knowledge objectives emphasize most of the psychological processes of remembering. The process of relating is also involved in that a knowledge test situation requires the organization and reorganisation of a problem such that it will furnish the appropriate signals cues, and clues which will most effectively bring out whatever knowledge is filed or stored.

Knowledge is then broken down into the following eleven categories :

1. Knowledge of verbal and non-verbal terminology.
2. Knowledge of specific data, facts.
3. Knowledge of ways and means of dealing with specific e.g. the ways of organising, studying, judging and criticising ideas and phenomena.
4. Knowledge of conventions.
5. Knowledge of trends and sequences.
6. Knowledge of classifications and categories.
7. Knowledge of criteria by which facts, principles and opinions are tested and judged.
8. Knowledge of methodology.
9. Universal and abstractions. Analysis of organisational principles (explicates well as implicit) structure underlying a communication unit.
10. Principles and generalisation and their thesis combining together of parts and elements so whole pattern or structure.
11. Knowledge of theories land structure and their applications. Synas to constitute a inter-relation.

INTELLECTUAL ABILITIES AND SKILLS

Abilities and skills refer to organised modes of operation and generalized techniques for dealing with materials and problems requiring no specialized or technical information but general information.

This objective stresses the mental processes of organising material to achieve a particular person. The material may be given remembered.

THE CATEGORIES

Comprehension. Here the stress is on the understanding of material and intent of material it includes behaviour of the following three types : (a) Translation. (i) From one level of abstraction to another. (ii) From symbolic form to another form and vice versa. (iii) From one verbal form to another. (b) Interpretation. (c) Extrapolation. It includes such behaviour as drawing conclusions, prediction etc.

Application. Here the stress is on remembering and bringing to bear upon the given material the appropriate generalisation and principles. Step 1. The problem is presented and perceived by the students as : (i) initially unfamiliar. The student searches for familiar element. (ii) immediately having familiar aspects to guide the action. Step 2. (i) the student uses familiar elements to re-structure the problem in a familiar context. (ii) There is some restucturing by the student to make resemblance to familiar model more complete. Step 3. The problem is classified as familiar in type. Step 4. The abstraction (idea, method, principle, theory) suitable to the problem is selected. Step 5. The abstraction is used to solve the problem. Step 6. The solution to problem is evident.

Analysis. Here there is stress on the breakdown of the material into it's constituent parts and of the way they are organised. It includes : (i) Analysis of elements. (ii) Analysis of relationships. (iii) Analysis of organisational principles (explicit as well as implicit structure underlying a communication unit).

Synthesis. It can be defined as combining (putting) together of parts and elements so as to constitute a whole, pattern or structure which was not clearly there earlier. It includes : (i) Production of a unique communication (conveyance of ideas, feelings or experiences) which can be even personal. (ii) Production of a plan or proposed set of operations. (iii) Derivation of a set of abstract relations.

Evaluation. It aims at making qualitative as well as quantitative judgement about the ideas, materials, methods, solutions, works and value etc. It consists of evaluation judgement in terms of : (i) internal evidence and (ii) external criteria.

AFFECTIVE DOMAIN

The domain is concerned with feeling and includes attitudes, appreciation, interest and values. The objectives pertaining to these characteristics are hard to define and evaluate. The objectives in this domain describe change in interest, attitudes, and values and the development of appreciations and adequate adjustment.

It has the following categories in heirarchial order each category is more abstract and complex than previous one

Receiving. It includes an individual's awareness of various sources of attention to making same response to a particular phenomenon or stimulus, information on science and recognising these resources which are encountered. Needless to say that it is the first and lowest level of affective domain.

Responding. It includes reaching about science and engaging in various science projects or extra moral activities.

Valuing. It indicates an internalisation of content to certain ideals and values and includes he objective of development of scientific attitude such as

(i) disregard of superstition,

(ii) prefering their formation culled from controlled experiments to the opinions of other people.

(iii) To suspend judgement until there is ample evidence.

Organisation. It refers to the building of a system of values. At this stage, value is conceptualised in the abstract and the conflicts between the values are resolved and inter-relations established. It involves the cognitive behaviours of analysis and synthesis. Naturally, the maturity level needed for this level is beyond that reached in the earlier years of formal education.

Value Set or Characterisation by a Value. This highest level of effective domain includes characterization of a person's behaviour by certain beliefs, controlling value or ideas and the integration of attitude and values into a world view or total philosophy of life.

PSYCHOMOTOR DOMAIN

It is the domain of doing the manipulation or motor skill areas. Presumably, it deals with areas involving varied types of muscular skills and coordinations such as those involved in clerical trades, mechanical work, physical training, surgery etc.

Although it is a very important domain, yet not much work has been done to define objectives in this area.

PROCESS APPROACH

The best example of this approach is the project 'Science-A Process Approach of AAAS Commission on Science Education. The primary aim in this case is to develop the child's skills in using science processes which are not developed by reading about science.

The Processes. The processes are the warp on which the woof of content is woven.

The following five processes can be taken up for primary classes :

(i) Observing

(ii) Classifying

(iii) Measuring

(iv) Communicating

(v) Recognising number relations.

The following integrated processes may be taken up in the classes 4th and 5th :

(i) Formulating hypotheses.

(ii) Making operational definition.

(iii) Controlling and manipulating vriables.

(iv) Experimenting.

(v) Interpreting data.

(vi) Free-floating models.

Heirarchail Charts. For each of these processes the heirarchies of skill were analysed and represented in the form of charts which are important components of the programme.

Samples of Exercises. In addition to the heirarchial charts the samples of exercises are also shown. Each exercise includes a number of suggeitions for evaluating children in the skills of handbag the science processes.

STATEMENT OF OBJECTIVES

Of late, the statement of objectives in behavioural or perfor-mancae terms has received closer and renewed attention. Robert F. Major has written a book 'Preparing instructional objectives this work is devoted entirely to the 'how' of writing good performance objectives'.

Again in A.A.A.S—Science—A Process Approach, for each lesson in the programme there are performance objectives.

STEPS OF WRITING

Major has suggested the following three steps for writing a performance objective:—

(i) Decide what the child should the doing when the instruction has been successful. (Determining of behaviour)—The performance objective is a statement of what the learner will be able to do at the end of the learning activity. It should not describel what the lesson is about.

In order to write good performance objectives, use a direct value describing what the child's action or activity will be. The verb should have one interpretation and not many vague interpretations.

Value open to many interpretations	*Value open to a few interpretations*
1. To appreciate	1. To compare
2. To believe	2. To contrast
3. To enjoy	3. To construct
4. To fully appreciate	4. To differentiate
5. To grasp the significance	5. To identify
6. To have faith in	6. To list
7. To know	7. To recite
8. To really understand	8. To solve
9. To understand	9. To write

(ii) Decide (Indicate) under what condition/conditions these behaviours will be observed and developed.

(iii) Decide/Indicate how well the child is expected to perform (What will be the expected level of performance?)

AIMS AND OBJECTIVES

The pupil acquires Knowledge of Biological terms, facts, concepts, principles, formulae etc.

(a) Recalls biological terms, facts, concepts, principles and processes.

(b) Recognises biological terms facts, concepts, specimens, principles, generalizations and apparatus.

The pupil Understands biological term, facts, concepts, principles, processes etc.

Specific Objectives : The pupil :

(a) translates biological terms, floral formulae, floral diagrams etc.

(b) illustrates a given biological phenomenon.

(c) detects errors in faulty statements, concepts, processes.

(d) identifies relationship between various facts, concepts, procsses etc.

(e) interprets charts, graphs, data etc.

(f) selects relevant terms, facts, data etc.

(g) compares biological facts, related concepts, processes etc.

(h) discriminates between closely related concepts, principles, processes etc.

(i) explains biological concept, principles, processes etc.

The pupil Applies knowledge of Biology in new situations.

Specific Objectives : The pupil :

(a) analysis the problem.

(b) makes hypothesis.

(c) suggests appropriate methods and materials for a given purpose.

(d) establish cause and effect relationship.

(e) gives reasons for a biological phenomenon.

(f) draws inferences and conclusion from the observed facts.

(g) predicts biological phenomena from the given data.

The pupil develops skill in :

(a) drawing diagrams;

(b) manipulating apparatus and instruments;

(c) collecting, mounting and preserving specimens;

(d) dissecting biological specimens;

(e) observing biological information, parts, structures etc :

(f) locating biological information from different sources;

(g) scientific expression.

Specific Objectives : The pupil

(a) draws accurate sketches and diagrams neatly;
makes diagrams with sense of proportion;
labels diagrams neatly, methodically and correctly;
draws sketches and diagrams at a resonable speed.

(b) arranges the apparatus systematically;
handles the apparatus with precision;
reads the instruments with precision;
maintains the apparatus and instruments in order;
impovises apparatus and models;

(c) selects the appropriate instruments for collection;
locates the right habitat for a particular specimen;
gathers the required specimens at the appropriate times.
uses the right preservative for different specimens.

(d) selects the appropriate specimen for dissection;
fixes up the specimen properly for dissection;
fixes or places the specimen in the right perspective ;
handles the instruments with specimen to dissect the specimen skilfully without damaging the parts;
displays the required parts of the specimen;
separates and removes the dissected puts of the specimen without any danger for detailed examination.

(e) notices the relevant detail the specimen carefully;

reads the instruments correctly;

discriminates between closely related structures, parts and specimens accurately ;

locates the desired parts exactly;

detects error in experimental set-up and procedures.

(f) taps different sources of biological information carefully.

uses the index card in the Library properly to get the desired information.

studies rightly the contents, table and index to collect the required information.

shifts the relevant material for his purpose efficiently.

refers accurately to the relevant bibliography for further reading.

(g) make use of correct biological terminology in describing a biological phenomena.

uses the appropriate terms at the proper places;

puts the ideas in clear, precise and unambiguous terms.

organises his thoughts systematically.

The pupil develops Interest in plants and animals in their study.

Specific Objectives : The pupil:

(a) collects, mounts and preserves plants and animals of his own;

(b) enjoys own observing, plants and animals' behaviour.

(c) actively participates in the activities of biological club.

(d) contributes biological material for school and other magazines.

(e) reads extra books and journals on biology and biologists.

(f) visits botanical gardens, zoo, museums and forests for getting additional information.

(g) improves biological apparatus and models of his own.

The pupil develop Science Attitudes towards biological phenomena.

Specific Objectives : The pupil:

(a) is curious to know the various biological phenomena.

(b) shows willingness to consider new interpretation of biological data.

(c) develops intellectual honesty in expressing and recording biological data.

(d) believes in cause and effect relationship in biological data.

(e) does not accept or reject views and conclusions without valid reasons.

(f) suspends judgement in the absence of proper evidence.

(g) shows perseverence in accomplishing various biological tasks.

The pupil Appreciates the biological phenomena in nature and the role of biology in human welfare:

Specific Objectives:

The pupil assimilates the knowledge of biology, derives pleasure in persuit of its study and realises the real significance of the:

(a) interdependence of animals and plants.

(b) wonders of nature as manifested in plants and animals.

(c) role of micro-organisms and their importance in daily life.

(d) role of biology in developing asthetic sense.

(e) struggle for existence in life.

(f) contrubution of biologists in human welfare.

(g) balance of life in nature.

(h) unity underlying diversity exhibited by plants and animals.

(i) complementarity of structure and function.

Questions

1. The following objectives in teaching Biology are stated. How will you change these to behaviourally stated objectives?
   (i) Show the parts of flower.
   (ii) Demonstrate the effect of electric shock given to the leg of a frog.
   (iii) Show a film on photosynthesis.
2. How will you conduct the behavioural objective testing of pupils of class IX of lesson on paramoecium?
3. Describe briefly the skills and techniques which science students should acquire.

6

BEHAVIOUR AND OBSERVATION

If you are keen in making lesson plans which may help you in achieving your identified objectives, they (the objectives) should be clearly stated. If objectives are not well defined, it is impossible to evaluate a student, a lesson, a unit, a course or a programme efficiently, and there is no sound basis for selecting appropriate material, content or instructional method. Unless the teacher (or programmer) himself has a clear picture of his instructional intent, he will be unable to select test items or frame questions that clearly reflect the student's ability to perform the desired skills or demonstrate his acquisition of desired information. With clearly defined objectives, the student knows which activities on his part are relevant to his success.

A meaningfully stated objective is one that succeeds in communicating to the reader the writer's instructional intent. It is meaningful to the extent it conveys to others a picture (of what a successful learner will be like) the writer has in mind. For example, if you provide another teacher with an objective, and he then teaches his students to perform in a manner that you agree in consistent with what you have in mind, then you have communicated your objective in a meaningful manner.

The best statement of the meaningful objective is the one that excludes the greatest number of possible alternatives to your objective. There are many needed words which are open to a wide range of interpretation. To the extent that you use such words, you have yourself open to misinterpretation, consider the following examples of words in this light.

Words Open to Many Interpretation—In order to understand, to really understand, to appreciate, to fully appreciate, to grasp the significance of, to enjoy, to believe, to have faith in, etc.

Words Open to Fewer Interpretation—to recite, to write, to identify, to differentiate, to solve, to construct, to list, to compare, to contrast, etc.

What do you mean when you say that you want a learner to know some thing? Do you mean that you want him to be able to recite, to solve, or to construct? Just to tell him you want him to know tells him little—the word can mean many things.

Though it is all right to include such words as 'understand' and 'appreciate' in a statement of objective, the statement is not explicit enough to be useful until it indicates how you intend to sample the 'understanding' or 'appreciating'. Until you describe what the learner will be doing when demonstrating that he 'understands' or 'appreciates' you have described very little if you want him to do at all. Thus, the statement that communicates best will be one that describes the terminal behaviour of the learner well enough to avoid misinterpretation.

THE CONCEPT

The most important characteristic of a useful objective is that it identifies the kind of performance that will be accepted as evidence that the learner has achieved the objective. The way to write an objective, that meets this requirement is to write a statement describing one of your educational intents and then modify it until it answers the question, "What is the learner doing when he is demonstrating that he has achieved the objective?" If the answer of this question is "YES" the statement of the objective will include the "Observable Behaviour" which the learner will be showing when he is demonstrating that he has achieved the objective. The objective written in this manner is called Behavioural Objective. As for example 'to be able to solve quadratic equation' or 'to be able to repair a radio' are behavioural objectives which include the observable behaviours 'solve' and 'repair' respectively.

Let us see another objective. 'To develop an appreciation for music.' Now ask the same question "what is the learner doing when he is demonstrating that he has achieved the objective?"

1. Does he sigh in ecstasy when he is listening to music?
2. Does he buy a stereo system and records?
3. Does he correctly answer 95 per cent multiple choice questions on the history of music?
4. Does he write an essay on five musical instruments?
5. Does he say 'Oh Boy! It's too much.'

For every question the answer is No. It is not a behavioural objective.

To state an objective that will successfully communicate your educational intent you will sometimes have to define terminal behaviour further by stating the conditions you will impose upon the learner which he is demonstrating his mastery of the objective. Here are some examples:

1. Given a list of
2. Given any reference of learner's choice
3. Without the aid of references
4. Given a standard set of tools
5. Without the aid of tools
6. Without the aid of calculator.

As for example in the behvaioural objective 'Given a list of 35 chemical elements, the learner must be able to recall and write the valencies of at least 30 'to recall and write' is the observable behaviour and 'Given a list of 35 chemical elements' is the condition. Similarly the behavioural objective 'Given a linear algebraic equation, the learner must be able to solve for the unknown without the aid of references, tables or calculating devices' has both – the observable behaviour as well as the condition.

For conditions you should ask yourself questions like these:

1. What the learner will be provided?
2. What will the learner be deprived?
3. What are the conditions under which you will expect the terminal behaviour to occur?

Very often, a good way to explain to the learner the conditions under which he will be expected to perform is simply to show him some sample test.

Example

(Behavioural objective stating observable behaviour and condition). The student must be able to demonstrate his understanding of the rules of logic by correctly solving problems of the following type:

Which of the following statements is illustrated by the diagram below:

(a) All animals are birds

(b) Some birds are animals

(c) All birds are animals

(d) No birds are animals.

Answer : (c)

THE STANDARDS

'What is it you want the learner to be able to do' gives the Observable Behaviour, and 'how will you want him to be able to do' given Criterion of acceptable performance. In order to include Criterion of acceptable performance in the statement of objective, indicate 'what the acceptable performance will be' by addition of words that describe the criterion of success.

Examples. (Behavioural objectives having criterion)

1. The student must be able to correctly solve at least seven simple linear equations within a period of 30 minutes.

Behaviour : Solve

Condition : within 30 minutes

Criterion : atleast 7

2. Given Human Skeleton, the student must be able to correctly identify by labelling at least 40 of the following bones; there will be no penalty for guessing (list of bones inserted here)

Behaviour : Identify

Condition : Given a human Skeleton

Criterion : at least 40

In order to test whether the statement of objective consists of *observable behaviour, condition* and *criterion,* the following questions may be asked:

1. Does the statement describe what the learner will be doing when he is demonstrating that he has reached the objective? (Behaviour)
2. Does the statement describe the important conditions (given or restriction or both) under which the learner will be expected to demonstrate his competence? (Condition)
3. Does the statement indicate how the learner will be evaluated?

Does it describe at least the lower limit of acceptable performance? (Criterion)

These are the 3 items for stating Behavioural Objectives.

THE FUNDAMENTALS

How can you write the behavioural objective having all the three items behaviour, conditions and criterion?

1. Identify the terminal behaviour by name, you can specify the kind of behaviour that will be accepted as evidence that the learner has achieved the objective.
2. Try to define the observed behaviour by describing the important conditions under which the behaviour will be expected to occur.

3. Specify the criteria of acceptable performance by describing how well the learner must perform to be considered acceptable.

Although each of these items might help an objective to be more specific, it will not be necessary to include all the three in each objective except observable behaviour.

1. A statement of instructional objective is a collection of words or symbols describing one of your instructional intents.
2. An objective will communicate your intent to the degree you have described what the learner will be doing when demonstrating his achievement and how you will know when he is doing it.
3. To describe the terminal behaviour (what the learner will be doing) :
   (a) Identify and name the overall *behaviour* act.
   (b) Define the important *conditions* under which the behaviour is to occur (given or restrictions or both).
   (c) Define the *criterion* of acceptable performance.
4. Write a separate statement for each objective; the more statements you have the better chance you have of making clear your intent.
5. If you give each learner a copy of your objectives, you may not have to do much else.

When stating objectives in behavioural terms, some keywords (called behavioural terms) are used. In the cognitive domain there are six categories of objectives—knowledge, comprehension, application, analysis, synthesis and evaluation. The teachers should practise in writing behavioural objectives in all these categories. For convenience behavioural terms for each category are given below:

Knowledge—define, describe, identify, label, list, match, name, outline, reproduce, select, state.

Comprehension—convert, explain, extend, generalise, give example, infer, paraphrase, predict, rewrite, summarise.

Application—change, compute, demonstrate, discover, manipulate, modify, operate, predict, prepare, relate, show, solve, use.

Analysis—break down diagrams, differentiate, discriminate, distinguish, identify, illustrate, infer, outline, point out, relate, select, separate, subdivide.

Synthesis—categorise, combine, compile, compose, create, devise, design, explain, generate, modify, organise, plan, rearrange, revise, rewrite, summarise, tell, write.

Evaluation—appraise, compare, conclude, contrast, describe, discriminate, explain, justify, interpret, relate, summarise, support.

When objectives are clearly defined and stated in behavioural terms, it is easy to develop test items (for multiple choice test items) for evaluation. Teachers should practise in constructing test items for identified objectives stated in behavioural terms. Some sample test items developed on some behavioural objectives are given below:

SAMPLES TEST ITEMS

Topic : Structure of an Atom

Behavioural Objectives

1. The students will identify the definition of atom with 100 per cent accuracy.
2. Given a list of material objects such as proton, positron, electron and neutron the students will identify the names of the particles of an atom with 100 per cent accuracy.
3. The students will write, how weights of electron, neutron and proton are related (weight of neutron is approximately equal to the weight of proton and weight of electron is negligible compared to the weight of proton and neutron) by memory with 100 per cent accuracy.
4. The students will write the charges of electron, proton and neutron (negative, positive, neutral) by memory with 100 per cent accuracy)
5. Given a diagram of atomic model the students will label the parts (shells) and necleus with 100 per cent accuracy.

6. Given the number of protons and electrons in an atom the students will write the charge of that atom with 100 per cent accuracy.
7. The students will write the position of protons, neutrons, and electrons in the atom by memory with 100 per cent accuracy.
8. Given the number of protons and neutrons, the students will write the atomic weight of the element.
9. Given the number of electrons or protons in an atom, the students will write the atomic number of the element.
10. Given the number of particular shell (1st, 2nd....last, next to last) the students will write the maximum number of electrons in that shell with 100 per cent accuracy.
11. Given the atomic number and atomic weight of an element the students will write the number of electrons in various shells and the number of protons and neutrons in the nucleus with 100 per cent accuracy.

Test Items

1. The smallest unit of elements is a/an

   (a) electron (b) atom

   (c) molecule (d) proton

2. The atom consists of all the following except

   (a) electron (b) proton

   (c) positron (d) proton

3. The weight of neutron is approximately equal to the weight of

   (a) electron (b) proton

   (c) twice the proton (d) none of them

4. The weight of an electron is

   (a) equal to the weight of neutron

   (b) equal to the weight of proton

   (c) negligibly small

   (d) more than the weight of proton or neutron.

5. The charge of a proton is
   (a) positive (b) negative
   (c) neutral
   (d) sometimes negative and sometimes positive
6. A negatively charged atomic particle is
   (a) proton (b) electron
   (c) neutron (d) nucleus
7. A neutral particle of an atom is
   (a) electron (b) proton
   (c) neutron (d) nucleus
8. 'A' represents
   (a) shell (b) nucleus
   (c) both a and b (d) none of them
9. 'B' represents
   (a) shell (b) nucleus
   (c) both a and b (d) none of them
10. If an atom has 17 protons in its nucleus and 17 electrons in the shells the charge of the atom is
    (a) positive (b) negative
    (c) neutral (d) none of them
11. The nucleus of an atom has
    (a) protons only (b) neutrons only
    (c) neutral (d) none of them
12. Which of the particles are found outside the nucleus in an atom?
    (a) neutron (b) electron
    (c) proton (d) none of them
13. An element has 11 protons, 11 electrons and 12 neutrons. The atomic weight of the element is
    (a) 11 (b) 12
    (c) 22 (d) 23

14. An element has 8 electrons, 8 protons and 8 neutrons. The atomic number of the element is

    (a) 8 (b) 16

    (c) 24 (d) 36

15. An atom has 8 electrons. The number of electrons in its 2nd shell will be

    (a) 2 (b) 6

    (c) 8 (d) 18

16. The atomic number of an element is 17 and its atomic weight is 35. All of the following statements are correct except

    (a) the nucleus will have 17 protons and 18 neutrons

    (b) the nucleus will have 18 protons and 17 neutrons

    (c) the first shell will have 2 elcctron

    (d) the third shell will have 7 electrons.

Answers

1. (b)	2. (c)	3. (b)	4. (c)
5. (a)	6. (b)	7. (c)	8. (b)
9. (a)	10. (c)	11. (c)	12. (b)
13. (d)	14. (a)	15. (b)	16. (b)

Questions

1. What do you mean by a "meaningfully stated objective"?
2. Write down words:

   (a) open to many interpretations

   (b) open to fewer interpretations.
3. What is the harm if we use words open to many interpretations, in stating our educational objectives?

4. What is the importance of :
   (a) behaviour
   (b) condition and
   (c) criterion in writing a behavioural objective?
5. Write down behavioural terms for stating specific objectives in the six categories of the cognitive domain.
   (a) Recognise a topic of a lesson in your field. Write five behavioural objectives to cover that content, which you can feel you can achieve at the end of the lesson.
   (b) Write a multiple choice test item for each objective.

7

Practical Importance

The aim of science education, along with satisfaction of intellectual curiosity, is the survival and welfare of man. Nothing has contributed more to human welfare, from his early animal behaviour, than the knowledge of plants, animals and of his own body. There are four chief ravages of human race :

(i) diseases (ii) wars, (iii) famine and now (iv) over population. From man's point of view life sciences is therefore, fundamental and important of all sciences. Developments in this discipline affect vital state policies on matters like conservation of natural and human resources, radiation experiments, population control, quarantine and health programmes life sciences also helps us answer such personal questions as What determines sex ? How are twins born? Why do babies resemble their parents? how do we acquire immunity against diseases? Why do we become enfeebled in old age? Sanitation, nutrition, pest control and other attributes of intelligent citizenship, all require a biological background.

ROLE AND PROSPECTS

We can discuss the role of life sciences in our lives and prospects of its education in future under the following headings : Population Explosion. Expanding population has been the root cause of unhappiness and war it is supposed that Japan joined second world war to find additional means for its population. Similarly Germany declared war with Russia as it had eyes on the vast wheat fields of Ukarine.

It is estimated that in the stone age there were only 10 million people in the world and around 4000 B.C. (when Mahabharata war took place) it was 1000 million. It increased to 200 million and Christ was born and today it has grown to more than 4000 million. In 2000 A.D. it is expected to be 5000 million. Every second three new babies are being born, which means 180 new months to feed every minute. In India an average couple has four children. It is estimated that with this rate of growth in population, in the next 600 years the population of the world will be 25 million of millions, with just about 5 square metres of land for each person to stand on. The situation is more tragic in the sense that rate of population growth is more in already populous countries like China and India.

The population cannot be allowed to increase indefinitely, if we are to survive. As biologists, we have a responsibility in educating our people. We have to devise methods of controlling high fertility. Several drugs have come to the markets but these have after effects of use. As thalidomide which was considered harmless sleep inducing drug, the women who used it gave birth to deformed babies although they themselves had no effects. So there is a need to develop safe contraceptive devices pregnancy termination methods and drugs, and educating the masses regarding the magnitude of the problem.

FOOD PROBLEM

With the increasing population of the world we must look for ways and means of increasing food supply. This requires an active role of agriculturists botanists, biochemists, zoologists and genetists. Attempts have been made to synthesize sugar artificially. The role of life sciences in connection with our food problem can be considered under the following heads.

Growiog Healthier Crops : In order to increase agricultural produce we need high yielding varieties, necessary fertilizers and earth surface to grow crops. As land surface cannot be increased, in order to increase our production we can use improved varieties of the crops fertilizers and better tools and techniques of farming. A lot of work has been done in the fields of soil chemistry, plant breeding and production of nitrogenous and other fertilizers artificially. But in India agricultural practices are traditional, so production is low. In America one farmer produces food for himself and 25 other people. In our country most of the population is engared in farming but people still starve at times. We can double or triple our grain production, without clearing more of our forests provided we have soundly trained biologists and agriculturists who can give better varieties of crops and can educate the masses about application of fertilizers and better agricultural practices.

New Sources of Food : Botanists have studied the process of photosynthesis in detail and it is estimated that out of the total light energy falling on plants, only 0.5% is utilized by crops on the average and only 2% by the best Crops. The problem is that most of the light falls on the ground and secondly much of the organic matter produced is unedible. In order to locate new sources of food experiments in America show that chlorella can utilize 20% of light energy falling on it and the whole of plant is edible. It is estimated that one acre of algae can produce 40 tons of dry matter out of which 20 tons is protein A. But farming of chlorella involves technical difficulties and is still impracticable. In this direction growing of Anabaena and Nostoe can be more useful as they can also fix nitrogen from the atmosphere. All this will require a change in our feeding habits.

Improving Live Stock : India's cattle population is the largest in the world but there is inefficiency in live stock management. A cow in Netherlands produces 10 kg. milk per day but in India it is 4 kg.. Religous sentiments demand retention of useless cows for the entire life period. Our poultry also needs improvement and scientific methods be adopted to grow fish and meat producing animals. More non-vegatarian eating habits require more land to be cultivated as it requires about seven times as much land to grow food in the form of meat, egg milk and poultry as it does to grow grain and vegetables which contain the same number of calories. If all people make adjustment much land can be freed from inefficient production of live stock and poultry.

CONSERVATION OF NATURAL RESOURCES

The forests buried millions of years ago provide us with the coal and oil that power much of our industry and home comfort. Today's forests give us timber for furniture, raw material for paper industry rubber, drugs, gums, resins, turpentine and camphor etc. Forests also help in distributed rains and check soil erosion and floods. But the forests have been cleared for making towns cities, forming and easy money making purposes. Recently the need of forests has been recognized by biologists and national policy makers. Now the Central as well as State Governments employ hundreds of men to conserve forests extensive areas are being replanted with trees, fire break, telephone systems, roads and lookout stations are being constructed and attempts are being made to eliminate insect pests and fungal diseases.

The clearing of forest has led to the extinction of several species of plants and animals as that of ferns, conifers, birds and mammals. In our country tigers, manned-lions and wild elephants are becoming extremely rare. Zoologists estimate that one species of mammal is becoming extinct every year some where in the world. Due to the importance of forests and wild life in the balance of nature most countries nowadays maintain wild areas designated as National Forests and National Parks where hunting and other similar activities, that interfere with animal life are banned.

BIOLOGY AND HEALTH

To live active and efficient life, it is absolutely necessary that we remain healthy and free from hazards of ill nutrition and diseases. In India average life expectancy is 41.2 years and there is maximum death rate due to several diseases like cholera, pneumonia, typhoid, tuberculosis etc. Twenty seven out of every one thousand children is born dead. We also find diseases due to ill nutrition on a large scale.

Life sciences have contributed a lot in the field of medicine as today we have several life saving drugs like antibiotics (penicillin, streptomycin, chloromycetin etc.) sulpha drugs, antiseptic surgery and blood : transfusions etc. We also know several vitamins and proteins that can be given to check deficiency diseases. But in our villages people still believe that diseases are caused by ghosts, witch craft and due to wrath of gods.

It becomes the duty of biologists and government personnel to educate people for sanitary habits and control of diseases and a scientific attitude towards their cause. In U.S.A and Denmark life expectancy is about 70 years and death rate has been reduced to one third. Trained biologists should be employed in sewage disposal and water supply departments and for checking food adult rations, so that health hazards in large cities can be avoided. Medical facilities should be extended to the villages and there should be education for the masses regarding sanitary habits and planned diet so that health of a large see-too of our population can be improved.

IMPROVEMENT OF PLANTS, ANIMALS AND MAN

There have been great advancements in genetics and plant breeding Hybridization and selection for disease, drought, frost resistance and for increased yield have become usual routine for agriculturists. The yield of maize, cotton, sugarcane, wheat, rice and of fruits and vegetables has nearly doubled since these practice were adopted. Breeding is a rearing process as newer high yielding varieties are in constant demand on the one hand and we need disease resistant varieties on the other, as strains of pathogens are developing constantly and one crop disease resistant today may fall victim to some pathogen tomorrow.

Induced mutations and cross breeding have also produced high milk, meat and egg yielding varieties of domestic animals. Genetists have employed sources like radiation and chemicals for induced mutations and inter species and intraspecies crosses are constantly, being tried

Like plants and animals we cannot improve human race by just-allowing healthier and intelligent people to produce children as it has social and legal implications. The science that deals with improvement of human race is called 'eugenics' and this has two approaches, positive and negative. Positive approach requires selected crosses and discourages the inferior ones. But in our social set-up it is not possible socially and legally. In negative approach, when it is expected that a child that will be born, has some disease or disorder, pregnancy termination is recommended.

BIOLOGY AND ATOMIC RADIATION

A very significant advancement in Physical Sciences during the 20th century has been exploitation of atomic energy. When this energy can be use for large scale generation of power and other economic purposes, it can also be used in preparation of Nuclear bombs which can explode in seconds and can destroy large cities like New York, Moscow and Calcutta in no time. Besides this destruction the radiation fall out is of more importance from biological point of view, as it causes genetic and physiological hazards in the organisms. In Japan deformed babies are still being born due to the effects of atomic explosions that took place in 2nd World War. There has been increase in radioactivity in our environment, since the nuclear tests were started. As experimental testing has been increasing radio-active pollution has increased. We find more radio-activity in organisms than ever before and it may reach the magnitude of affecting human race genetically and physiologically. Necessity or studying organisms in relation to radio activity has given out a new discipline-Radiation Biology.

RELATION TO SPACE TRAVEL

Today space travels are mainly employed for military purposes. It is thought that satellites and rockets can be used for communication, geophysical survey and fast travel. While in the space ships the human passengers face several difficulties like that of low pressure, high temperature, natural radioactivity, gravitational force, jerks, food and oxygen etc. Life science have contributed to overcome several of these difficulties. In order to avoid draining of blood in upper and lower part of the body during landing and take-off, people should lie parallel to the direction of flight so that heart may function normally. Pressurized cabines and pressure-suits are recommended for high altitudes. For high temperature and radioactivity, insulators are used. Compact food material and compressed oxygen is today used in space travels but attempts are going on to provide closed ecosystems in the spaceships in which algae like chlorella can recycle the human wastes and provide food and oxygen in the space.

Questions

1. Developments in the field of life-sciences education have affected National Policy making all over the world. Discuss.
2. Discuss the role of life-sciences in relation to
   (a) Conservation of wild life.
   (b) New resources of food.
   (c) Health programmes.
   (d) Atomic radiation.
   (e) Space travel.
3. How is Life-Science related to the lives of the people? Discuss with suitable examples.

8

CONCEPT OF TEACHING

What do we teach in Science? Why should we teach what we teach in Science? How should we teach Science? Why should we teach the way we teach Science? How should we evaluate that students have understood what we taught them. These are some very important points to be considered by those who are concerned with science teaching. They may be science teachers, educators, researchers and curriculum developers. This is what is usually taught in Science Method Courses.

BASIC PRINCIPLES

What we teach in science is 'content'. Now the question arises, *'what is science'*? Science is a way of describing and explaining some aspects of the world around us. To the extent that a lot of human effort has already been expended in developing such explanations, our students do not have to 'start from scratch'. A large and ever-increasing body of scientific knowledge already exists, and evidently part of the task as teacher is to pass on some of it to the students. But this is only part of the job, for science is also a package of processes by which we can increase our knowledge of external world. Teaching science implies involving our students in investigation, so that they become 'scientists for the day'. There are facts, theories, concepts and also a way of working, which together constitute 'the subject science.' Thus science is not just content. Science is content plus processes. This is dual nature of science.

Content. One of the things you will be doing as a science teacher is familiarising your pupils with theories, helping them to develop concepts and appreciate the structure which connects them. However, so extensive and powerful are these networks of concepts that there is a tendency never to put pupils in the position of scientists. Thus, pupils come to believe that science provides no opportunity for the expression of differences of opinion, for imagination and for creative work. They feel that there is no scope for personal contribution, that knowledge is embodied in the natural world waiting to be discovered and, once discovered, must be accepted without question. But scientist makes his own observations and deduces generalisations from them.

Content to be taught at a particular level should be carefully selected. It is a hard task. Scientific knowledge keeps on increasing. It doubles every decade. Our students are to keep pace with increasing scientific knowledge. We should teach them what they really need at a particular level. If it is more to be completed in a classroom in the allotted time, we should develop some techniques so that students could learn a part of content on their own outside the classroom.

Presentation of Content. 'What we teach' should be compatible with:

1. cognitive level of students,
2. identified objectives, and
3. existing classroom conditions.

The 'content' presented to the student should be such that he could understand it, and not just memorise. Learning is understanding, and not memorising. In every class there is some content in science, which most of the students memorise without understanding. Such content should not be included at that level, but shifted to a level where students can really understand it.

The content in the textbook should be presented in such a way that pupils like it. They take interest in it. Sometimes the content given in the syllabus is compatible to the cognitive level of pupils, but it is presented in the textbook in such a way that the pupils have difficulty to follow it. Therefore they do not like to read such textbooks. According to Professor Jack Carter of University of Colorado, USA and Director of B.S.C.S. Project (AISTA Silver Jubilee Conference, New Delhi, December 1981), "the content presented in our science textbooks is just like a scientific paper which is meant for those who are experts in science, rather than for those who are students in science."

Syllabi given by the education departments or education boards are usually outlines. Therefore different authors go to different depths for the same content when writing the textbooks. If our science syllabi are well defined in the form of 'objectives written in behavioural terms' the authors will know exactly what they are to write, students will know what they are to learn and teachers will know what they are to teach, and paper setters will know what is to be evaluated. All of them will be on the same track, and will not go astray.

Science Processes. The current innovations in schools emphasise the processes of science, the ways in which scientists advance their knowledge and solve problems. Science should be presented to pupils as a way in which they can conduct an inquiry into the nature of things as well as a body of information built by other people. In the past, the processes have been neglected, and school science has been concerned almost exclusively with the 'body of information, the concepts, principles and techniques developed by scientists; too rarely have pupils been made 'scientists for the day,' encouraged to become personally involved in solving problems, in discovering some science for themselves.

The teachers' guides of most recently developed school science programmes in United States and United Kingdom suggest ways in which pupils can become involved in scientific inquiry. They ask to follow the stages : Problem-Hypotheses—Experiment—Result, in solving problems. If you as a science teacher, are to engage your pupils in the processes of science, it is important that you should have thought carefully about what these processes are. The sequence of development of the thirteen science processes is as follows:

1	Observing	2	Classifying
3	Using numbers	4	Measuring
5	Using space-time relationships		
6	Communicating	7	Predicting
8	Infering	9	Defining operationally
10	Formulating hypotheses	11	Interpreting data
12	Controlling variables, and	13	Experimenting.

Nature of Science. Science is a broad based human enterprise that can be defined differently from different viewpoints The layman might define science as a body of scientific information, the scientist might view it as a method by which hypotheses are tested, a philosopher might regard science as a way of questioning the truthfulness of what we know, All these views are valid, but each presents only a partial definition of science, only collectively do they begin to define the comprehensive nature of science. Therefore, science should be viewed as a way of thinking in the persuit of understanding nature as a way of investigating claims about phyenomena and as a body of knowledge, that has resulted from inquiry.

Science as a Way of Thinking. Science is a human activity that can be characterized by the thinking that occurs in the minds of people who participate in it. The mental work of scientists illustrates human kind's curiosity and desire to understand phenomena. These individuals possess attitudes, beliefs, and values that motivate them to answer questions and solve problems. Scientists are driven by enormous curiosity imagination and reasoning in their quest to figure out and explain natural phenomena. Their work, as viewed by many philosophers of science and cognitive psychologists, is a creative activity whereby ideas and explanations are constructed.Therefore, the thinking and reasoning of scientists as they go about their work offer important causes regarding the nature of science belief. The tendency for scientists to find out seems to be motivated by their belief that a set of laws of nature can be constructed from observation and explained by thought and reasoning.

Science as a Way of Investigation. Science as a way investigation illustrates many approaches to constructing knowledge. Science has many methods which demonstrate human kind's investigation for seeking solutions to problems. Some of the approaches used by scientists rely heavily on observation and prediction as in astronomy and ecology other approaches rely on laboratory experiments that focus on cause and effect relationships such as those used in microbiology and other sciences. Among the many processes associated with science and inquiry as discussed above are observing, classifying, using numbers, measuring, using space-time relationships, communicating, predicting defining operationally, inferring, denning operationally, interpreting data, controlling variables, and experimenting.

Science as a Body of Knowledge (Product). The body of knowledge produced from the scientific disciplines represents the creative products of human invention that have occurred over the centuries. The enormous collection of ideas pertaining to the natural and physical world is organized into astronomy, biology, chemistry, geology, physics and so on. The result is a compilation of carefully catalogued information containing many types of knowledge, each of which makes its own unique contribution to science. The facts, concepts, principles, laws, hypotheses, theories, and models from the content of science. These ideas poses their own specific meaning, which cannot be understood apart from the processes of inquiry that produced them. The facts of science serve as the foundation for concepts, principles, and theories.

According to '*The Columbia Encyclopaedia*' (1963), "Science is an accumulated and systematized learning, in general uses restricted to natural phenomena. The progress of science is marked not only by an accumulation of facts, but by the emergence of scientific method and of the scientific attitude".

From the above definition three basic principles of the nature of science can be identified (1) an accumulated and systematized body of knowledge, (2) the scientific method of investigation, and (3) the scientific attitudes or ways of thinking. The first point indicates the product of science, while second and the third points indicate the process of science. In other words, Science is both a product and process.

Thus Science has a dual nature.

1. Content of science. 2. Process of science.

Why to Teach ?

It can be discussed into two parts:

(i) Why should we teach science?

(ii) Why should we teach what we teach in science at a particular class level?

Why Should We Teach Science? It is very unfortunate that we as science educators never practically think at 'why.' The principal goal of science education is to create men who are capable of doing new things, not simply of repeating what other generations have done – men who are creative, inventive and discoverers. If that is why we teach science, then how far our science education is compatible to achieve this goal?

METHODS OF TEACHING

The key to national prosperity lies in the effective combination of three factors – technology, raw materials and capital, of which perhaps the first one is the most important. Since the creation and adoption of new scientific techniques, technology can, in fact, make up a deficiency in natural resources and reduce the demands on capital. But technology can only grow out of the study of science and its applications. Technology serves man. It gives individuals and nations roots, a frame of reference, horizons, a world view and inner freedom. Science and technology are used to promote the establishment and furtherance of the community of man to the community of nations. We teach or learn science for a variety of reasons.

1. Science is fundamentally concerned with exploring and interpreting the physical world through the three fundamental areas of Physics, Chemistry and Biology. Physicists are concerned with the exploration of energy and general properties of inanimate materials, chemists with the particular properties of inanimate materials, and biologists explore the behaviour and properties of animate materials. The physical and biological world is of fundamental human interest and man has a basic

motivation to understand and control the physical world in which he has his being.

2. We live in a scientific and technological age and no citizen can function effectively in a developed society without a basic scientific literacy and certain elementary skills. Every citizen needs to live a healthy life with proper sanitation and clean surroundings. The knowledge and skills required by a modern householder in dealing with electrical, plumbing, and human first-aid may be cited as some justification for teaching science to all children in school.

3. We depend upon scientific knowledge and understanding for economic and material advancement. Science has provided so many aids for 'the good life' from bicycle to jet aircraft, antibiotics to heart surgery, radar to colour television, and fertilisers to plant growth harmones. Although we are beginning to realise many follies in the large-scale application of science and technology in terms of a net environmental damage, the fact is that we will need science again to rectify these follies (like application of science and technology in a better way which would not affect the environment adversely) and to enable more people to live on this planet in conditions which do greater justice to the dignity of man. The priority which the developing countries like India are giving to basic science education for public health and agriculture can clearly be seen.

4. Science cannot be used in society without a body of men and women who have been specially trained for science-based vocations in industry, research and teaching. A vocational justification is, therefore, possible for science teaching.

5. Science, if studied properly, develops power of thinking, reasoning, curiosity, open-mindedness, and ultimately develops scientific attitude or scientific temper. Thus science could be aimed as an instrument for social change towards a better society.

6. Professor Yashpal (1992) is of the opinion that, instead of considering science as an extraneous activity or as a tool for providing the means to a good life, usually borrowed from outside, we should treat it as a part of the culture of society, integral to our living and thinking and connected to the deepest questions we ask in regard to who we are and where we come from. Although, the tools that technology provides in the form of increased means of productive goods and services, means of communication and transport are important, but if we make science as a part of our culture, they would all come, much more naturally, more creatively and more in tune with our living.
7. Science is essential for helping us to comprehend and establish connections with the physical and biological world around us. It familiarizes students with the empirical modes of investigation. Understanding its conceptual structures and methodologies are an important part of an educated person. It can help in the development of intellectual skills and motor abilities like comprehension and application of understanding to new contexts and accurate observation of phenomena. Scientific knowledge not only influences our thinking about human, political and social affairs but also affects our thinking about ourselves. Its importance for arousing scientific curiousity and in developing scientific attitudes, as well as educating people for science based vocations in industry, research and training cannot be over-emphasized. The scientifically literate person has a knowledge base of facts, concepts, conceptual networks, and processes, which enable the individual to continue to learn throughout life.

Why Should We Teach What We Teach in Science at a Particular Class Level? Who decides what is to be taught in science at a particular class level *i.e.* science syllabus for various classes (I-V, VI-VIII, IX-X, XI-XII)? Perhaps those who never taught those classes. Science teachers who teach those classes are not empowered to make such decisions. Therefore some topics become too difficult to be understood by the children. It will be advisable that syllabus framers should also involve concerned science teachers when they frame science syllabus for various classes. Syllabus framers should be answerable, why they put this science content in the syllabus. They should objectively say, "We put this science content in the syllabus because children need it, children will understand it and children will enjoy it."

"To learn science is to do science, there is no other way of learning science," D.S. Kothari. This is how we should teach science. Do we actually do so?

Several methods of teaching science are taught in B.Ed. classes but what B.Ed. students mostly practise are 'lecture method' or lecture-cum-demonstration method' during their practice teaching. And so they usually use the same two methods when they become regular science teachers. They should practise all the methods which they learn in theory. Then they will be able to use what best fits in the actual classroom conditions.

Our science courses are mostly content-oriented. When content worship is becoming old fashioned in developed countries, our country is still behind it. Whenever the courses are updated more content is added. Courses become heavier and heavier while time allotted in the school time-table remains just about the same. Thus students are to cover much more content in comparatively much lesser time. Moreover classes are crowded and teachers are heavily loaded. Thus inspite of sufficiently available science equipment for experiments and demonstrations, content is covered by asking students to read books, or giving lectures to cover more content in lesser time without demonstrations and experiments.

Under such classroom conditions we are to devise some self-learning techniques in teaching science. Programmed Instruction is one such device. When Self-learning Modules, Programmed Instruction Materials in science or Adjunct Programmes on various science textbooks are used, students will be able to cover a part of the syllabus on their own, and teachers will get some time for individualised instruction. If one were to list expressions that best describe science education for the twenty-first century 'Individualised Instruction' certainly has to be included. The Programmed Instruction and Modular Approach are some of the efficient ways of providing individualised instruction. If our science teachers could have well-sequenced programmed materials and self-learning modules, it would be great help to them since they are heavily loaded. Also if the programmed materials and self-learning modules provided activities of 20-25 minutes duration, students would have more opportunity to do the experiments themselves, even in smaller periods.

Constructivism : A Dominant Perspective about How Children Learn Science. Constructivism is a general name given to the dominant perspective on learning and especially in science education. This approach of teaching learning is quite different from traditional views.

"I hear and I forget, I see and I remember, I do and I understand", must be a familiar phrase for you, but this phrase shows the intent of constructivism. Constructivism is not entirely new. Contemporary researchers from various countries have updated the theories and methods and synthesised several dominant perspectives on learning. This perspective is evolved from the research and theories of Piaget, Vygotsky, Bruner and philosophy of John Dewey. There is a consensus among many philosophers of science, psychologists, science educators, scientists and people concerned with the children's learning that learners must construct and reconstruct their own meaning of ideas about how the world works.

Joseph Novak (1986) defines constructivism as the notion that humans construct or build meaning into their ideas and experiences as a result of an effort to understand or make sense of them. According to Duckworth (1989), all people have their own understanding, one cannot make them believe anything unless they construct it by themselves.

There is no one constructivist theory of learning. Therefore students can be encouraged to learn by reinventing the wheel for themselves, so that the learner does the discovering by forming mental connections. The understanding or conceptual clarity is deeper and retention is greater. The teacher mediates the learning environment and thus plays an important role. The hands on activities in science, manipulative skills, process based learning share some common intentions with costructivism, which is becoming popular in education. The constructivist teacher must fulfill many roles, helping the learner to think critically and use information creatively to construct scientific ideas, concepts and largely function as a facilitator of knowledge construction in order to help the learner how to learn. This conceptual clarity through construction of knowledge is ultimately reflects through their attitudes. This should be the constructivist role of a teacher.

There are various methods of teaching science "When a particular method is to be used," is very important

In science there are some concepts and some skills "Temperature" is a concept, and "Measuring temperature or reading a thermometer," is a skill. 'Weight" is a concept and "Weighing by a spring balance, weighing machine, physical balance or chemical balance, ' is a skill. "Photosynthesis" is a concept, and "setting up and performing photosynthesis experiment," is a skill.

By researchers it has been found that concepts are best learned by Child Centred Approach (CCA), and skills are best learned by Teacher Centred Approach (TCA).

If you want to develop "creativity ' and "scientific temper," do not give them readymade answers, use "Scientific Method" or "Problem Solving Method". Similarly you can think of when a particular method of teaching science is to be used.

THE ASSESSMENT

During Teaching. When teaching science in a classroom, we ask some questions before we start the lesson. The answers of these questions give us some idea, whether the students have the previous knowledge or entry behaviours for the lesson. We ask some questions during the lesson and also encourage students to ask questions if they do not understand anything. Answers to such questions give us the idea whether the students are understanding what we are teaching them. We also ask some questions after the lesson, just to know whether students understand what we taught them in the lesson.

In Examination. Let us look at our examination system. If we analyse the examination questions very critically, we find mostly knowledge questions are asked and very little emphasis is given to comprehension, application and skill questions. Our examination questions should test all the objectives—cognitive, affective as well as psycho-motor. Clearly defined objectives help us in effective and objective evaluation. Therefore we should identify our objectives before-hand and state them very clearly. If our objective is just knowledge, we should not ask comprehension, application or skill questions; and if our objectives are knowledge, comprehension, application and skill, we should test all the objectives and not just the knowledge as it is usually the case. If our objective is 'to develop the skill of reading a thermometer, our test should be, 'Give a thermometer to the student and ask him to read, instead of how will you read a thermometer? Explain with the help of a diagram. Our education is examination-oriented. Though we identify several objectives but they are just on paper. We try to achieve only those objectives which are usually tested in examination. So our examination system has a big hand of providing quality science education to our children.

SCIENTIFIC ATTITUDE

Let us examine the present situation of science education in our country. First of all let us have a look at the objectives of science teaching as stated by Prof. B. Sharan of NCERT, which are as follows:

1. To make aware of those aspects of science that are environmental based and life centred.
2. To emphasise the scientific method which has helped in solving problems.
3. To train students in the use and maintenance of science equipment.
4. To make students creative.
5. To develop the mental faculty of open-mindedness.
6. To prepare children for change of life.

Now you can yourself examine, how far our existing science curricula, teaching methods and evaluation techniques are compatible to achieve these objectives.

The curricula have been drawn up and textbooks written by those who perhaps have never taught in schools. They have tried to compress in the textbooks, a variety of topics some of which have little utility or relevance. In spite of the Ishwarbhai Patel Committee on Curricula Reforms for the ten-year school submitted in 1977, the curricula have not been updated. Even the Minister of Education presiding over the annual general meeting of the NCERT on March 11, 1981 regretted that attempts at improving the quality of education in terms of upgrading curricula were not heartening.

One of the recommendations of the Education Commission under the chairmanship of Prof. D.S. Kothari (1964-66) was that science should be made a compulsory subject in school education. The recommendation was accepted and science was made compulsory upto class X in several states and Union Territories. 10+2 Education Scheme started in July 1975. Science courses at 10+2 stage were framed in a hurry and they were implemented without any try-out. When framing the courses, not many teachers who actually teach the students at this level were involved, and editorial boards were made of people from Universities and Institutes of Technology. Ishwarbhai Patel Committee for reviewing Class I-XII courses was asked to submit its report within two months' time. Therefore ad-hoc deletions were made. Sometimes diagrams were deleted while content related-to those diagrams remained.

In the old 3-years Higher Secondary Scheme (IX-XI) about one-third of students who were really interested in science used to take science in class IX. But now science is also a required course like other subjects upto class X. Therefore majority of the students (about two-thirds) who perhaps do not have the interest and aptitude for science have to take it. Now the question arises, must every student be forced to learn a subject for which he has no aptitude or a special science course be developed for such students so that they are also attracted toward learning science.

The former Prime Minister Morarji Desai, while addressing the members of the Review Committee on the curriculum for the ten-year school at New Delhi stated, "The books that I did carry in College are being carried by School students today. The students are burdened by how many books, I do not know." Knowledge of science almost doubles every decade. We are to keep pace with this new development. Then the problem is how much knowledge in science should be given to a child at a particular level, so that he is not burdened.

The goals and expectations of the science education change with time and with them the curriculum. Updating, revising, reorganising, or adopting science curricula are not sufficient to reduce the present state of fragmentation and narrowness, what is necessary is the design of science programmes for the-non-specialist, the common man.

The social imperatives of education and specially science education have recently been attributed new importance and urgency. The long-term social problems of : (1) environmental pollution, (2) food shortages, (3) limitations on available energy, and (4) expanding population demand, change the curriculum emphasis and modes of teaching. Students are not only to be informed about these social problems, they also need practice in making decisions, so that as adults they will be wiser in individual and collective decision-making. Since these social imperatives do not conform to the traditional academic boundaries of the sciences, or even of any subjects commonly taught in schools, new curricular patterns must be generated, developed, tested, and evaluated for evidence of effectiveness. Relevant research is needed not only in the development and testing of these new instructional materials, but more basic studies are required on the ways, means and amounts of various experiences which modify the attitudes and enhance decision making skills.

It is time that the country's intelligentsia, educational planners, educational administrators, educationists, politicians, teachers and parents should give some serious thought to what direction the country's education system should go, and what should be the place of science in the curriculum. They owe it to their children and to the future generations. The time seems to be ripe for a serious national debate on the 'future of science education' taking into a serious view of its past and present.

We always say that we should teach science in such a way that we are able to develop scientific attitude and scientific temper among our students. This remains our objective of teaching science. How far we are able to achieve this objective? What is scientific attitude? What is scientific temper? Is there any relation between these two? Can scientific method help us to develop scientific attitude and Scientific temper among our students?

Before talking about scientific attitude let us discuss what is attitude. Attitudes are mental state or individual outlook towards people, objects, events etc. Attitudes are developed and learned/ they are not inborn. Attitudes can be changed through experiences especially in children. They are the result of experiences.

Scientific attitude refers to an individual's outlook towards life. It means a willingness to adopt scientific approaches and procedures for resolving issues/ assessing ideas or information. Robert Ebel (1997)/ defines attitude as a mental condition/ a stabilized mental set which expresses itself in a tendency to react to any member of a class of stimuli in the same general way. Scientific attitude predisposes a person to engage in responsible action after weighing the possible consequences of alternative options/ using rational arguments based on evidence. She distinguishes between scientific evidence and personal opinion and between reliable and unreliable information, remains open to new evidence and the tentativeness of scientific knowledge and recognizes that science and technology are human endeavours. Some other manifestations of the scientific attitude are/ questioning/ suspension of judgement, appraisal of different sides of an issue, verification of knowledge, curiousity and appreciation of the natural and human-made world, open mindedness/ intellectual honestly/ cooperation and tolerance of the point of view of other people.

The complex interactions of science with society need to be understood by individuals and applied in everday decision making. For improving the quality of life through economic and material development/ we depend on the knowledge of science. Developments in science have prepared the way for a more effective/ practical mastery of the environment and the technological innovations in agriculture, industry and medicine have produced transformations in traditional patterns of social living. In the words of Indira Gandhi (1982). "Science has not only radically altered man's material environment/ but what is of still deeper significance/ if has provided new tools of thought and has extended man's mental horizons. It has thus influenced even the basic values of life/ and has given to civilization a new vitality and dynamism".

Scientific attitude or Scientific temper

1. open-mindedness

2. objective decision making
3. critical thinking
4. not believing what other people say unless convinced what is being said is correct
5. desire for accurate knowledge
6. confidence in procedures in seeking knowledge
7. expectation that the solution of the problem will come through the use of verified knowledge
8. using scientific method (problem, hypotheses, experiment, conclusion) in decision making

Recognising a person having scientific attitude (Scientific Temper) through the following episode in which there are four main characters – principal science consultant physics teacher and science students

A Science Consultant went to a school. As soon as he entered the Principal's office, Principal requested him to go to Ms X Physics class as she does not do anything and we have lot of complaints against her. The Science Consultant went to her class and observed her lesson. Here are his remarks "The teacher was teaching waves by lecture-demonstration method. She was demonstrating longitudinal and transverse waves, crests and troughs, rarefaction and condensation, nodes and antinodes, frequency and wave length with the help of a SLINKY. It was a very lively class. Students were really enjoying and participating. There was very healthy teacher learner interaction in the class. Questions between and after the lesson were thought-provoking. Homework copies and practical notebooks were checked up to date. The physics lab was well set for the day practical work. "The Principal was shocked to listen to these comments She spoke to the Science Consultant, "Are you sure, these are your comments." "Yes, these are my comments. She is an outstanding physics teacher. How did you know that she does not do anything. Who was complaining against her, the science consultant asked. Some teachers were telling, the Principal replied "Do not believe what others are saying, unless you are convinced that what they are saying is correct," the Science Consultant advised the Principal.

1. Who has scientific temper – Principal or Science Consultant ? Justify your answer
2. Do all science teachers have scientific temper ?
3. Do you have scientific temper?
4. Do non-science teachers also have scientific temper?
5. Do science or non science principals have scientific temper?
6. Do scientists have scientific temper?
7. Do non scientists have scientific temper?
8. What is scientific temper?
9. How will you recognise whether a certain person has scientific temper?
10. Does she have (a) scientific attitude (b) scientific temper?
11. Which of the above characteristics show that she has : (a) scientific attitude, (b) scientific temper?
12. Do you find any difference between scientific attitude and scientific temper? IV. How to develop scientific attitude or scientific temper?

Try for the following:

(i) satisfaction of curiosity.

(ii) to get rid of superstitions.

(iii) proper way of teaching with no ready-made answers.

(iv) utilising co-curricular activities like working on investigatory science projects

(v) open classroom environment.

(vi) inspiring for the study of scientific literature.

(vii) encouraging day to day problems by scientific method.

(viii) develop in students well defined abilities such as the : (a) spirit of inquiry, (b) creativity, (c) objectivity, (d) courage to question, (c) problem solving and decision making skills.

(ix) self example by the teacher.

Answer the Following Questions

(a) Will these help in developing scientific attitude or scientific temper ?

(b) Which of these are not needed in developing scientific attitude or scientific temper

(c) What more will you like to add for developing scientific attitude or scientific temper

(d) Are the answers of these questions same or different for scientific attitude and scientific temper? Justify your answer.

A 15-year old boy Saurav ended his life in East Delhi's Nirman Vihar on Sunday night (February 16, 1997) fearing failure in the forthcoming CBSE Class X Examinations. (*The Times of India*, February 18,1997)

Rahul (Bombay) was punished for not studying regularly. At times, he was made to stand in the bitter cold outside his house. Fed up by his parent's expectations and fearing that he would fail in the Class XII Examinations he committed suicide.

On February 13,1997, 21-year old Chemistry student, Mousumi (Bombay) was found hanging in her hostel room. She was afraid she would not get a first class. Her academic record was very good. She committed suicide due to fear.

"I am tired and frustrated with life as I have to study all the time," were the last words of 16-year old Chandrakant (Bombay). Tired of studying by rote, he immolated himself and died of burn injuries in hospital in February 1997.

Saurav, Rahul, Mousumi and Chandrakant are not alone. A good number of students throughout the country end their lives after not performing well as expected in examinations.

Some educationists feel parental and peer pressure, more than school syllabi, put unfair pressure on students. Air Force Bal Bharti School New Delhi, Principal K.K. Mohindroo blamed it on parental and peer pressures. "Parents want their children to score above 90 per cent in all subjects (Physics, Chemistry, Biology, Maths). This, at times, makes students panicky," said Mr. Mohindroo. Delhi Public School R.K. Puram New Delhi Principal Shyama Chona, too had similar views. "The class X (science and other subjects syllabus) is minimal. It is mainly parental and peer pressure which affects the students," said Ms. Chona.

School authorities blame parents for putting undue pressure on children to excel, and parents hold schools and school education boards for the inability of wards to cope with syllabi.

It is time the school education boards revamp the existing system and base it on the three H's of education-head, heart and hands. We need to tackle this issue seriously so as to bring back the simple joys of going to school and to strengthen the bonds between the teacher and the taught. When the syllabus is prescribed by NCERT and various school education boards, not much consideration is given to how much a student of a particular age-group can comprehend and apply.

Many of our students are first generation learners, hence their parents are not able to give any help at all. Many parents put their children in English-medium schools even though they have no such background, and the subjects taught become too difficult for them to understand. The teacher is weighed down by quantity, not quality. The poor child is the silent sufferer-sometimes he breaks down, sometimes he gives up and sometimes he ends his life.

Delhi University educationist Krishna Kumar felt public school students were more vulnerable to pressures. "Prestige is an obsession with most elite public schools. Students are subjected to inhuman pressure. This sometimes takes its toll," said Mr. Kumar. Mr. Kumar felt syllabi were another culprit. "The Yashpal Committee suggested major changes, particularly in science and mathematics. The overall situation could have been much better if the recommendations were implemented," he added.

Parents and Teachers Associations should be empowered and sit down to discuss those problems and put pressures on School Education Boards, NCERT and SCERTs to do some rethinking.

NEW TRENDS

Now Science is for all upto Class X. Then what type of science curriculum our children need to be functionally literate, as well as achieve optimally in science. Several children, parents, teachers, principals and administrators were interviewed. Here are some suggestions for restructuring school science curriculum at all levels.

(i) For children to do well in science, we need to identify the basics in science. Once the basics have been chosen and implemented, children will have key facts, concepts, and generalisations to achieve. Teaching science will be more professional once the basics have been identified. A sower (the science teacher) that goes out to sow will then reap not ten nor twenty fold, but hundred fold. Why so? Time spent in teaching science will be spent on the relevant basics, and not upon the irrelevant.

(ii) Basics are to be stated in measurable terms. There is no reason for keeping the children in the dark as to what they are to learn. Measurably stated objectives, announced clearly to children, will assist them to achieve as much as possible. Children achieve poorly in science if the evaluation techniques are not matched with the precise objectives.

(iii) Science instruction should be based on the interests of children. Good science teachers find out what children are interested in, and bring these interests into each lesson. Good training (pre-service and in-service) makes good science teachers. Good science teachers make good science students. If these good science students are permitted to give their input into the science curriculum, they will bring many many items of science to make science interesting.

(iv) Research data indicates how important parents are in helping their children learn. If parents assist their children in learning, achievement continues to rise. Teachers, administrators and parents should learn to work cooperatively to increase children's achievement in science. There would be some parents whose input might be taken into the science curriculum.

(v) We need to stimulate children to identify and solve problems within the science curriculum. Subject matter may become outdated due to new research findings in science, but problem solving is always to stay. We should not focus so much on the content of science, but on processes of science.

(vi) In the past the slow learners received an inferior science education. Science teachers should be trained to identify slow learners and teach them science in such a way that they also enjoy science like normal children.

Now we entered twenty-first century. What types of Teaching of Science Courses we are going to have? It all depends upon what type of "Science Education" we will have in Twenty-first century. Let us study the existing Teaching of Science Courses, so that they could accordingly be revised for the Twenty-first Century.

Teaching of Science Courses for Universities. At present there are different Teaching of Science Courses, in various universities of the country. As a sample few of them are given here for study (Appendix F).

I Syllabus Outline for Science Method Course

II Syllabus Outline for Integrated Science Method Course

III Syllabus Outline for Secondary Physics Method Course

IV Syllabus Outline for Senior Secondary Physics Method Course

V Syllabus Outline for Secondary Chemistry Method Course

VI Syllabus Outline for Senior Secondary Chemistry Method Course

VII Syllabus Outline for Secondary Biology Method Course

VIII Syllabus Outline for Senior Secondary Biology Method Course.

IX B. El. Ed. (4 years) Science Course

Syllabus Outline for Science Method Course

Paper – 1. Natural Science

Paper – 2. Pedagogy of Environmental Studies

Paper – 3. Pedagogy of Natural Science

Syllabus Outline for Science Content Course

Paper – 4. Physics I

Paper – 5. Physics II

Paper – 6. Chemistry I

Paper—7. Chemistry II

Paper—8. Biology I

Paper—9. Biology II

Teaching of Science Course for **DIETs.** In some universities Teaching of EVS (science) course is also introduced. This course is for teaching at primary (I-V) level. The syllabus for this course is given in Appendix-B "How to Use This Book in DIETs?" One District Institute of Education and Training (DIET) is to be started in each district of the country. So far (1997) 425 DIETs have been established. These are coming up since 1988-89. NCERT has developed 2 years Elementary Teacher Education Diploma Course for Pre-service Teacher Education (PSTE) students of the DIETs. In 1st year they are trained to teach primary classes (I-V). NCERT developed DIETs syllabus includes a good Teaching of EVS (science) course (Appendix—B). This may be adopted or adapted by universities if they introduce this course at B.Ed. level.

In 2nd year DIETs' PSTE students are trained to teach upper primary or middle classes (VI-VIII). NCERT syllabus for DIETs also includes a good Teaching of Integrated Science Course (Appendix B). This course may be compared with "Syllabus Outline for Integrated Science Method Course (Appendix-F II)/' and adopted or adapted by universities when they introduce this course at B.Ed. level.

PROBLEMS AHEAD

Science Teaching today is not so simple as it was in early fifties. But even in those days use of audio-visual aids was quite common, though students and parents were not as demanding as they are now. In those days there was not so much competition, there was not so much load on students, and therefore there was no need of rote memorisation. Now with the loaded curriculum students cannot escape the drudgery of mugging textbooks and learning without tears and fears. Now in the existing school and classroom conditions Science Teaching is a Challange, which a science teacher alone is to face, but he cannot do much unless he has support from the Principal, Education Officers, SCERTs, IASEs, School Education Boards, DIETs, Parents as well as NCERT, NIEPA and NCTE.

Some Teachers, Students, Parents, Principals, Education Officers, and school Managers were interviewed. What they feel about Today's Science Teaching – A Challenge, is given below.

1. We should have 24-30 periods a week with no substitution periods so that we could get enough time for planning, evaluating copies, preparing demonstrations and experiments.
2. Well-equipped Science Labs, with enough audio-visual aids for demonstrations and experiments.
3. Lessons to be observed and necessary guidance be given for better science teaching.
4. Giving some demonstration lessons with up-to-date educational technology.
5. To be trained in the latest techniques of teaching science and in new science content enrichment (pre-service and in-service).
6. To be trained in continuous and comprehensive evaluation.
7. Qualified and well trained Lab. Assistants.
8. Good science teaching, every difficulty to be removed in the class, teachers should not proceed further unless all students understand, to avoid private tutions, so that we could have good marks in X and XII to get admission in higher studies.
9. Less homework, more work in school.
10. Less Course, useless course to be removed.
11. Two Science Courses in X-B-Course for those who will not take science in XI-XII; A-Course for those who will take science in XI-XII; A-Course should cover all Entry Behaviours for XI-XII Science (Physics, Chemistry, Biology).
12. Coordination in Theory and Practical, not as we have now – Theory in IX and Practical in XII.
13. Less Extra Classes, in Extra Classes only Remedial and Enrichment Work, Courses to be completed in regular classes.

14. Maximum and Effective use of Audio-Visual Aids, Hardwares and Softwares in Science Teaching, Science Teaching should be Activity Based—Demonstrations, Experiments, Field Trips, Investigatory Science Projects.
15. Use of computers to teach some portion of Physics, Chemistry and Biology.
16. Use of Self-Learning Multimedia Packages-printed, audio, video, audio-video, computers.
17. Make Science Teaching enjoyable at least less Boring.
18. Good Teaching-No Need of Private Tutions.
19. Remedial and Enrichment Extra Classes.
20. Excellent Results in X and XII to get admission in higher studies without outside coaching.
21. Intensive Training in Educational Administration, Planning and Management—Pre-service and In-service.
22. Needed support and guidance from officers of education departments.
23. Science Textbooks should be tried out and revised before implementation—Formative Evaluation Before Summative Evaluation.
24. Officers of education departments should also be given proper training to guide and supervise the work of Teachers and Principals, and give some concrete suggestions for improvement of science teaching.
25. Science supervisors of education departments to be very active for giving proper guidance to Science Teachers for quality science Education and good science results.

ROLE OF ADMINISTRATION

1. All teachers should teach and all students should study.
2. 100 per cent results with All First Divisions and Distinctions.
3. Effective use of Audio-Visual Aids and Educational Technology.
4. Use of computers in Learning Science.

5. B.Ed. Courses should be restructured to enable science teachers to teach science very effectively in existing classroom and school conditions, one science teacher should be able to teach full science upto class X.
6. Timely Need-Based and Effective In-service Training of Science Teachers to enable the teachers to teach science very effectively to give good results.

All these issues are to be very seriously taken up by concerned people and agencies to face the challenge in Science Teaching.

(i) Science Teaching is to be made participatory, joyful and relevant for all type of students.

(ii) Environmental Approach is to be used in science teaching like Science Through Kitchen, Exploring Our Body, Science Experiments using Low Cost Teaching Aids prepared by the Material Available in the Environment.

(iii) Students are to learn science by observing, experimenting and participating.

(iv) Home is to be used as Science Lab.

(v) Scientific Method is to be used in Science Teaching to develop Scientific Temper which is a Basic need for survival Today.

Education Policies come and go, but it looks that our children still are to follow the education system invented by Macaulay, and they are to mug up so many things, without understanding. This has become a painful experience for our children. "There is no joy in mugging. Joy lies in understanding, in finding out things on our own" Professor Yashpal. If we link education of a child with his immediate environment, then education will no more be a burden on the child, and the child will be encouraged to create his own knowledge. There is no dearth of resources, human or material in our country. If we are ready to face the challenge, nothing is impossible. When there is a will there is a way, with the right will we can make education and science education more relevant and enjoyable for our children. This is also a challenge for our science teachers. They can do and make others do. Then our Schools will be joyful places for Learning Science. If Children are taught in a Joyful manner, they will leam faster and retain much more.

"It is our solemn duty to do what the children want us to do. Children are a challenge to policy makers and the challenge has to be recognised and accepted" Arjun Singh, says the former Minister of mhrd. Let's make his dream true.

Questions

1. What is the place of : (a) Science, (b) Physics, (c) Chemistry, and (d) Biology in school curriculum? Discuss.
2. What should we teach in science – content, processes or both? Discuss with due importance and reasoning.
3. "To learn science is to do science, there is no other way of learning science." Discuss taking into consideration the existing classroom conditions.
4. How science is being taught in our schools? Are you satisfied with the way it is being taught? If not, discuss how it should be taught in the prevailing classroom conditions?
5. How should we evaluate whether students have learned what we have taught them in science?
6. Discuss the present situation of science education in our country. How can we have better science education programmes for our schools?
7. Describe nature of science at school level.
8. (a) Why should we teach science?
   (b) Why should we teach what we teach in science at a particular class level?
9. (a) How should we teach science?
   (b) Why should we teach the way we teach science?
10. (a) What is scientific attitude?
    (b) What is scientific temper?
    (c) What is the difference between scientific attitude and scientific temper?
    (d) What are the characteristics of a person having scientific temper?

(e) How will you recognise that a particular person has scientific temper?

(f) How will you develop scientific temper among your students?

(g) What is scientific method? How is it related with scientific temper?

11. "Our students are frustrated with the existing science courses and the examination system." How far do you agree with the statement? Justify your answer.

12. How can we restructure the existing science courses so that learning science may be a joyful experience for our students?

9

TEACHER'S GROWTH

The beginning life sciences teacher should be concerned with how he can keep himself in touch with the new developments in the subject matter and teaching methods of life sciences. Professional growth of a teacher requires that he should continue to learn throughout his profession. A teacher should feel responsible to find the best way to permit his growth professionally. Participation in in-service training workshops, getting enrolled for higher studies and attending professional meetings are some of the activities which help a teacher to keep himself aware of new developments in his field.

SOME ACTIVITIES

Activities in the School : Certain in-service courses can be offered to aquaint the teachers with new approaches and methods such as D.S.C.S. biology and the new curriculum developed by N.C.E.R.T. (India). These courses can be of varying duration after school hours. Some University course can be taught in the school premises by some university teacher Science teacher's club activities may also involve meetings to improve curriculum, sharing thoughts on methods of teaching sequencing the content, activities resources and scope or-the courses. Seminars can be orgnized on particular topics like co-curricular activities, techniques of teaching evaluation and life sciences curriculum improvement.

Some other activities like exhibitions, experimental projects, demonstration lessons and extension lectures etc. can be organized in the school. Life sciences teacher from various schools of a district or state can assemble at two or three times in a year to discuss various problems and share their experiences on methods, material curricular activities and evaluation. Local problems can be discussed and solved.

Higher Studies : Many school systems require their teacher to enter further studies. Government Education Departments send their teachers for in-service training and research work. It is seen that several school teachers are either registered for research work or doing post graduate studies in the field of education of in other subjects. In India N.C.E.R.T. and other institutions organize refresher courses for professional growth of the teachers. Recently U.G.C. has devised a scheme of "teacher fellowship" under which college teachers can under take research work with full pay plus fellowship with leave for the duration he pursues research work. School teachers are also allowed leave if they desire to undergo some training or undertake further studies in the field related to his profession but some more facilities are needed in this direction.

In-service Training : The Directorate of Extension Programmes for Secondary Education has been organizing a large number or in-service, programmes for working teachers. The in-service programmes lesson planning and evaluation etc. Several extension centres also organize workshops to aquaint teachers with the implications of the revised syllabi introduced in their states. Workshops include certain courses that are conducted by qualified teachers or university personnel. They involve more active participation on the part of individuals who are enrolled. Generally a workshop is centered around a particular theme like curriculum construction planning for teaching and construction of tests. All this has brought a keener awareness along science teachers about the new concepts and techniques in science teaching. Government of India also has a science teachers' exchange programme in order to pool their abroad experiences in the field of science education.

Summer Institute is a programme of in-service training of school teachers for a period of 4-(weeks, sponsored jointly by N.C.E.R.T., the U.G.C. and U.S.A.I.D. The teachers attending these institutions learn new way of teaching science that leads students to discover things. In 1965 we had 43 such institutes out of which 8 were devoted to biology. Upto 1966-76 biology teachers had been benefited by this programme.

Professional Organization : In a democratic set-up, professional personnel are allowed to have associations and the teachers also have several associations at state an national level. In India only a few associations of teachers have their ethical codes published and these are least concerned with the improvement in educational standards.

Teacher associations can publish various magazines, bulletins and pamplets that can contribute to improve the status of teaching in different subjects. Some other activities that can be organized by teacher associations are meetings, lectures, reading of papers, round table discussions, demonstration of techniques and material and pooling of the experiences of teachers.

Most of the teacher associations in India only stress on facilities and pay scales. The associations hold their meetings only to agitate against the administrations either for their self interests or to meet some political end.

Writing for Professional Growth : writing is an important means of continuing professional growth for the life sciences teacher. By this he can improve his ability to communicate and express his ideas. The teacher can write about his classroom experiences and techniques and methods developed by him. He can also contribute his views about curriculum, methods of evaluation etc. The teachers can also contribute his articles and reports of the projects undertaken by him, to some journal or magazine and that may bring him name. By this the teacher may also subscribe to one or two journals and this will keep him in touch with the-views of others.

Other Means of Professional Growth : There can be several other means of professional growth as contact with other teachers, travel and visits, science hobbies, research and readings. A new teacher-when he comes in contact with other teachers learns a lot of intricacies about the profession. These contacts may be through visits, conferences and meetings. Beginning teachers should also observe experienced teachers in action. Where travel provides relaxation and pleasure, it also helps in gathering information, experience and material that may help the teacher in his classroom teaching; visits of a life sciences teacher to fields, museums, aquaria, gardens, exhibitions and Industries give him a practical knowledge of organisms.

A life sciences teacher may have interest in insect collection or bird , watching as hobby. Such hobbies not only help to enrich the curricular activities but also stimulate pupils interest in undertaking certain projects when they see their teacher actively interested in his hobbies.

Life sciences teacher may specialize in a particular branch of this field, biology, education or psychology and undertake research work in the field of working. This will add to the existing stock of knowledge and professional status of the teacher. Readings also contribute a lot to professional growth of a teacher. The life sciences teacher should contribute to one or two famous periodicals of his subject in order to keep himself in touch with the new developments in his field.

To summarize we can say that the following activities contribute to the professional growth of a life sciences teacher :

(a) Membership of a professionals organization.

(b) Attending in service institute, workshops, district or state sponsored school programmes to provide experience in using new material and equipments.

(c) Involvement in trial use and evaluation of new material methods and text books.

(d) Higher study at colleges of universities.

(e) Participation in job experience programmes and research work in college, university, industrial laboratory, public or private agency.

(f) Contribution to some famous journals and writing in the field of life sciences education.

(g) Field trips and visits to places of biological importance.

INSTRUCTIONAL MATERIAL

Life sciences teacher should contribute to some journals and periodicals. He should be aquainted with some important literature related to his field and some sources of instructional material. Given ahead are some suggeston journals, periodicals, books and instructional material that may help the teacher in his classroom instruction and professional growth.

JOURNALS

Indian

(a) Every day Science.
(b) Junior Scientist.
(c) Science Reporter.
(d) Science Today.
(e) Vipan Lot.
(f) Vigyan Pragati.
(g) World Science News.
(h) Journal of Indian Education (N.C.E.R.T.)
(i) Indian Educational Review (N.C.E.R.T.).
(j) School Science (N.C.E.R.T.).
(k) Vigyan Shikshak (A.I.S.T.A.).
(l) Primary Teacher (N.C.E.R.T.).

Foreign

(a) Bio-Science.
(b) Nature.
(c) Natural History.
(d) Scientific American.
(e) American Biology Teacher.
(f) Biology Teacher.
(g) Journal of Research in Science Education.
(h) The Science Teacher.

(i) Journal of Biological Education.

(j) Science Education.

BOOKS

1. Biological Science : Molecules to Man. B.S.C.S. (Blue version) Houghton Mifflin Boston 1968.
2. High School Biology, B.S.C.S. Rand Me Nally &; Co. Chicago 1968.
3. Biological Science :. An Inquiry into Life. B.S.C.S. (Yellow version). Harcourt Brace Jovanovich Inc. New York 1968.
4. Biological Science, Interaction of Experiments and Ideas: Prentice-Hall Inc. Englewood Cliff, New Jersey.

Questions

1. What is the need of professional growth of a life-sciences teacher? Discuss the ways and means of professional growth of a life-sciences teacher.
2. Discuss the role of journals and instructional material that can contribute to the professional growth of a life-sciences teacher. List some of the journals, books and instructional material.
3. Write short notes on the following:
   (a) Supplementary reading material in life sciences.
   (b) Professional growth of life-sciences teacher.

10

TEACHING PLAN

Lesson plan is a teacher's own guide to control the teaching learning process under the conditions he finds himself in. Lesson plans differ from teacher to teacher but the teachers should be able to frame lesson plans which provoke productive thought and action among the, students.

A unit is a group of lesson plans that cover a particular topic and that is to be taught in a specified time. The name lesson plan is generally used for daily lessons but unit planning involves deciding upon the unit or a complete topic that is to be taught in a week or so and this is done by daily lesson plans.

THE IMPORTANCE

We plan for lessons because this is important according to the following considerations :

(1) We can present the subject matter in a logical, systematic and organized way keeping in view the intellectual development of the students.

(2) We can obtain adequate subject matter for teaching in order to achieve the aims and objectives of teaching the subject.

(3) The number, type and the time to use teaching aids, is decided in advance and confusion about their use during teaching is avoided.

(4) A writen lesson plan provides a feeling of security, especially for the unexperienced teachers.

(5) Lesson planning also helps the teacher in recapitulation, evaluation of his teaching and knowing about the effectiveness of presentation of the subject matter to the class.

(6) Planning lessons for a unit teaching presents the unit in a systematic and clear way and that helps sequential development of concepts in the students.

CRITERIA FOR SELECTING A LESSON

The lessons that are planned for teaching in the class should

(a) fulfil the objectives of teaching that lesson,

(b) suit the age, intelligence, aptitude, social development and interests of the students,

(c) induce activity and critical thinking among the students,

(d) be of the nature that it can be taught by utilizing local or school resources,

(e) be presented in ascending order of difficulty and involve learning from concrete to abstract as far as possible.

PLANNING THE LESSON

When writing a lesson, it is better for the teacher to divide it into certain parts and each part adequately stressed. Generally we divide the lessons into the following parts :

Preliminary Information: This part includes information about the lesson such as subject, unit, lesson class, date, number of students, duration, average age of the students and the name of the school etc.

Aims and Objectives: Here the teacher furnishes statements regarding the aims and objectives of teaching that lesson to the class. These can be divided into two parts such as

(i) General aims

(ii) Specific aims.

Teaching Aids: The teacher, in this part, writes the aids he will be using during the presentation of the lesson to the class. Teaching aids can also be divided into two categories such as

(i) General aids and

(ii) specific aids.

The general teaching aids include the things like chalk, black board and pointer etc., that are commonly used during teaching, but the specific aids include charts, models, specimens or glass wares and instruments that are required while teaching that particular lesson only.

Previous Knowledge Testing: When the teacher goes to the class to teach something, he always has a mind, or expects, that the students have knowledge in that discipline upto a particular extent. In this part of the lesson he furnishes statements about what he expect tne students to know *(Assumed Previous Knowledge)* and for satisfying himself about the level of knowledge on the part of students he puts certain question to the class *(Previous Knowledge Testing)*. In the beginning the teacher should ask general questions and later he should direct his questions towards the particular topic that is to be discussed in the class.

Introduction: After testing the level acknowledge possessed by the students the teacher asks certain questions related to the daily life activities of the students and later some questions related to the topic that he wishes to teach. Some questions may be even from the content of the topic. When the students are not able to answer some questions from the content of the topic or related to that, or the answers are not clear, or only a few students answer the questions, the teacher announces the topic to be taught that way. So this part of the plan includes the questions that the teacher puts to the class and a statement for announcement of the topic.

Presentation: In this part of the lesson the teacher writes the actual subject matter that he wants to teach. The subject matter is written in organized systematic and logically coherent manner. Generally presentation of the topic is divided into three parts.

(a) Method of Teaching, which includes questions the teacher puts to the class from time to time during the presentation of the subject matter and the activities that the teacher undertakes before the class.

(b) Matter to be taught, includes the total subject matter that the teacher gives in answer to the questions he puts and that is inferred from the activities, the teacher undertakes.

(c) Black Board Work includes the work, to be done by the teacher, on the black board and this may include writing of difficult terms, definitions, generalizations and drawing of certain diagrams. The order of presentation of questions and activities come under ,the heading Method of Teaching, so this part needs special consideration. It is not always necessary that presentation should be divided into three parts sometimes. Only two parts Methods and Activities and Black Board Work can serve the purpose as is done in Mathematics classes.

Generalizations : After the lesson is over the teacher generalizes his topic. He makes one or two statements that summarize the whole topic that the teacher taught that day. Suppose the teacher gave demonstrations to show that water, light, chlorophyll and carbon dioxide take part in the process of photosynthesis and starch and oxygen are the end products. At the end he may generalize. "In the process of photosynthesis chlorophyll, utilizing water, carbon dioxide and light, synthesizes food and oxygen is released."

Applications: This part of the lesson includes some statements about the applications of the generalizations or principles that the teacher had taught. Application of the biological knowledge can be in further learning, in explaining other biological phenomena or in solving the problems which the students come across in their daily life.

Recapitulation: After the lesson is over the teacher asks some questions in order to know how far the students are able to recollect the things or whether they have understood the subject matter or not. In this part of the lesson the teacher writes those questions that he will be putting to the class after he finishes his lesson. The questions should be representative of the whole subject matter taught and these should be well structured and organized.

Self Evaluation: After the lesson or the unit is over, the teacher can give a class test in order to evaluate the way he organizes and presents the subject matter to the class but this does not essentially make a part of the lesson plan.

SPECIMEN LESSON PLANS

LESSON PLAN I

(Parts of a Flower)

Method of Teaching: Lecture Demonstration Method Name or Roll No of the P.T. :

Subject : Life Science **Class:**VI

Unit : Reproduction in Angiosperms. **Section :** A

Topic: Parts of a flower **No. of students :** 30

Duration:45 minutes

Average age of students : 11 +yrs.

Name of the School : Govt. Sr. Sec. School, Kurukshetra.

General

(1) To develop scientific method of working and scientific attitude in the students.

(2) To give knowledge of biological things to the students.

(3) To develop interest of students in natural things.

(4) To develop skills in handling of apparatus and manul observations.

Specific : To give students the knowledge of parts of typical flower and their importance;

Teaching Aids

(a) General : Blackboard chalk, duster and pointer.

(b) Specific : Flowers of China Rose and Mustard or of Gulmohur, slides, microscope, needles, watch glasses petri dishes and a chart showing parts of typical flower.

Previous Knowledge (Assumed)

Students know some plants by names and their different parts. They also know certain flowers for their colour and smell.

Presentation

Method	*Material*	*Black Board Work*
What is a flower? (Now the flowers are distributed among the students)	Flower is the modified part of shoot and is meant for sexual reproduction	Flower is the modified part shoot which is meant for sexual reprodution in plant.
With which part is the flower attached to stem?	Pedicel :	Pedicel (Thalamus) The flower is attached to the stem with the help of a stalk called pedicel. The uppermost part of the pedicel is somewhat flattened (thalamus) on which different parts of the flower are attached.
Display the chart	Calyx : (showing the outermost whorl of the flower). What is the part of the flower called?	Calyx. The outer most whorl of the flower is called calyx. It is generally green in colour and protects the flower at bud stage.

Contd.

Method	*Material*	*Black Board Work*
What is one member of the calyx called?	Sepal : Single member of the calyx is calledsepal.	Sepal (Draw a diagram of Calyx with pedicel) Sepals may be free or jointed. Number of sepals may differ from plant to plant.
	(Showing the second whorl in the flower) What is this part of the flower?	Corolla : The second Corolla whorl of the flower is called corolla. It is gererally colorued and attractive. Corolla attracts insects which help the plants in their sexual reproduction.
What is one member	Petal : Single member of of the corolla called?	Petal (Draw diagram of the the corolla is called petal corolla.) The mumber of petals may vary from plant to plant. may also be free or jointed. The shape of the flower is generally determind by the petals.

Contd.

Method	*Material*	*Black Board Work*
(Showing the third whorl of the flower and asking them to look it in their flowers)	Androecium : The third whorl of the flower is called androecium. One member of the androecium is called stamen. The stamens may What is the third whorl of the flower called? What is the name of single member of androecium? What are different parts of a stamen? (Show some pollen grains)	Androecium, Stamens, stamens, Fillament, Anther lobes connective, Pollen grains. (Draw labelled diagram of a stamen and draw some be free or jointed and their pollen grains.) number also differs from plant to plant. Each stamen can further be divided into filament, anther lobes connective. The anther lobes are connected together with the help of connective and these in turn are connected to the thalamus with the help of filament. The anther lobes contain pollen gratns which take part in the sexual reproduction. Androecium makes the male part in the flower.

Contd.

Method	*Material*	*Black Board Work*
(Showing the central part of the flower) What do we call this part of the flower? What is one member of gynaecium called? What is the structure of a carpel? (Show a section of ovary undrr dissectingh microscoper).	Gynaecium : The fourth or central whorl in the flower is called gynaecium. One member of the gynaecium is called carpel. The carpels may be jointed or free or there may be only one carpel in the flower. The number of carpels also differs from plant to plant. A carpel has three parts, the uppermost is called stigme, middle one, tubular is called style and the lower most most swollen pat is called ovary. The ovary contains ovules. Gynaecium forms female part female part in the fower and takes part in sexual reproduction. On development the ovary the ovary forms fruit and ovules turn into seeds. Sometimes flowers either do not have and roecium or gynaecium, these are called incomplete flowers, and are said to be females or male flowers respectively.	Gynaecium. Carpels. Stigme. Style. Ovary. Ovules. Sexual. Sexual reproduction. Complete flowers. Incomplete lowers. Male flowers Female flowers. Fruits. Seeds. (Draw a labelled diagram of carpel and a section (T.S) of ovary.

Previous Knowledge Testing

(1) Name some plants that you have seen.

(2) What are different parts of a plant?

(3) Which is generally the most attractive part of plant?

(4) Name some colours of flowers.

Introduction

(1) What is the coloured part of a flower called ?

(2) What is the outermost whorl of the Bower called ?

(3) With which part is the Bower attached to the stem '?

(4) What are different parts of a Bower and

(5) What do you knew about their functions?

(Students will not be able to answer some questions or the last question).

Annouocement of the Topic

"Well students today we will be discussing about 'the parts of typical Bower and their functions".

Generalization

A typical flower has four whorls, calyx, corolla, androecium and gynaecium which are formed of sepals, petals, stamens and carpels respectively. All the parts of flower contribute to the sexual reproduction in plant.

Recapitulation

1. What is a flower?
2. Name the different whorls in a flower and their individual parts.
3. What is the structure of a stamen?
4. What is the structure of a carpel?
5. What are the functions of sepals, petals, stamens and carpels?
6. What do you mean by complete and incomplete flowers?

Home Work

Draw a labelled diagram of flower and describe its parts.

LESSON PLAN II

(Structure of cell)

Method of Teaching : Lecture Demonstration Method.

Subject : Life Sciences. **Name or Roll No. of the P.T. :**

Unit : Organization of Life. **Class :** IX

Topic : Structure of Cell. **Section :** A

Duration : 45 minutes. **No. of Students :** 25

Average age of the students : 13+yrs.

Date : **School :**

General

(1) To add new information to the existing stock of knowledge of the students.

(2) To develop certain skills and interests of the students in Life Sciences.

(3) To develop scientific method in the students.

Specific : To give students knowledge of structure of typical cell.

Teaching Aids

(a) General : Black-board, chalk, duster and pointer.

(b) Specific : 3 Charts showing structure of typical cell plant and animal cells and different types of cells. Microscope Slides, petridishes, needles, onion, scale leaves etc.

Assumed Previous Knowledge

(1) Student know difference between living and non-living things.

(2) Students know that plants and animals are made up of cells.

(3) Students also have an elementary idea of structure of typical cell.

Method	Material	Black Board Work
How was the knowledger of cell structure discovered?	History of scientific events tells us that Robert Hooke (1665) saw a thin slice of cork under his self-made, microscope and noticed numerous compartments in that and assigned them the name 'cells'.	Cells Robert Hooke (1665).
	Anton Leeuwonbock (1632-1723) saw different living structures like bacteria through his crude microscope.	Leeuwonbock (1632-1723).
	In 1833 English biologist Robert Brown described the cell nucleus. In 1838 M.J. Schleiden and Nucleus. Schleiden and T. Schwann told that every organism is made up of cells and they formulated cell theory. Later on details of cell structure were known by their minute details.	Robert Brown (1833). Schwann(1838).
What is cell Theory?	In 1838 Schleiden and Schwann formulated cell Theory, which is as follows: (a) Cell is the structural unit of all organisms. (b) Cell is the functional unit of all organisms. (c) The new cells come from pre-existing cells.	Cell Theory (a) Cell is structural unit of all oraganisms. (b) Cell is the functional unit of all organisms. (c) The new cells come from pre-existing cells.

Contd.

Method	*Material*	*Black Board Work*
What do you know about the shapes and sizes of different cells?	Cells have different shapes such as square, rectangular, round, fibrous and thread like The size of cells is measured in microns and one micron is one thousand of a millimeter. Some bactrial cells are only 0.5 microns while some plant fibres are 20 to 550 mm. (Utricaceae) in length. Ostrich egg cell is 5 cms. in diameter.	(Display chart with different cells or draw diagrams.) Rectangular, Round. Fibrous. Threadlike. Micron(μ) = $\frac{1 \text{ mm}}{1000}$ Bacterial cells 0.5 microns. Fibres-20 to 550 mm. Ostrichegg cell-5cms. diameter.
What do you know about the structure of a cell? *(Show some onion scale peel cells under microscope.)*	If we see plant cell under microscope we find cell wall as the outermost part. Next to this we see cell membrane which encloses the cytoplasm. In the centre there is nucleus. Cytopolasm other than nucleus is called protoplasm. Protoplasm is jelly like substance and we find vacuoles and certain cell organelles like chloroplasts, mitochondria and other plastids. In animal cells we also find centrole with centrosomes above the nucleus. In electronmicroscopic structure of the cell we can also see ribosome, endoplasmic reticulum and Golgi bodies.	

Contd.

Method	*Material*	*Black Board Work*
What is the difference between a plant and an animal cell? *(Mount a plant cell and an animal cell under different microscopes and show them to the students.)*	We find the following differences in plant and animal cells: (a) There is a cell wall in plant cells but it is not found in animal cells. (b) In plant cells we find larger and more in number, the vacuoles as compared to animal cells. (c) In plant cells we find centrioles with centrosomes which we do not find in animal cells.	*(Display a chart showing differences in plant and animal cell sturctures.)* **Plant Cells** (a) cell wall (b) chloroplasts (c) Vacuoles **Animal Cells** Centriole with centrosomes.
What are the funtions of different cell organelles?	We can state the functions of differerent cell organelles as : In plant cells, cell wall gives difinite shape to the cells and protects these. Cell membranae in both plant and animals is of semipermeable nature and it regulates the entrance and exit of different substances in the cell. Chloroplasts of plant cells participate in the process of photosynthesis. Centriole and controsomes in animal cells help in cell division.	**Cell Wall:** Shapek protection, **Cell membrane:** regulation of entrance and exit of substances **Chloroplasts:** photosynthesis **Centriole Centrosomes** cell-division **Mitochondria-Respiration**

Contd.

Method	*Material*	*Black Board Work*
	Mitochondria, both in plant and plant and animal cells, participate in respiratory reactions and release of energy. Nucleus contains hereditary material and regulates the activities of the cell. Golgi bodies give out certain secretions, ribsomes help in protein synthesis and endoplasmic reticulum helps in transport within the cell. Vacuoles act as sinks and maintain turgidity.	**Nucleus**-Heredity material and cellular control **Golgi bodies**-Protein secretion **Reticulum.** Transport within the cell. **Vacuoles**-Exeretion, turgidity.

Previous Knowledge Testing and Introduction or the Topic

1. What is the structural unit of the wall of the room?
2. What is the structural unit of organisms?
3. How do you categorize organisms based on the number of cells they are made of?
4. What is cell theory ?

Generalizations

1. There has been contribution of several biologists in exploring the cell structure.
2. There are different shapes and sizes of cells and plant and animal cells differ in their structure to some extent.
3. Different cell organenes, cell wall, cell membrane, nucleus, mitochondria, chloroplasts vacucles, centriole, Golgi bodies, ribosomes and endoplasmic reticulum perform different functions in the cell and the cell acts as structural and functional unit in the organisms.

Applications

1. How did the knowledge about cell structure grow up ?
2. What is Cell Theory?
3. What do you know about shape and sizes of different cells?
4. What do you know about the structure of typical cell ?
5. What are the differences in the structure of plant and animal cells?
6. What are the functions of different cell organenes ?

Home Work

Draw a labelled diagram of typical cell and point out differences in structure or plant and animal cells.

HOW TO JUDGE A LESSON ?

In judging the lesson and evaluating the teaching the following points should be taken into consideration

1. Preliminary information regarding the topic and the class etc.
2. Testing of previous knowledge and introduction of the topic. Appropriateness of the time and smoothness in announcement of the topics.
3. Black-board writing of the teacher. Whether black board work was enough or not and the summary of the topic was systematic or not.
4. Presentation of the subject matter. It should be presented to the class in logical coherent manner.
5. Fluency of expression and confidence on the part of the teacher.
6. The way of questioning adopted by the teacher and response from the class. Individual attention paid to poor students and the distribution of questions over the class.
7. Whether the teacher sought students' participation or their involvement in the process of teaching.
8. Correlation of the topic to the previous knowledge of the student and to their daily life activities.
9. Number of teaching aids used their suitability to the class standard and in the topic and organization and appropriateness of time of use.
10. Suitability of the topic regarding the age group and understanding of the students.
11. Class discipline attention and interest of the students in teaching.
12. Whether generalizations were given and applications etc. told.
13. Recapitulation : whether systematically done and the response from the class. Structuring and distribution of questions can also be considered.
14. General behaviour, appearance and attitude of the teacher towards the class can also be considered.
15. Whether home task was given or not.

Questions

1. Discuss the importance of planning in teaching.
2. What steps will you follow in lesson planning for sciences teaching life
3. According to what criteria will you judge a lesson ? Explain.
4. Draw a lesson plan on anyone of the following topics for class VIII :
   (a) First lesson on compound leaves.
   (b) Pollination.
   (c) Balanced diet.
   (d) External adaptation in fish.
5. You have to teach a lesson on "Balanced Diet" to class VIII or "Tapeworm" to class VII. Draw a lesson plan for a period of 40 minutes.
6. Prepare a lesson plan for IX class on any topic of your choice in life-sciences.
7. Discuss the importance of general and specific objectives of teaching life-sciences in a daily lesson plan or a unit plan.
8. Prepare a lesson plan of 40 minutes for secondary students on anyone of the following subjects and also indicate the class for which the plan is suitable :
   (a) Respiration in plants.
   (b) Living and non-living things.
   (c) Circulatory system in frog.

11

TEACHING METHODS

Teacher's main job lies to teach. There is not a method or the methods of teaching science which could suit in all the situations. All teachers are different. No two children are alike. Teachers differ in personality. Children differ from family to family and from locality to locality—even in respect of their mental and physical development. Thus a teaching method is largely governed by these three factors—environment, teacher and pupil. It will be advisable to lay down a series of methods of science teaching, so that the teachers could select from them according to their need.

MAKING A CHOICE

There are some guiding principles for determining our teaching methods. They are as follows:

1. Every method we use should be based on an understanding of the pupils in our classroom, and not on an understanding of children we have read about.
2. Every method we use should be one which we thoroughly understand and believe will be successful with the pupils

in our classroom and not merely one which we have heard is successful.

3. Every method we use should lead the pupils to a sense of achievement through interest and purpose.
4. Every method we use should stimulate the pupils to think and cooperate actively.
5. Every method we use should be based on the realisation that the word education derives from a Latin word 'educo' which means "I bring up" or "I nourish." Education is a "drawing out" and not a "putting in."

Mindful of the above points there are certain vital instincts which stimulate the child to learn and through which he acquires knowledge and skills. They are instincts of play, imitation, curiosity and competition. These are the instincts which are principally concerned with the educational development of the child and which we must consider when planning our methods of teaching science.

Beside these vital instincts from which the impulse to learn springs, there are some physical agents which enable a child to acquire skills and knowledge. They are as follows:

1. The hands – Learning by touching and doing.
2. The eyes – Learning by seeing
3. The ears – Learning by hearing.
4. The mouth – Learning by saying.
5. The nose – Learning by smelling.
6. The tongue – Learning by tasting.

These senses should be utilised as much as possible in our method of science teaching for creating effective teaching learning situations

DIFFERENT METHODS

Traditional Methods

1. Lecture Method (8 4)
2. (Improved) Lecture Method (8 5)
3. Demonstration Method (8 6)

4. Concrete to Abstract Approach (8 7)
5. Lecture Demostration Method (8 8)
6. (Improved) Lecture Demonstration Method (8 9)
7. Laboratory Method (8 10)

Discovery Methods

8. Scientific Method (8 11)
9. Project Method (8 12)
10. Investigatory Project Method (8 13)
11. Problem Solving Method (8 14)
12. Heuristic Method (8 15)
13. Inquiry Approach (8 16)

Other Methods

14. Discussion or Interactive Approach (8 17)
15. Programmed Instruction Method (8 18)
16. Multimedia Package Approach (8 19)
17. Individualized Instruction Method (8 20)
18. Modular Approach (8 21)
19. Teacher Centred versus Child Centred Approach (8 22)
20. Activity Approach (8 23)
21. Process Approach (8 24)
22. Environmental Studies (EVS) Approach (8 25)

LECTURE METHOD

This is one of the most popular methods of teaching in our schools. This is a teacher structured method, and the students are just passive listeners most of the time. Very few teachers allow questions during the lecture, though some of them give some time to their students to ask questions after the lecture. Many students forget their questions by the time the lecture is over. So their questions remain unanswered. Teachers talk most of the time without using any teaching aid though some of them use blackboard. For them the lecture method is talk and chalk method. Sometime the back benchers cannot even read what is written on the blackboard. Students take notes of the lecture, and slow writers miss many points.

Research studies have been made on what actually happens in classrooms where teacher is teaching by lecture method. 'Step into a classroom and what do you hear. The chances are better than 60 per cent you will hear someone talking. If someone is talking the chances are that it will be the teacher more than 70 per cent of the time. The teachers talk more than all the students combined.

The teacher is the main actor 85 per cent of the time. Pupils receive recognition, praise and encouragement only 1-2 per cent of the time." According to Flanders, N.A. "We want to encourage our pupils to learn to express themselves fluently, yet on average there are two speeches by each pupil each day in class, and the mean length of these is 8.4 words."

Students dislike lectures. In an adult education class those who had heard only 15 minutes of a radio talk could score 41 per cent on a factual recall test while those who listened to the 30 minutes of the lecture could score only 25 per cent on the same test. In other words, the second period of 15 minutes proved to be for less productive as it reduced the listener's ability to recall the first 15 minutes. It may be due to fatigue set in which students lost the concentration. The span of concentration seems to be less for the child than for the adult. Children switch their attention rapidly from one subject to another.

It implies that the teacher should not lecture continuously for more than a very limited time, say 15 minutes with an average secondary school class. After that a change of activity, to practical work, watching a film, writing or working in small groups, or discussion could be submitted. Lecture method has some advantages and disadvantages.

Advantages

1. It is quick, and a lot of knowledge can be imparted in quite a lesser time.
2. It is highly efficient if teacher teaches in systematic and logical manner.
3. It is convenient and easy and a teacher is free to develop his own style of teaching.

Disadvantages

1. Students' involvement and participation is nil or quite less.
2. Students' previous knowledge or entry behaviours are usually not taken into consideration.
3. Developing scientific skills are neglected.
4. Teacher needs a lot prior knowledge to prepare a lecture.

It is wise to have notes (in points) available while lecturing for ensuring correct sequencing of ideas and figures, but word by word reading from notes should be avoided. Listening to your tape recorded lecture or comments of your colleagues on your lecture will enable you to find out the limitations of the lecture method as well as to enable you to improve your further lectures.

Lecture Method is perhaps as old as appointment of the first lecturer in our country, as lecturer is one who lectures, and uses Lecture Method in his class. But old is Gold. It is correct that in Lecture Method, no audio-visual aids are used, and we do not need audio-visual aids all the time. If our students have enough experience of what is to be talked about in we do not need to use audio-visual aids in the lesson, and the lecture can be improved (enriched) by adding Teacher-Learner Interaction (TLI) and Learner-Learner Interaction (LLI), into it. Involve your students into your Lecture with the two interactions—TLI and LLI. Adding these two interactions with the lecture, some of the disadvantage of the lecture (8.4) can be removed, and the lecture can be improved.

Encourage your students to ask questions (NPE 1986). You should also ask questions to all types of students (average, below average and slow learners) and not just the above average during your (improved) lecture. Sometimes ask some open question, for which first students had to have LLI, before answering.

DEMONSTRATION METHOD

Demonstration means to show. In lecture method, the teacher just talks but in demonstration method he also shows and illustrates certain phenomenon and applications of abstract principles through demonstration of experiments. Demonstrations provide concrete experiences to students. Demonstrations may also include use of films, slides, overhead projector or the micro-projector.

While using the demonstration method the teacher can:

1. provide significant, rich and worthwhile experiences to students enhancing their power of observation.
2. illustrate abstract ideas in concrete form.
3. co-ordinate laboratory work with theory and highlight safety methods.
4. pose a problem to students and gather their hypotheses based on their experiences.
5. provide concrete experiences for the solution of a problem.
6. add additional demonstrations after its review, if considered necessary.
7. do those demonstrations which are dangerous for students to perform themselves.

Characteristics of a Good Demonstration

1. It should be clearly visible to all students, even to the batk benchers.
2. It should be pre-tested so that it may be convincing, striking and clear-cut.
3. Children should also be involved.
4. Results should not be known to students.
5. If there are more than one demonstration in a lesson they should be well-spread.
6. In a demonstration only one idea should be taken at a time. Too many ideas in one demonstration may confuse the children specially the young ones.

Points to be Noted

1. For large scale demonstration, the teacher must spend a good deal of time in thinking and devising experiments to make principles quite clear, and in showing various types of experiments necessary to clarify the numerous difficult concepts of the science course.
2. The teacher should carry out the experiment in such away that the students should learn how to carry it out by themselves.

3. When carrying out demonstration experiments the teacher should make sure that everything is in order before the lesson begins. He should be certain that the demonstrations will prove his points. The table should be well illuminated either by day light or by electric lights. The background should preferably be white or black so that the apparatus and other materials are clearly visible.
4. The teacher should see the general order and tidiness of the demonstration table. Nothing looks worst than a demonstration table litered with books and other material not to be used. The demonstration table should have only apparatus and materials relevant to the lesson.
5. In this method students are placed in a passive role which may be frustrating or boring for them unless the teacher involves them in thinking behind the experiment and in the manipulation.

This problem can be minimised if the demonstration is assembled ready for action before the lesson and there is every expectation that it will work. Demonstrations need to be rehearsed. For effective demonstration the following questions should be kept in mind:

(a) Is the apparatus clearly laid out from where the students view?

(b) Do instruments have large enough dials to be read by all the students in the class?

Overhead projector has made it possible to modify some demonstrations so that they are more easily seen and students can take readings and plot graphs while demonstration is proceeding. Under such conditions the teacher can involve their students in making predictions, speculations about causes, and thinking of ways of testing ideas.

Advantages

1. There is a possibility of using more sophisticated apparatus.
2. More difficult experiments can be undertaken.
3. More hazardous experiments may be attempted.

4. Expenses may be minimised compared to laboratory method.
5. There is a possibility to demonstrate manipulative and allied practical skills.
6. There is possibility to draw the attention of all the pupils of the class simultaneously.
7. It takes less time compared to laboratory and other innovative methods.
8. This method is more efficient in a way compared to laboratory method as a teacher is more competent than students to handle apparatus.
9. All students can see the same operation and techniques simultaneously.
10. Teacher is in a position to explain each and every step and to ensure that all students see and interpret all the work in the same manner.

Disadvantages

1. All students do not experiment with their own hands. It is a substitute for laboratory work.
2. When the demonstration is complex or there are too many demonstrations in one lesson, students feel difficulty in understanding the basic concepts, principles and skills.
3. Various details of the apparatus, significant reactions and other essential steps undertaken by the teacher in drawing conclusions are not necessarily visible to all the students of the class equally well.
4. It deprives students of many of the advantages of laboratory method such as handling of the apparatus and other materials as well as making their own interpretations.

Whenever you plan a lesson, ask yourself whether you really need audio-visual aids, as sometimes you do not need audio-visual aids. If your answer is "yes" then ask yourself of what type of audio-visual aids. Edger Dale has arranged the various audio-visual aids, from more concrete in nature to comparatively more abstract (5.4).

1. Direct Purposeful Experiences (5.5)

2. Contrived Experiences (5.6)
3. Dramatic Participation (5.7)
4. Demonstrations (5.8)
5. Field Trips or Excursions (5.9)
6. Exhibits (5.10)
7. Motion Pictures and Television (5.11)
8. Radio Recording and Still Pictures (5.12)
9. Visual Symbols (5.13)
10. Verbal Symbols (5.14)

This will help you to select right type of audio-visual aids for your lessons. This arrangement should not be considered as rigid divisions or watertight compartments.

This is a method generally used by our science teachers. Students cannot learn science either by lecture or by demonstration used in isolation. Even most effective demonstration cannot guarantee learning in science. This may also be true for the lecture-demonstration method. It can succeed when lecture is based upon concrete experiences of the students' environment and a demonstration focuses them into scientific phenomenon, while discussion between teacher and students goes on in a permissive atmosphere. Demonstration method when combined with a well directed discussion is a successful teaching technique. It can be modified by allowing limited students participation and by problem solving at times. It fits well into the regular method of uniform class procedure for all students but does not permit of very wide individualisation. If widely individualised and modified, it approaches to a method usually called the problem solving or project method.

Through contrived situations in this method students themselves form concepts. Therefore lecture-demonstration method should achieve the advantages of both lecture and demonstration methods, and minimise their disadvantages. Lecture-demonstration method though widely used in our science classes has a limited role in the teaching-learning process. This is because all students do not participate actively.

Advantages. Lecture-demonstration method, has all the advantages of a demonstration method plus one more that the teacher can also involve the students in discussion.

Disadvantages. Disadvantages of a lecture-demonstration method are the same as of demonstration method.

Like lecture, Lecture-Demonstration Method (8.8) can also be improved. Here along with Teacher-Learner Interaction (TLI) and Learner-Learner Interaction (LLI) two more interactions, Teacher Material Interaction (TMI) and Learner-Material Interaction (LMI) are to be added in Lecture-Demonstration (8 8). Addmg all the four mteractions—TLI L1L TML and LMI with the Lecture Demonstration (8 8) some of the disadvantages of the Lecture Demonstration (8 8) can be removed. TLI and LLI will improve the Lecture part, and TMI and LMI will improve the Demonstration part of the Lecture Demonstration. This will be (Improved) Lecture Demonstration Method, much better than the Lecture-Demonstration Method of Teaching.

When demonstrating involve students with you instead just teacher demonstrating (TMI) involve also students individually or in small groups in handling the equipment and doing the activities themselves (LMI). During TMI and LMI involve students in TLI and LLI just like you do in (Improved) Lecture. Thus using (Improved) Lecture-Demonstration method students will understand and enjoy the lesson much better.

LABORATORY METHOD

In this method students perform laboratory experiments or laboratory exercises by their own hands individually or in small groups. So here they are more active and involved unlike demonstration method, where teacher was performing experiments involving few students and most of the students in the class were just passive observers.

Unless students carry out experiments by themselves, they will never get to know what science really is. In this method they get an opportunity to do experiments individually or in small groups. In our schools set up there is a provision of separate science labs but in the West like in USA in most of the schools there are classroom cum labs. There is a provision for 55 to 60 minutes class periods. It is upto the teachers, they can utilise this time for theory or practical or both. They carry the needed equipment and material in the classroom-cum laboratory in trolleys, students pick up the material from trolleys, take it to their work tables, and return it to trolleys after doing the laboratory work.

In our schools at secondary and senior secondary stage students go to science labs to do practical work. Usually in every school there are three science labs—Physics Chemistry and Biology For lab work two continuous periods (of about 30 minutes each) are given. At secondary stage students go to lab work once a week If one week they do Physics, the second week they will do Chemistry and the third week they will do Biology, and the same cycle is repeated. Thus for each subject (Physics, Chemistry and Biology) the turn comes every three weeks. At senior secondary stage students go to lab work twice a week m every subject—Physics, Chemistry and Biology. Usually students work in groups of about 20. If there are 40 students in a class, they are divided into 2 groups (if one group is doing Physics, the other will be doing Chemistry or Biology) so that the teacher may supervise their students work (in a smaller group) more satisfactorily as well as to guide them individually or in still smaller groups.

Generally lab experiments are of five kinds :

1. Experiments to illustrate scientific principles
2. Experiments to find numerical results
3. Experiments to produce something as preparation of gases or biological slides.
4. Experiments to verify experiments carried out by other scientists.
5. Original work or investigatory science projects or open-ended experiments.

In our science courses there are usually the first four types of experiments. Now a little importance is also being given to the fifth type, the investigatory experiments, at senior secondary stage. Usually there is no coordination between theory and practical work.

The science courses in USA like PSSC, BSCS and CHEM study have employed a more heuristic approach with the practical work embedded right in the middle of the theory. A cycle of events is envisaged. The pupil is given a laboratory problem and his observations give rise to discussion and hypotheses. These hypotheses are tested by experiment, and so the cycle ends where it started at the laboratory table.

Open-ended experiments, are more difficult to organise and supervise than the traditional ones. The heuristic approach (8.15) demands that the pupils should be allowed to stop and think, discuss and suggest modifications for further experiments.

Objectives. When teaching science by laboratory method, the following objectives should be kept in mind:

1. To develop manipulative skills.
2. To arouse and maintain interest in science.
3. To encourage accurate observations and careful recording.
4. To make biological, chemical and physical phenomenon more real through actual experience.
5. To be integral part of the process of finding facts by investigation and arriving at principles.
6. To train the students in science processes and scientific method.
7. To give training in problem solving. To verify facts and principles already taught in theory.
8. To elucidate the theoretical work so as to aid comprehension.
9. To prepare the students for practical examination.

Advantages

1. Learning by doing.
2. Opportunity to handle materials.
3. Learning to follow directions carefully.
4. Learning skills in performing experiments, recording observations and results, summarising data and drawing conclusions.
5. Opportunity for critical thinking.

Disadvantages

1. More expensive if separate equipment is provided to each student.
2. Difficult to schedule in the school timetable when double periods are provided.
3. More time consuming compared to demonstration method as students are unskilled workers and or not as competent to handle apparatus as their teachers.
4. No guarantee that the students will learn to solve problems or think scientifically.

When there are more students and the equipment is not enough for each student to do experiments, then a large number of experiments should be arranged, and different students could do different experiments at the same time. If possible typed instructions should be given to students for each experiment. This-will facilitate, students to work on their own and teacher will have time to go to students who need him most.

SCIENTIFIC METHOD

Scientific method is one of the methods for discovery. Training in scientific method necessitates discouraging traditional demonstrations and laboratory experiments. When teaching by scientific method, the students do not perform the prescribed list of experiments in which emphasis is on the verification of some already known science principles and laws. Instead they are involved in investigatory problems whose solutions are not available either in textbook or lab manuals.

Steps of Scientific Method

1. *Problem*. What does a student want to learn?
2. *Hypothesis*. What does a student think the answer would be?
3. *Experiment*
   (a) Testing of Hypothesis by an Experiment. How could a student tell the answer would be what he predicted?
   (b) Collection of Data

(c) Interpretation of Data. What happened when a student tested his hypothesis?

4. *Conclusion.* What do the results of the experiment show? Is the hypothesis accepted, rejected or needs modification.

Advantages

1. Students do their own learning under the guidance of their teacher.
2. They learn to propose, formulate and structure problems.
3. They learn to collect varied pieces of information relevant to the problem from different sources.
4. They collect the evidence to prove or disprove the identified hypotheses.
5. They learn to solve everyday problems.
6. They are more closely familiar with various things, their applications and relationships instead of having mere knowledge.
7. They establish a healthy and favourable relationship with their teachers.

Disadvantages

1. This method is very slow, long and time consuming. Therefore the syllabus (knowledge and information) could not be covered in the allotted time. Thus a different syllabus is needed for this method as in some American science programmes like PSSC, BSCS and CHEM Study of which formulation of hypotheses and their testing is the dominant feature.
2. There is too much emphasis on practical work which may give a wrong concept of the nature and philosophy of science in general. Learning science is a joyful process but too much practical work may make it dull and routine type of affair.
3. Most of the teachers are perhaps not able to teach by this method, as they have not practised teaching science by this method.
4. All students are not capable to learn by this method.

PROJECT METHOD

A project is any purposeful activity. It may or may not involve investigation. If it involves investigation it will be investigatory project. In progressive schools students are allotted some projects during summer holidays. It may be a curricular or enrichment activity. Teacher try to cover a part of syllabus by this method. Parents also help their wards when they work on their projects. Titles of some projects generally given to students are as follows:

1. Indian Scientists
2. Story of Wheel
3. From earth to moon

Here students read some reference material, talk to some professional people and the public, observe what is going on around them and so on. This is how they gather data. Then they analyse their data, and prepare their project reports. The report may be hand-written or typed and it may include pictures, charts, graphs, models and so on. Students learn a lot when these project reports are discussed in the Class. Project Method is an example of Assignment Method.

The Investigatory Project Method involves investigation, discovery and finding out something which was not known to the student before. An investigation is much more than the repetition of a standard experiment. Here the student is to decide what experiments are necessary and how he is going to carry them out. He may have to design his own apparatus, if that is not available in the laboratory. He has to search for the appropriate principles, laws, formulae, apparatus and data; and originate solution to a problem. The student will act like a scientist.

This method involves the steps of scientific method:

1. Problem
2. Hypotheses
3. Experiment
   (i) Testing of hypotheses by experiments
   (ii) Collection of data
   (iii) Interpretation of data
4. Conclusion.

This is the least used method of teaching science in our schools. In USA, Canada and UK teachers try to cover a part of syllabus by this method. In this method a group of students select a problem in consultation with their teacher/ and then through discussion develop the plan of action and design the type of equipment needed to carry out the experiments to reach the conclusion. Students thus are trained in science processes and scientific method.

Advantages

1. It creates interest in science.
2. It develops understanding.
3. It develops self-confidence, cooperation, leadership and emotional stability.
4. It promotes curiosity and develops scientific temper, interest and appreciation.
5. It develops abstract and concrete scientific skills.
6. It develops interest in scientific hobbies in the right use of leisure time later on.

Limitations

1. This is the most difficult method for the teacher, requiring more planning and more effort of execution.

   Though it is the most difficult method for the teacher requiring more effort and planning, the lack of this effort is one of the reasons for much of the mediocre teaching that is done. The results of this method, when it is properly executed, are more than compensate for the extra work that is required.

2. If properly operated it calls for somewhat more materials and equipment than in the strictly demonstration method.

   The necessity for more materials and equipment is generally an excuse rather than a reason for not using it. he problems and experiments can be so devised that they will require nothing that cannot be had at little or no expense.

3. The amount of time consumed by the projects may be so great as to make it impossible to cover a wide variety of topics thus resulting in an incomplete course.

   Also to the economy of time, there is much doubt as to whether time spent upon less subject matter might not be worthwhile to the student than the same time spent in hurrying over more subject matter.

4. It may result in a task of proper coordination of subject matter when individualised, since students may be working upon different problems or projects.

   The lack of coordination which sometimes is the result of individual work is little more than the result of poor planning and less execution upon the part of the teacher.

5. Difficulties of method increase when there are more students in large classes and more periods per day of the teacher.

   In no other method there is equal provision for the essential factors demanded by our objectives. The solving of problems is essential to the training in scientific thinking and the following of projects is a vital part of the production of those attitudes which should be the outgrowth of science teaching. Proper planning will provide for group or even class participation as a means of diminishing the problem of number of students and number of classes that must be taught and will still make possible a sufficient amount of independent work to provide for the necessary individualisation.

PROBLEM SOLVING METHOD

Problem is not a problem if a child can solve it by his previous knowledge. Problem solving takes place only when student's previous knowledge is insufficient to enable him to provide an acceptable solution, and solution becomes possible only when he acquires new knowledge which he does not have before. A method to solve a problem is called a problem solving method.

Steps in Problem Solving Method

(i) Identification of problem after problem survey;

(ii) Statement of the problem – a clear description;

(iii) Explanation of the problem – discussing with students ensuring that they clearly understand what the problem is;

(iv) Delimitation of the problem – isolating only those parts of the problem which are within the reach of students.

These are the four steps of scientific method. Scientific method is a problem solving method.

In problem solving method step III may be eliminated, and for testing the hypotheses information from some other sources (reference books, journals, newspapers, discussion with some experts etc.) may be taken.

Sometime even steps II and III both may be eliminated in problem solving method, and information from some other sources (mentioned above) may be used to find the solution of the problem.

Advantages. Its advantages are the same as of Scientific Method or Project Method of teaching science.

Disadvantages or Limitations. Its limitations are also the same as of Scientific Method or Project Method of teaching science.

HEURISTIC METHOD

Heuristic means discovery in Greek. Professor Henry Edward Armstrong of Imperial College, London, was a strong advocate of Heuristic Method. Professor Armstrong tried his best to place his students in the position of original discoverers. He involved his students in finding out by themselves instead of telling them. Laboratory work was compulsory for every student where they could discover instead of being told. His method was quite simple. He used to provide instruction sheet to his students concerning the problem and students were expected to take observations and conduct experiments according to these instructions. Students used to record their observations in their record-books. From these observations they were asked to draw their own conclusions. Thus, they were introduced to reasoning from their own observations and experiments.

Heuristic Method demands that the students should be allowed to stop and think, discuss and suggest modifications for further experiments.

Advantages and Disadvantages. Heuristic Method develops spirit of enquiry in students, but this method can never be the main method for science teaching. This method is a time consuming process by which students gain less worthwhile and significant knowledge in more time. Students are not expected to rediscover all the knowledge which already exists; they are expected to know at least a part of it.

INQUIRY METHOD

Example. One day an electric bulb blew out in the class. "What happened" asked the students. The teacher took out the bulb from the bulb holder, and showed it to the students. The students gathered around the teacher. He passed it around them and said, "Look at it and try to develop a hypothesis about what happened." "What is inside the bulb" asked one of the students. "I do not know," said the teacher. "Is there air inside the bulb," asked another student. "No," said the teacher. "Is there any other gas inside the bulb," asked another student. "No," said the teacher. The students were puzzled and they started looking at one another. Finally one student asked, "Is it vacuum inside the bulb"? "Yes," said the teacher. "Is it complete vacuum," someone asked. "Almost" replied the teacher. "What is that little wire made of," asked another student. "I do not know," said the teacher. "Is that little wire made of some metal," asked some students. "Yes," the teacher said.

Such Yes-No Answer questions continued between teacher-students interaction, till students identified the material of the wire inside the electric bulb, and the events that took place without teacher's readymade answers. Finally students began to formulate hypotheses about what happened. After the students formulated some hypotheses, they started searching through Reference Books (in the library or at home) in order to verify them.

This is an example of Inquiry Approach of teaching science. Students are trained for inquiry. Inquiry begins with a puzzling event like "an electric bulb blew out in the class." Students inquired (what happened—a problem) when they were puzzled.

After the puzzling event is presented to the students, they ask the teacher some questions. The teacher should answer the questions in "Yes" or "No." The answer of each question may be a small hypothesis.

Inquiry Approach of teaching science may have the following steps.

1. Encounter with the Problem.
2. Formulation of Hypotheses.
3. Data Gathering – Experimentation and Verification.
4. Conclusion – Solution of the problem.

DISCUSSION METHOD

When teaching science by lecture method or lecture-demonstration method, if students are involved in discussion (interaction) they are in a much more better situation of learning science. As discussed under lecture method, the teacher should not lecture contmuously for more than a very limited time so that the teacher should not lose the concentration of their students. For this he can do a change of activity, and discussion (interaction) is one of the several activities in which students can be involved very actively. So by using lecture-cum-discussion method some of the disadvantages of the lecture method can be taken care of.

Similarly when lecture-demonstration method is combined with a well directed discussion (interaction), it may prove to be a successful technique of teaching science.

In our schools lecture method and lecture-demonstration method are most commonly used. If we add "discussion" or "interaction" into it, these methods may come out to be much more effective,

There may be 4 types of interactions.

(i) Teacher-Learner Interaction (TLI)

(ii) Learner-Learner Interaction (LLI)

(iii) Teacher-Material Interaction (TMI)

(iv) Learner-Material Interaction (LMI)

When teacher is lecturing, TLI may be initiated. When children are discussing in small groups, like tutorials, LLI may be initiated. When teacher is demonstrating, he is using some teaching aids (material) he can use TMI along with TLI for more effective teaching. When children are doing some experiments in small groups, LMI will be of better use along with LLI and TLI.

PROGRAMMED INSTRUCTION METHOD

Programmed Instructional Materials as discussed in the elsewhere, provide self-learning units. Such units may prove to be very useful when our science teachers are heavily loaded, and they do not have time to interact specially those students individually, who really need them.

There are some topics in every field of science (Physics, Chemistry and Biology) which the students can leam on their own if programmed learning units are available on these topics. But in our country programmed" learning units are not available in the market. So the only choice remains that some innovative science teachers should write some programmed units on selected topics to be used by their students. These guidelines may be used when writing programmed units. Such units when written, may be shared by other science teachers in their classes. Self-Learning Modules are as good as Programmed Instruction Materials for self-learning.

Like Programmed Instruction, Self-learning modules and Multi-media Packages if available on some topics, may also be given to students to cover part of syllabus on their own. Multimedia packages can also be developed by teachers. Such packages once developed may be used again and again. This is Multimedia Package Approach of teaching.

INDIVIDUALISED INSTRUCTION METHOD

Not all students are alike, but we teach them the same thing by the same method. In a classroom there are students of different science background. Most of them perhaps do not have aptitude for science, if they have a choice perhaps they will not offer science. But we are to teach the same science to all of them, and we usually use the same method to teach all students, without taking into consideration their individual differences.

Usually we can classify our students in three groups – average, below average and above average. When we teach science we assume some pre-requisites or entry behaviours of our students, we assume that this much they already know, and men we start our lesson. When we do so, we take into consideration only the average students, and forget about the below and the above average. The result is that only the average students are satisfied and the below and the above average are frustrated. The only solution remains that some individualised instruction and some other self-learning materials be developed and used to satisfy all the students.

Programmed Instruction is one way of individualised instruction. Self-learning modules, slide-tape programmes, and multimedia packages are some other means. Though such materials are not available in the market, yet they can be developed by some innovative teachers for the use of their students. Then their materials can also be shared by other science teachers in their classes.

Use of self-learning modules in teaching is another form of individualised instruction. This is called Modular Approach of teaching and learnmg. If self-learning modules are available on some topics, they can be given to students as assignment for self-learning. Teachers can also develop such modules on some topics. Such modules once developed can be used again and again.

Teacher Centred Approach (TCA). If we observe classrooms, we find it is the teacher who speaks most of the time, and the children either given no opportunity to speak or a very little opportunity to speak—ask questions or interact. This is a Teacher Centred Approach of Teaching.

Example. In a study about 1000 classes were observed (I-XII) in all subjects and in all types of schools, and it was found that on an average 95 per cent of the time teacher was speaking and 5 per cent of the time the children were speaking. This is an example of Teacher Centred Approach of Teaching.

Lecture Method and Lecture Demonstration Method are Teacher Centred Approaches of Teaching. Teacher Centred Approach is a very effective method for teaching skills (processes). Reading a thermometer, reading a spring balance, preparing gases like hydrogen, oxygen and carbon dioxide, salt analysis, volumetric and gravimetric exercises, setting up a microscope, making a slide and seeing it through a microscope, setting the experiment for photosynthesis etc., are all skills. Until a child perfectly learns a skill, the teacher is very much involved in telling the child "what to do" and "how to do." The teacher has to use Teacher Centred Approach. Cooking; sewing; driving a scooter, a motor cycle or a car; repairing; playing musical instruments; dancing etc., are all skills. Teaching each of these skills, a teacher is needed who teaches these skills by Teacher Centred Approach.

Example. Reading a thermometer is a skill. According to a study children and even teachers not taught this skill by Teacher Centred Approach, generally read the thermometer wrong. If the reading was 46°C, they read 40.6°C. Then came the teacher to teach this skill. He pointed at 40 and asked "What is the reading?" The child said "40°C". Then he pointed at 50 and asked "What is the reading?" The child said, "50°C". Then the teacher asked, "How many marks are there between 40°C and 50°C?" When the child failed to answer, the teacher himself counted—1, 2, 3, 4, 5, 6, 7, 8, 9,10. Then the teacher asked "How much is one mark?" Then the child replied "1°C." (This is actually the least count of the thermometer which the child was not knowing, and therefore he read 40.6°C instead of 46°C). Then the teacher asked, "How many marks is the mercury above 40°C"? And the child counted, "1, 2, 3, 4, 5, 6." Then the teacher asked, "Now tell, what is the reading of the thermometer?" And the child again counted, "41, 42, 43, 44, 45, 46," and then said," Thermometer reads 46°C and not 40.6°C".

Now look at the approach, teacher used to teach the child to read the thermometer correctly. In this approach the teacher was more involved than the child, and therefore this is Teacher Centred Approach. Reading a thermometer is a skill. Therefore Teacher Centred Approach (TCA) should be used to teach skills (processes) to the child.

Child Centred Approach. Some innovative teachers themselves speak less in the class, and give opportunity to their children to speak more. Here the science teacher acts as moderator (leading and moderating discussions) and a guide (helping slow learners). This is Child Centred Approach. In teaching science by Lecture Method or by Lecture-Demonstration Method, these innovative teachers involve their children in interaction and question-answer sessions that even their lecture and Lecture-demonstration become child centred. Inquiry Approach, Problem Solving Approach, Laboratory Method, Scientific Method, Project Method and Investigatory Project Method are Child Centred Approaches.

Example. A teacher is teaching a concept "Air has weight" by scientific method. It involves *"weighing"* by a spring balance, which is a *skill (process)*. The teacher teaches the skill (process) of weighing to the children by Teacher Centred Approach before he teaches the concept "Air has weight."

Then he starts the lesson with a:

Problem. Does air has weight? (This is TCA). Then children formulate their own

Hypotheses. (i) Yes, (ii) No. (This is CCA). Then children (as already know the skill of weighing or reading a spring balance) test their hypotheses themselves with an experiment.

Experiment. weighing an empty football bladder, and the same football bladder full of air. (This is CCA). Then they themselves draw the conclusion.

Conclusion. that air has weight. Hypotheses "yes" is right, and hypotheses "*no*" is wrong. (This is CCA).

Here step – 1 is Teacher Centred as teacher asks the question or poses a problem. Steps – 2, 3, 4 are Child Centred. Therefore Scientific Method is 25 per cent teacher centred and 75 per cent child centred. Thus as a whole Scientific Method is Child Centred Approach (CCA).

Note "weight" is a concept and "weighing" is a skill. When skill of "weighing" already taught by the teacher to the children by Teacher Centred Approach, the concept of "weight" is to be taught by Child Centred Approach. Do not tell to the child "air has weight," let him find out himself whether or not "air has weight" by the Child Centred Approach (CCA).

Remember

1. Teach skills (processes) by TCA, and
2. Teach concepts by CCA.

ACTIVITY METHOD

"Believe nothing because you have been told about it. Don't believe what your teacher tells you merely out of respect for the teacher."

Who said this? When this question is put to science teachers in seminars the reply is 'some scientist'. Actually it is the statement of Lord Buddha.

Many times teachers teach and children do not understand. This is because children are conditioned in accepting and memorising what teacher tells them, without questioning and understanding.

In science there are many facts, principles, laws, concepts and skills, which children memorise without understanding. Have you ever thought why is it so?

Cognitive Development of Children. There are three types of children:

Formal operational -- They can understand science without activities.

Concrete operational – They can understand science only if they do activities by their own hands.

Pre-operational – They can understand science if they do activities repeatedly by their own hands.

This is the way Piaget categorised the children. These are the children's cognitive stages of development.

Example. Siddiqis worked with Piaget at Florida State University (USA) in 1970 when he came as a Visiting Professor. He went to the neighbouring schools to demonstrate how children at these cognitive stages look at things, think and response. There it was found that only 5 per cent children at primary level (I-V) were at formal operational stage, the remaining 95 per cent children were either concrete operational or pre-operational.

By using Piagetian tasks, Siddiqis conducted Research Studies on 1206 Primary school children in Delhi from all type of schools during 1975-77. The average interview time with each child was about 15 minutes. So it took about 300 hours to complete the task. It was found that only 4.4 per cent children at primary level (I-V) were at formal operational stage. In Class V formal operational were 9.4 per cent, concrete operational 69.3 per cent and pre-operational 21.3 per cent.

Even at Upper Primary Level (VI-VIII) a good number of children will be at concrete operational stage. This shows that specially at primary and upper primary levels, if children are not involved in doing activities or get first-hand observations, the concepts do not become clear. They may memorise and recall without understanding. When the concepts are not made clear in lower classes, their cumulative effect is seen in higher classes. Other than this there are new concepts at secondary and senior secondary levels which can be clarified through activities or relevant demonstrations.

Generally in our schools, science is taught by giving Lectures, and sometime by demonstrating few experiments. Children are not really involved in doing activities by their own hands. Teachers should also learn a lesson from the following saying:

"I heard and I forgot,

I saw and I remembered,

I did and I understood "

This is not just a saying. As hypotheses these were tested by Siddiqis and they were found correct.

If our objective is that the child may remember the content for sometime. Lecture Method may be relevant without even using Audio-Visual Aids. If the objective is that the child may remember for longer duration. Lecture will not work. But Lecture-Demonstration will be more effective. Care should be taken that every child is able to observe what is being demonstrated using all the 5 senses (see, touch, smell, taste, hear).

But if the objective is that the child must understand then doing is the only method for pre-operational and concrete operational children. Lecture and Lecture-Demonstration are not going to work. The children will have to be involved in doing activities by their own hands.

Thus Activity Based Science-Teaching is the only way of teaching science, if we want our children to learn science. Learning science is understanding science, and not just memorising.

Sample science Activities for primary, upper primary and secondary classes have been given. Some of the activities from this list may be selected according to the science topics to be taught by you in various classes. These activities may be demonstrated by you, or may be done by your students by their own hands, in science classes. These activities will make science teaching quite interesting and learning science by Activity Approach will be a fun for students.

Another important aspect of Activity Based Science Teaching is Teaching with Process Approach.

"If you will teach content, then who will teach science" D.S. Kothari. Science is not just content. Science is content plus something. That something is Process. If our stress shifts from content to process, content will automatically be included and much more meaningfully.

American Association for the Advancement of Science (AAAS) has identified 13 science processes — observing, classifying, using numbers, measuring, using space-time relationships, communicating, predicting, inferring, defining operationally, formulating hypotheses, interpreting data, controlling variables and experimenting.

If we teach science through process approach, it automatically becomes activity based. If a child learns science through process approach, he learns lot of science on his own. Thus Process Approach is one of the best ways of teaching science, as it motivates the children, and they get involved in doing activities.

Certain competencies are to be developed in children while teaching science like spirit of inquiry; objectivity; courage to question; problem solving; decision making; investigating; developing scientific attitude or temper; using scientific method; reducing all sorts of prejudices based on sex, caste, religion and language etc. " These are also the objectives of NPE — 1986. These competencies may be developed in children through Process Approach of Teaching Science, more meaningfully.

Although one has to devote a little more time when teaching science through Process Approach, but teaching-learning process becomes more interesting and effective. There are teachers who use Process Approach for teaching science in their classes, and for their children learning science is fun.

Use materials (like plants, animals, human body, living-non-living, natural-manmade, wind, hails, snow, dew etc.) and phenomena (like rains, lightning, day and night, seasons, dispersion, rainbow, photosynthesis *etc.*) of the environment around you (like family, house, neighbourhood, school, earth, sky, human body etc.) as teaching aids, when teaching science. Involve students in discussions based on what they observe in their environment in and outside classroom.

Make an exhaustive list of materials and phenomena available in your environment. Add more items whenever you see some more, in your list. Classify them according to the topics you teach in science, and use them again when teaching science. Your students will enjoy learning and you will enjoy teaching science by EVS approach.

Questions

1. State five guiding principles when selecting methods for teaching science.
2. How do the vital instincts and senses of a child pay their roles in teaching-learning process?
3. (a) Discuss the weaknesses of a lecture method for teaching science. Defend your answer with some research findings.

   (b) How can a lecture be made more effective in teaching science?

   (c) Write some advantages and disadvantages of a lecture method.
4. (a) What is the difference between a lecture method and demonstration method for teaching science?

   (b) What are the activities a science teacher can do while using demonstration method for teaching science?

   (c) What are the characteristics of a good demonstration?

   (d) What are some key points to be noted by a science teacher when using demonstration method?

   (e) Write some advantages and disadvantages of a demonstration method.
5. (a) What is the difference between demonstration method and lecture-demonstration method for teaching science?

   (b) Write some advantages and disadvantages of lecture-demonstration method.

   (c) How can this method lead to problem solving?

(d) How can you use the steps of Scientific Method when teaching science by lecture-demonstration method? Illustrate your answer with some examples.

6. (a) What is the difference between demonstration method and laboratory method?

   (b) What is the difference of laboratory work in India and that in USA?

   (c) What are the five kinds of experiments that are usually done in the laboratory? Which of them are done in your practice teaching school?

   (d) What are the objectives of teaching science in the laboratory?

   (e) Write some advantages and disadvantages of laboratory method for teaching science.

7. (a) Differentiate between teacher-centred-teaching and learner-centred-teaching in science. Illustrate the situations in which the two approaches of teaching science should be utilised.

   (b) Name five discovery methods. What steps are common in these methods? Write down advantages and disadvantages of each discovery method.

8. (a) Describe scientific method for teaching science, taking a topic in your field.

   (b) How can the steps of scientific method be taken up when teaching science by lecture-demonstration method?

9. Discuss investigatory project method for teaching science, taking a topic in your field. Compare this method with Scientific method for teaching science.

10. (a) Identify a topic in your field and explain how will you teach by problem solving method.

    (b) Compare this method with scientific method and investigatory project method for teaching science.

12

TEACHING APPROACHES

It is essential that a teacher should be acquainted with various methods of teaching, in order to achieve the set aims and objectives of teaching a subject. Some ways of teaching life sciences can be discussed as follows :

TRAINING IN SCIENTIFIC METHOD

A procedure or method of solving a problem in a scientific way is called scientific method.

Scientific way of working is doing the work systematically that ultimately leads to the solution of the problem. The scientific method involves the following steps, which can be stressed while teaching for training in scientific method :

Recognizing and Defining the Problem : A problem is located intentionally or it is hit upon incidently. The problem is clearly stated. Here the teacher can open a new field of investigation for the students or the questions put by the students can be organized in such a way that students' curiosity is aroused and they feel interested in solving the problem After the problem is located it is defined in an orderly way. The class may discuss the problem and later on a statement about the problem is laid down. If required, limitations of the problem or field of study can be stated.

Making Observations and Collection of Data : Here the problem is viewed from all possible angles and study is undertaken to collect data and procedures regarding the solution of the problem. Students collect information from their past experiences, discuss with other people and take down information from the books. If the problem involves some natural phenomena, it is observed critically in its natural setting.

The data so collected can be interpreted and analysed and only the information related to the solution of the problem can be retained.

Making Hypothesis : This step involves laying down of possible solutions of the problem. The teacher encourages discussions in the class and every student give his views regarding the ways in which the problem can be solved. Some possible solutions of the problem are recorded.

Testing the Hypothesis-Experimentation : This is the most difficult step in scientific method and needs systematic execution. Here the hypothesis or hypotheses are tested experimentally. The possible solution laid down in the above step, is experimentally verified. If one possible solution does not hold good other one is tested. Every experiment should have one controlled experiment in order to establish the exact cause.

Drawing Conclusion and Making Generalizations : This step involves evaluation of the results of experimental findings. Those results that support the hypothsis are retained. If none of the proposed hypotheses is supported by experimental results other hypothesis or hypotheses are laid down and tested. Generalizations about the retained hypothesis are made. If the generalization holds good in other situations also or it can be applied to the solution of similar problems, it become a principle.

Application : This step has nothing to do with the solution of the problem but the generalization drawn, as a result of problem solving activity, is applied in the solution of similar problems. The generalizations can also help in related studies to broaden the horizon of scientific discoveries.

We can see the problem solving activity, which can lead to the development of scientific method in the students in the following example.

The teacher with his sixth class students goes for nature study in the school garden. While moving about in the lawn one of the students overturns a piece of stone lying in the lawn and finds a yellowish patch of grass under that stone. Now the student reports it to his teacher. *(The problem is hit upon)*

Thinking it to be a problem that can be solved scientifically the teacher leads other students to that spot. Now the teacher asks the students, what they see, after telling the incident. *(The problem is now stated)*

The teacher now asks the students about the possible causes of the colour of grass patch. *(Induces discussion)*

Now the students recall their past experiences and discuss among themselves, they can also be given time for collecting information regarding the cause. *(Collection of data)*

Suppose the students give three possible causes of yellowish colour of the grass patch. *(Laying down hypothesis)*

(1) One group of the students supports that this colour is due to the pressure of the piece of stone on the grass.

(2) Second group says that the grass turned yellowish because it could not get air under the piece of stone.

(3) Third group states that the grass turned yellowish as the patch could not get light.

Now the three groups of the students are encouraged by the teacher, the test, the three possible causes, experimentally. The students are asked about the procedures, to test those possible causes. Here the teacher can also help the students in devising the procedures. *(Experimentation)*

Suppose the class conducts the experiments as follows ·

(1) The first group puts a glass plate at one place and a piece of stone at another. The weight of the two should be equal and the grass patches should be in equal conditions. After some fixed days the students find that grass patch under the glass plate did not turn yellowish. *(First hypothesis rejected)*

(2) Now the second group puts a piece of black cloth or a black sheet of paper at one patch of grass and the piece of stone at another patch. After certain days the students find both patches of grass yellowish. Air is not the cause. *(Second hypothesis rejected)*

(3) The third group puts a black cloth or a sheet of paper at one spot, and piece of stone at another and a very thin white cloth at another patch keeping other conditions equal. They find that the patch under white cloth did not turn yellowish. *(Third hypothesis supported)*

Now the class generalizes that for normal growth of the plants light in essential or in the absence of light the plants turn yellowish. *(Drawing conclusion)*

For normal growth of the plants we should expose them in sufficient light. *(Application)*

The overall procedure of this activity should be recorded sidewise. Points which should be observed while teaching for training in scientific method:

(1) A democratic atmosphere should prevail in the class during discussions about findings, defining and making hypothesis, about the problem.

(2) The teacher should act as co-worker and channelize working and interest of the students towards the finding out of the solution.

(3) If more than one hypothesis are to be tested, the students an be divided in groups and they should be convinced to set up different experiments.

(4) A complete record of the activities undertaken should be maintained.

(5) The problem should be presented in general terms and students should be encouraged through group discu-ssions to plan the experimental procedures.

(6) Have students compare results with each other, after-wards and lead discussion on discrepancies and the reasons for discrepancies.

(7) Consider how the experimental procedures could be modified and improved, let some students repeat the modified versions of experiments and report results to others.

(8) Lead students' discussion concerning why certain conclusions are valid and others are not.

This method of undertaking teaching activity aims at decentralizing the teaching learnings process. Learning is under controlled guidance, students structure and formulate problems and their solutions, it leads to de-emphasis on text-books. This method also helps students solve their everyday problems.

DEMONSTRATION EXPERIMENTS

In demonstration experiments, the teacher performs experiments in the class and goes on explaining what he does. To some extent this method of teaching can also involve active participation of the students.

In teaching life sciences demonstrations can be organized in two ways:

(1) Illustrative

(2) Investigative.

ILLUSTRATIVE DEMONSTRATIONS

In this sort of demonstrations the teacher first teaches the topic or some phenomena and after that he performs experiment, before the class in order to illustrate that.-As for example, first day the teacher taught respiration-in the class and next day he goes to the class with some apparatus to demonstrate that. The teacher fills two test tubes about half of water and puts one drop of phenol-red indicator in each test tube (Phenol red indicator gives red colour in alkaline solution and yellow colour in acidic solution.) Now the teacher tells the class that when CO_2 dissolves in water it produces carbonic acid. After this the teacher illustrates the phenomena of release of CO in respiration. He blows through, with some pipe, in one test tube and the students see that the solution turns from red to yellow but colour of the solution in second test tube remains unchanged. Students can also be asked to carryon the experiment.

INVESTIGATIVE DEMONSTRATIONS

In this the teacher goes to the class with required apparatus and fills two test tubes half full of water and adds a drop of phenol-red indicator to each. Now he blows in one test-tube. The colour of the solution (experimental) gets changed from red to yellow and that of other (controlled) remains unchanged. By this the curiosity in the students is aroused. The teacher asks the students how that happened. What from exhaled air causes colour change here. The students are asked to collect information about the constituents of inhaled and exhaled air and the dissolution of these gases in water. *(collection of data)*

Now more solutions are prepared and one is blown in with CO_2 and other with O_2 and the third one is kept as such. *(experimentation)*

It is noted that solution of the test tube blown with Co_2 gets changed from red to yellow and in others remains unchanged. From this the students generalize that we exhale Co_2 during breathing or Co_2 is produced during respiration. *(Drawing conclusion)*

We can organize our class room demonstrations in three phases :

(a) Preparation Phase

(b) Presentation Phase

(c) Evaluation phase.

Preparation Phase : In preparing for carrying out demonstrations the teacher should make a brief written plan that includes:

(i) A statement of instructional objectives.

(ii) Material required and the diagrams.

(iii) Questions to be put to the class.

(iv) General procedure.

(v) Time allowed etc.

It should be kept in mind that all material required for demonstrations is available and the demonstrations should be simple and understandable. Before presenting the demonstration to the class, it should be rehearsed.

Presentation Phase : The teacher, while conducting the demonstration in the class, should observe the following points :

(i) Make sure that demonstration is visible to the whole of the class. If the experiment involves use of small material, use microprojector, otherwise use large containers as petri dishes, test tubes etc. Have a slightly higher demonstration table. If the number of students in the class is large set up two or three demonstrationals.

(ii) Voice of the teacher should becloud enough to be heard by every student.

(iii) Pace your presentation. Do not be in a hurry but also do not stretch the demonstrations for longer time as it mars the interest of the students. If the demonstration does not work, do not feel irritated. Leave the problem to the-class and present the demonstration on the next day.

(iv) Make use of the black board and develop a summary of the procedure, draw equipments used and write the results etc.

(v) Students' participation, as far as possible, should be sought while performing demonstration.

Evaluation Phase : Here the learning outcomes of demonstration are evaluated. This can be done by oral questioning. The teacher can ask some questions to the class after the demonstration is over. The teacher can also induce discussion in the class about the procedure, generalizations and application of generalizations, involved in the demonstration.

In written questions the teacher can give fill in the blank, completion type questions, writing down of the account of observations or principal ideas involved in th demonstration.

Demonstration experiments as a method of teaching is economical as it requires lesser apparatus, psychologically sound as it involves learning from concrete to abstract but the students do not get chance for individual work or learning by doing.

INDIVIDUAL PRACTICALS

Some investigators and writers put individual practical work up as it involves maximum activity of the students and here potentialities of learning are high. If individual practical method is to produce maximum effect, in teaching learning process, it must be planned, directed and and controlled by the teacher as is done in demonstration method of teaching.

Individual practical work or laboratory work involves the same steps that are followed in scientific method of working i.e. defining the problem, collection of data, making hypothesis, testing hypothesis (experimentation) and drawing of conclusions.

Individual practical work can be organized at three levels, depending upon the level of the students.

First Level : The problems and procedures are given and student are to find out the solutions of the problems.

Second Level : Problem is given but method as well as answers are left open.

Third Level : Problems methods and answers are left open.

The approach to individual practical work can be illustrative (1st level) where the phenomenon is already discussed in the class and students just verify it by doing practicals. It can be investigative (2nd and 3rd level). Where the students are given problems and procedures or problems only, the students carry out practicals for the results or solutions of the problems.

In our schools, illustrative approach is generally followed which involves preparation for the procedures at home (writing the practicals in the note-books) and performing the practicals in the laboratory. Here the students take down observations and calculate the results.

Some practicals that the life-sciences students do at school level are identification of organisms and their parts or organs, dissections of organisms, analysis of food and other organism products for their chemical constituents, taking observations on some physiology experiments and identification of stages of cell division etc. By following illustrative approach we just help students' learn thing by doing and develop certain skills but these phenomena can also be taught by, demonstrations. For developing scientific method and scientific attitude we shall follow the investigatory approach in conduting the laboratory work where ever it is possible.

The trditional illustrative practicals can be re-organized in the form of problems and students can be given these problems for solution in the, laboraory. Depending on the level of studnts we can follow one out of the three aprroaches. We can give the problems and procedures or problems only and students can be asked to follow scientific method of working and solve the problems. The teacher can give some instructions and precautions and he may assist to some extent in adopting procedures.

Some points that should be observed while organizing individual practical work in the laboratory :

1. The objective of any arrangement of the students for the programme of laboratory work should be to obtain maximum participation of all students.
2. In complex experiments, requiring care of experimental material, taking down observatiom and extensive data collection, groups of students should be small.
3. The teacher should be available in the laboratory to encourage and help the students.
4. The teacher should demonstrate before hand, handling of living animals injecting, pithing or cutting, making of cultures and preparation of solutions etc.
5. Students should be informed about handling of dangerous organisms, equipment and materials they might be using.
6. Students should be made responsible for returning of microscopes and other materials. They should leave the glassware washed and table cleaned. Students should be asked to keep accurate records of all experimental procedures and results in a note book.
7. Keeping of record is one of the most important requirements of experimental work. The students' note books should keep complete and running account of observations hypotheses, calculations and ideas from other sources etc.

Individual practicals or laboratory work as a method of teaching has several merits. It involves learning by doing and learning from concrete to abstract. It develops scientific method of working in students and students can work at their own pace. But it is a costly method of teaching and requires much planning on the part of the teacher. There are chances of copying the results among the students. Individual practical work can be employed as a method of teaching only in Higher Secondary classes while well supervised by the teacher.

Recommendations of First Asian Regional Conference

1. Emphasis should be on practical laboratory work and field study in order to give the pupils experience in scientific enquiry. For proper implementation of these the following points are suggested ;
   (a) Observations to be made should be guided by a list of questions.
   (b) In planning practical work existing facilities should be taken, into consideration and improvisation should be encouraged.
   (c) Laboratory experiments should be planned to fit the level of pupils being taught.
   (d) As much as possible local biological material should be utilized.
   (e) Emphasis should be laid on quantitative measurements. Accurate and systematic methods of recording and presentation of observations should be practised.
   (f) Interpretation and conclusions should be discussed in the class under the guidance of the teacher.
2. Group discussions and active participation by pupils should be encouraged to the maximum. Lecturing by the teacher should be minimized.
3. As much as possible practical applications of biological principles should be emphasized.
4. Teaching aids such as specimens (preferably living) models, charts, films, slides, film strips etc. should be used to help percent the lesson more interestingly.
5. Written and practical examinations should be designed to provide-the teacher with relatively accurate evaluation of the effectiveness of his teaching.

6. Biological gardens and museums are useful means of effective instruction and should be availed of.
7. Auxiliary readings to supplement the text should be encouraged.
8. Pupils should be given incentive to collect information on topics of biological interest from sources other than books and should be encouraged to present this information in the class room.
9. In case educational TV is used there should be close co-ordination between procedures and programmes and materials should be orderd to bring about maximum effectiveness.

Questions

1. What is scientific method? What points would you observe for developing scientific method in students while organizing your teaching in life-sciences?
2. Our demonstrations in teaching life sciences are illustrative. Comment. How will you organize your teaching by under taking investigative demonstrations? Discuss with some examples.
3. At what stage of schooling, should individual practical work to be allowed? How will you organize individual practical work for teaching life-science?
4. What do you understand by demonstration method? What points would you keep into mind to make your demonstrations a success?
5. Discuss the advantages and difficulties for the Demonstration method for teaching life-sciences.
6. Describe the lecture-cum-demonstration method of teaching life-sciences. What objectives of teaching the subject are best served by this method and how?

13

INQUIRY APPROACH

Inquiry technique, as the word implies, relates to the inquiry about the topic. In this method the student is an active learner. He subjects every information or fact to ruthless inquiry in order to know the fact for himself and to test its validity. He puts to prove the theories proposed by his teachers.

THE ADVANTAGES

(i) Teaching science through inquiry methods leads to unfoldment of child's mind. Teaching science through inquiry methods leads to unfoldment of child's mind instead of stuffing it with dead material. Curiosity is an innate urge of human beings. Whether young or old educated or illiterate everyone has the desire to know the unknown. This urge of curiosity has been responsible for all discoveries and inventions. Newton witnessed the fruit falling down to earth instead of getting into the sky. This led him to the famous law of gravitation.

(ii) Inquiry teaching has a supplementary character. Inquiry technique supplements the existing set of knowledge by throwing open flood-gates of knowledge to be picked in both hands by the students. The knowledge gained in this way is much more superior and everlasting than that got through the sermons of the teacher.

(iii) Inquiry technique supplies impetus to work with double zeal. The students feel themselves in extra-ordinary high spirit with the topic. They take lessons just like play.

(iv) Inquiry technique blesses the students with extra energy to face new challenges. This technique blesses the students with added strength to face all the challenges and vicissitudes during the lesson and discovery with stamina, vigour and joy.

(v) It is both rewarding and gratifying. It is only through this way of teaching that ever developing judiciously taught.

(vi) Inquiry technique ensures sublimation of natural endowments. Inquiry technique helps it the sublimation of natural instincts.

(vii) Besides being responsible for growth of civilization, spirit of inquiry infuses bits of good moral values. Inquiry technique helps to develop the spirit of co-operation, team spirit, mutual discussion, other good habits and sacred values which chisel a student into an honourable citizen.

MOTIVATING INQUIRY

(i) The spirit of inquiry invokes joy, thrill and excitement in the learner. The central purpose of teaching science is to awaken in the students a sense of joy and thrill over the discovery and the excitement to manipulate things.

(ii) How to arouse inquiry? There is no single and ultimate method to arouse inquiry. Each child is unique in its way of putting up an inquiry. Similarly the method of arousing inquiry will depend upon the age group because different age groups have different modes of inquiry. Let us take an example of rolling ball. A child of two years takes it for a play thing and enjoys its movement. For a child of six years the ball is rolling because the surface is smooth. A child of twelve years will try to move because or in rolling and discover that it was because of some external force.

(iii) Novelty and familiarity which ensure inquiry should not be to this extreme. Too much of either jeopardises the initiative to inquire. The problem meant for arousing inquiry should be novel to the extent that the learner should feel that his past experience would not help him solve it fully. The objects or problems chosen for the purpose must be familiar with the student's previous knowledge.

ROLE OF TEACHER

In this method the teacher does not give ready made notes. He does not dominate the stage and lecture to the students. He becomes a spectator, guide and at the most a computer. He becomes a promptet to guide his students from the wing instead of coming to the forefront. He motivates and pricks the curiosity of the students and then goes into the background. Even then his role is very important in the following ways :

(i) He should make available all the responsive environments.

(ii) He should provide opportunity for developing further skills.

(iii) He should guide the learners at the different stages of solving problem.

(iv) He should make available reading material, pictures, diagrams and other teaching aids necessary for manipulating and exploring the given problem.

(v) The teacher should see that the learner does not become a parasite upon him. The students should not treat the teacher as ready-reckoner .

(vi) The teacher should allow the students to undergo various somersaults and to hit and get during the process of inquiry.

(vii) He should manage the material in such a way as the learners themselves get answer to their own question.

(viii) The teacher should insure that the learners work harmoniously on common problems and exchange notes.

(ix) He should help the learners to verify their own experimental results and findings against established facts and principles.

Questions

1. What do you mean by Inquiry method approach or technique?
2. How can you motivate inquiry ?
3. What is the role of the teacher in the Inquiry Method Approach Technique ?

14

ACTIVITY APPROACH

Life Sciences teacher, with his students, can undertake some activities while teaching the subject, these activities should involve developing of knowledge, skills, scientific attitude and scientific method of working in the students. The cooperative working of the students may also lead to some material products.

Some activities in teaching life sciences can be discussed as below:

PROBLEM SOLVING

There can be various definitions of problem solving method.

Problem solving is a planned attack on a difficulty in order to find out a satisfactory solution. We can also say that it is a method of solving some problem with the application of scientific method. In whatever words we define it, the procedure involves systematic way of solving the problem. A problem can solved by two methods:

(a) Inductive method

(b) Deductive method.

INDUCTIVE METHOD

Here an array of facts or a series of informational material leads to the formulation of a generalization or principle.

Procedure : An individual confronted with a new situation or with the modification of an existing situation so that a problem is presented to him. When the problem is to be solved the individual surveys the situation as thoroughly as he can. He recalls his past experiences and tries these out to have a solution to the problem. If he succeeds, he goes his own way but if he fails he tries other possibilities and after the solution of the problem some generalization is drawn.

The following sequence of activities usually makes up the problem solving behaviour :

Defining the Problem : Students are asked to identify, state or formulate a statement of the problem.

Collection of Data : The problem is critically examined and students collect all necessary information relating to the problem.

Laying Down Hypothesis : Here the students are asked or encouraged to lay down the possible solution or solutions of the problem.

Experimentation or Testing the Hypothesis : Here the students undertake experimentation to test the proposed solution or solutions of the problem and observations are noted down. If none of the possible solutions is verified other possible solutions are stated and tested. Experimentation may be directed by the teacher and it is better to have one controlled experiment.

Drawing Conclusion : Ultimately the students are guided by the teacher in formulating a conclusion or generalization based on the experimental evidences.

In a problem solving activity the teacher should be able to provide a situation, or perform some demonstration that leads to the formulation of some problem. He should guide in designing the experiments and should help in generalizing the conclusion as a result of problem solving activity.

For example 8th grade life sciences teacher wishes to have his pupils develop the following conclusion as a result of problem solving activity. During the process of digestion certain chemicals in the mouth help to change starch into sugar.

The teacher narrates the / following incident to the class John wanted to eat sweet biscuits with milk but there were no sweet biscuits. Then his mother advised him to take unsweetened biscuits and chew, he would get sweet taste. John did so and to his astonishment he found his mothers statement true. *(Providing situation)*

Now the teacher gives unsweetened biscuits to the students and asks them to chew those for some time and tell the taste. The problem is now stated. "Why do we get sweet taste after chewing unsweetened biscuits ." *(Defining the problem)*

After this the teacher asks the students to get the knowledge of chemical composition of biscuits. How are starch and sugar tested chemically. What flows in our mouth when we chew something? *(Collection of data)*

Now the students are asked to propose some solutions for the above said problem. Suppose some proposed solutions are :

(i) We secrete some sugary material in the mouth when we chew the biscuits.

(ii) Something in the saliva changes starch, component of biscuits into sugar.

(iii) There is something sugary in the biscuits but we taste it later when it dissolves into saliva. (Laying down hypotheses)

The next step is to test the above laid solutions. Here the teacher gives some rubber pieces to the students and asks them to chew those and collect the sliva, so released in a beaker. The teacher dissolves some biscuit material in water and displays chemicals like iodine solution, Fehling's solution A and B. He now asks the students to, undertake the experimentation to test their proposed solutions.

(i) We did not taste sweet while chewing rubber pieces. Saliva collected is boiled with some Fehling's solution (A+ B). No red spot. (First hypothesis rejected)

(ii) Take the biscuit material in solution form and boil it with Fehling's solution (A+B) : No red spot. (Third hypothesis rejected)

(iii) Take three test tubes and put equal quantity of dissolved biscuit material to two of these and in the third equal quantity of water (controlled). Now add drop of iodine solution to all the three test tubes. Blue colour in two test tubes shows presence of starch. After this add some quantity of saliva to one of the test tubes containing biscuit material and to the one containing water. Leave the test tubes as such for some time. The blue colour in the test tube, to which sliva was added, disappears but no change in the colour of solutions of other two test tubes. Starch disappears in the first test tube. Now add some Fehling's solution (A+B) to all the three test tubes and boil, Red precipitate only in that test tube, from which starch disappeared, shows the presence of sugar. Observations are recorded side wise. First hypothesis retained. (Experimentation)

Now it is concluded that certain chemicals in the mouth help to change starch into sugar. We can also say that digestive juices in mouth help to change starch into sugar. *(Drawing conclusion)*

DEDUCTIVE METHOD

When applications of a generalization are made in terms of testing the power to predict, it involves solving of some problem. This means we apply some generalization or principle, already concluded, in explaining some phenomena or solving some problem. If application of one generalization does not help other generalization the principles are tested.

Procedure : In this method also we define the problem after locating it. We apply the previously known principles to have the possible solution of the problem. So generalizations drawn by inductive method of problem solving are used again and again when the same or similar problem arises. Affinities between related problems are recognized and established solutions are used or are modified as needed. Here we are more concerned with the applications of principles or known facts.

For example students have been taught that starch is not soluble in water, some enzymes (amylase) convert starch into sugar and there are certain enzymes that can convert sugar into starch (phosphorylase etc).

Now the class is presented with the problem that underground potato contains much of starch but starch is synthesized in leaves.

Starch is not soluble in water, then how is it translocated to under ground parts ?

"How does the transportation of starch from leaves to underground arts of the plant takes place ?" *(Problem stated)*

For the solution of the problem already acquired knowledge of facts principles and generalizations is applied : In this case the above said facts, and generalizations are applied and the solution of the problem can be elaborated as "Starch in the leaves is converted into sugar by certain enzymes, now it dissolves into water and comes to the underground parts of the plant, here the sugar is reconverted into starch stored." If some generalization does not fit in the solution of the problem some other is tried. *(Problem solved)*

A new generalization can be drawn, such as Starch after changing into sugar moves down to underground parts of the plant and is reconverted into starch. *(Drawing conclusion)*

When full solution of the problem is not reached and no generalization can be drawn, the judgement or solution is suspended till further knowledge in this field comes in.

Merits of Problem Solving Method : In this method of teaching, students are asked to identify problems, propose hypotheses, experiment to test those, evaluate the consistency of the solutions and finally draw conclusions and apply these in new situations. By teaching students with this method we can develop scientific methods of working in the students and a scientific attitude towards ideas and events. Learning is from concrete to abstract. Certain laboratory skills and problem solving skills in the students are developed. Students get training in planning, formulating problems and reporting their results to other people effectively. A training in problem solving helps students solve their daily life problems.

SETTING AND MAINTENANCE OF AQUARIUM

The class can undertake the activity of setting up an aquarium and its maintenance. Also students' active participation can be sought while making observations on the aquarium. An aquarium proves to be a good teaching aid as we can study various phenomena and also can use several plants and animals for laboratory studies.

The importance of having an aquarium can be elaborated as follows :

1. We can make observations on the size and number of plants and animals teat can be put in the aquarium. Growth and development in relation to time can be studied.

2. In microscopic examinations we can use Hydrilla leaves or Elodea internode cells for protoplasmic movements, various cell types, cell division and structural contents of the cells can be studied.

3. Eggs of different animals such as of frogs and snails can be studied to their full embryonic development.

4. Animals and plants from the aquarium can be used for anatomical and histological studies. Some organisms can also be used for physiology experiments.

5. Various micro organisms like protozoans, bacteria and algae can be identified and, studied.

6. Various plants and animals can be cultured in a balanced aquarium .

7. Process of photosynthesis, can be studied, we can notice the bubbles coming out of water. The effect of light, temperature and other factors can be studied on photosynthesis.

8. Organisms can be tested for their chemical composition. Presence of starch protein and sugars can be tested.

9. Change in the soil (substratum) composition can be tested from time to time. Interdependance of plants and animals can be studied. We can also note seasonal fluctuations in the behaviour of plants and animals.

Due to the above noted advantages of an aquarium it becomes almost necessary for us to have an aquarium for teaching life sciences. If the teacher intelligently undertakes the activity of setting up an, aquarium with his class he will be able to have an aquarium for the class alongwith the learning outcomes.

Setting up of an Aquarium : The requirements and procedure for setting up an aquarium can be discussed as below :

The Aquarium Tank : A commercially built aquarium tank of about 5 gallon capacity may conveniently be used but it is not of absolute necessity. Any type of container with, regard to size and shape can be utilized. Some suggested sizes of aquarium tanks arc 18" X 9" X 9", 30" x 12" x 12" and 48" X 16' x 16". Some other water tight containers such as fruit jars glass jars wide mouthed pickle jars. buckets and barrels can be made use of.

*The Substratum:*An inch or so of sand or soil should be added to the tank as substratum. This will serve as a source of mineral and a medium in which plants may become anchoraged and animals can burrow. Marble pieces for animals that hide and well washed sand for those that burrow can be used. There should also be some mud in the aquarium.

The Water : Ordinary tap water, well water, water from ponds, pools and streams can be used satisfactorily. A glass lid may be used to prevent excessive loss of water from the aquarium. The water used for aquarium should be free from chlorine.

The Plants : Hydrilla, Elodea, Vallisneria are good submerged plants that can be introduced in the aquarium. Other plants like some algae, floating angiosperms. Salvinia. Azolla can also be put, if wanted for culture. The above mentioned submerged plants grow rapidly and are good oxygenators. These make a good food for fishes. Care should be taken that there be no dense mat of floating or submerged plants in the aquarium.

The Animals : To maintain a balanced aquarium we can use a number of small fishes that breed rapidly. A general rule is one inch of fish to a gallon of water. Some snails, insect larvae and small crustaceans can also be added. Some protozoans such as Amoeba, Paramaecium etc. can also be introduced.

Location of the Aquarium : The aquarium should not be exposed to direct sunlight. Place the aquarium where sunlight xemains for a short time or at a place that is well illuminated by transmitted or refracted (through window pane) light. When light is not sufficient electric bulbs of 100-150 watts can be used. Where temperature drops down at night, electric aquarium heater can be used.

Maintenance of Aquarium : Followings things should be observed in proper maintenance of aquarium :

1. Check at times the population of organisms. It should not go out of balance. There should be enough of plants to sustain the animal population.
2. With change of seasons, temperature of the aquarium should not fluctuate much. If the temperature falls down in winter an aquarium heater should be used.
3. From time to time remove plant and animal debris care should be taken to eradicate diseases if any develops in the organisms.
4. If the plant growth attains a thick mat sort out some plants.
5. Care should be taken that the aquarium remains in refracted or transmitted light for most of the day time. If light, is not enough artificial sources of light can be arranged.
6. Water should be added to the aquarium at times to meet loss due to evaporation.
7. Some artificial food should be given to aqurium animals and water should be aerated artificially if we are to keep a larger population of animals in the aquarium.

Questions

1. Discuss with suitable examples the inductive and deductive methods of solving problems in life sciences.
2. What are the educational values of having an aquarium for life sciences laboratory. Discuss the common requirements for setting up an aquarium.
3. Write short note on :
   (a) Setting and maintenance of aquarium.
   (b) Discovery Method.

15

PROBLEMS IN TEACHING

In India, particularly, teaching of life sciences faces several problems. Some of these problems can be discussed regarding curriculum, text books, laboratory work, teachers, methods of teaching and evaluation.

In India teaching of life sciences has been oral in character with some demonstrations thrown in. At lower stages, in schools there are either no experiments or these are performed according to set rigid rules. Aims and objectives have been talked much about but most of these are not implemented. The curriculum is not organized psychologically and text books are written traditionally without keeping in view the process of learning. Methods of teaching life sciences are dull and generally ineffective. Teaching is aimed at performance by the students in examinations and not at real learning of the subject matter learning in scientific method of working, problem solving, creative thinking and development of scientific skills, interests, attitudes and application of the knowledge remains in the state of neglect. There is lack of research in teaching life sciences, the contents are old and the condition is still deteriorated by the different media of instruction throughout the country.

Problems that we come across in teaching life sciences in Indian school conditions can be discussed as under :

CURRICULUM

In India there are different kinds of school courses, High schools (two years course after eighth class or middle stage), Higher secondary course (three years course after eighth class). The new organization 10+2 is still in its way of implementation. In High Schools there is no life sciences curriculum as such but it forms only a part of General Science curriculum. The students learn little beyond gaining some familiarity with a few plants and animals and an elementary idea about digester, respiration and photosynthesis. There is no laboratory work, only a few models, slides, charts and specimens etc. are shown while teaching in the class room. This curriculum does not fulfil the aims and objectives of teaching life sciences.

In Higher Secondary Schools of eleven year duration we have general science curriculum upto middle stage and the condition of teaching upto this stage is as that in high schools mentioned above. At Higher Secondary stage the old syllabus was divided into Botany and Zoology, included too much of technical terms and definitions, limited to morphology and anatomy, so imbalanced. There were no topics relating to human body working or relating to daily life activities and to the future careers of the students who discontinue their studies after this stage.

N.C.E.R.T. developed a modernized traditional curriculum for Higher Secondary classes in which biology was elective subject for science students. Here the subject matter is dealt according to the major groups of plants and animals and the classical branches of biology. The curriculum was balanced to some extent but did not include knowledge regarding the daily life activities and for some vocation, for the students terminating their studies after Higher Secondary stage.

Biology was not taught in Indian Schools till as late as 1940's. It was taught in Intermediate colleges representing the first stage of degree course. When Higher Secondary system was adopted the then existing course for Intermediate classes was condensed to 80% and prescribed for Higher Secondary classes. Later N.C.E.R.T. provided the new curriculum for Higher Secondary classes 10+2 System of schooling, in which general science is taught compulsorily upto 10th class and students can elect this subject in 11 th class, is in its way or implementation. Life Science forms a part of general science curriculum upto 10th class. N.C.E.R,T. has developed new curriculum-from 6th to 10th and upto 12 class. The curriculum is balanced but it is criticised as it places too much burden on the students. Scrutinizing and rewriting of the syllabi is going on and a final form of the curriculum is yet to be decided.

TEXT BOOKS AND READING MATERIALS

The content of the textbooks is determined by the type of curriculum. There were available, only college books of Botany and Zoology for Higher Secondary classes till N.C.E.R. T. produced a text-book of biology. The content of the earlier books was too much dominated by the use of technical terms and definitions and subject matter was not organized according to the learning processes of students at this stage. The Higher Secondary system was shown apathy in its implementation and hence in teaching, the new text book of biology. The book was available in English, later translated in Hindi also but not in regional languages. The new books under 10+2 system have large volume of content matter and these books have not been favoured publicly so condensing and rewriting of the subject matter is in process.

The problem regarding text-books is further aggravated by the production of made easy and matter of facts books in the markets and students incline more on these. These books contain nothing more than definitions and brief notes on the more important topics which the student can memorize.

There are no guide books for the teachers and help books for students regarding laboratory work and further reading. The existing stock of book leaves much room for improvement regarding printing and illustrations.

LABORATORY WORK

Most of our schools lack physical facilities for teaching life sciences. There is also much over simplification of laboratory work.

Field work and experimentation have no place in it. There is more emphasis on bookish knowledge and students are often not aquainted with the beautiful fauna and flora of their own locality. In most schools, at higher secondary stage students attend the laboratory twice a week for 70-80 minutes on each turn. They spend most of their time in observing and dissecting the various plants and animals included in their syllabus in making labelled diagrams of the entire or dissected specimens, in copy 'ng figures from charts and books and in looking through the microscope. They also get some chance to observe the set up of a few experiments in plant physiology. Since the laboratory work is of short duration the students rarely have the opportunity of seeing any experiment to its completion. The teacher who has to look after a class of 30-35 students generally without a laboratory assistant to help him, cannot manage to demonstrate the experimental results on a quantitative basis. So there is no scope for students to find out something for them selves through experimentation. Most of the laboratory work recommended for higher secondary classes, includes morphological and anatomical studies of some plants and animals included in their theory syllabus, and a few experiments in plant physiology. No field work, projects or work in laboratory techniques has been recommended.

THE TEACHER

Secondary Education Commission in India (1952-53) recommended that students in higher secondary schools should be taught by post-graduate (M.Sc.) trained teachers. However the salaries of teachers, throughout India, are not adequate to give them the wgnity and status which their work demands. Their chances of promotion are very few. Teaching profession therefore attracts the least promising men and women and there is an actute shortage of really good trained teachers. In some school teachers who do not have any biological background teach life sciences upto middle stage and in many schools science graduates teach this subject for all the three years at higher secondary stage. Heavy duty (30-35 periods of 40-45 minutes each per week) and poor remunerations prevent the teachers from putting their heart into the work. They are often on the look out for non teaching more prosperous jobs. Our training institutions also do not produce well trained teachers as the training remains stereotyped and they are not told about new methods ,of teaching, techniques of evaluation, proper use of teaching aids and organization of co-curricular activities or undertaking of projects and problem solving. Our teachers are also not well, at laboratory techniques.

METHODS OF TEACHING

Even where post-graduate teachers for higher secondary classes and graduate teachers for lower classes are available, the teaching remains stereotyped and sometimes even unbalanced. Post graduate teachers are specialized in classical biology-either botany or zoology. Depending upon his specialization, he may do full justice to one branch but may do a step motherly treatment to the other and it may influence the future choice of the subject by the students studying under him. The teacher's initiative is often crushed by the traditional curriculum and his teaching becomes dull and lifeless due to the pressure of dead weight of examinations which often demands little more than good memory.

In teaching, only lecture method or lecture demonstration method is utilized. In demonstrations also performance in the class rooms remains poor. The teachers do not employ investigatory approach while working in the laboratories or undertaking demonstrations. Some methods of teaching like problem solving project method or undertaking field work and excursions are not at all utilized. So we are not able to develop in students, scientific method of working, which we aim at inculcating in them while teaching life sciences.

THE EVALUATION

We do not have any standard tools for measuring the learning of the subject matter in Life sciences at different stages of schooling. The teachers generally employ essay type tests and some questions are set from so called important parts, or topics of the books. The essay type examinations are not valid, reliable, objective or sometimes even practicable. These tests can be employed for testing depth of knowledge, comprehension, application but there are chances of learning by rote memory, without adequate understanding of the subject matter. The new type tests or objective type tests are becoming popular due to their high validity, reliability, objectivity and these are easy to practise. These objective type tools are also not foolproof and cannot be employed where we want to test depth of knowledge, power of comprehension and application of the knowledge and there are chances of copying and guess answering.

DEFECTS IN PRACTICAL EXAMINATIONS

Our practical examinations also suffer from certain defects. In these examinations, examiners are generally influenced by personal relations of them are sometimes prejudiced. Students' performance is evaluated on the basis of practical note books which contain neatly copied diagrams and sketches. The skills of taking observations handling of apparatus and drawing etc. should be evaluated by at the spot checking.

Questions

1. Enumerate the problems that we face in India, regarding teaching of life-sciences at school level.
2. As a policy maker for teaching life-sciences at school level what improvements would you seek in upgrading the standard of teaching this subject?

16

TECHNOLOGY IN TEACHING

Before, five centuries, when the first book was printed, no longer did students need to cluster at the feet of their teachers to listen and memorise what was read to them from a precious, laboriously produced hand-written manuscript. The printed book was a form of automation, a kind of teaching machine. Each student could have his own copy of the text to study. It seemed that the teacher has been permanently replaced, but the teacher increased in importance. His function changed. Relieved of the chore of reading to his students, now he had time to counsel and to explain and expound, to interpret and correlate the mass of information and knowledge that books made available to all.

For centuries the teacher's chief job has been that of presenting information and testing students to see whether they can remember it on cue or not. But now it is clear that assignment of lists of non-functional facts to be studied and remembered is out of place. Changes in a society usually bring changes to its institutions including education. The educational institutions are also affected by rapid increase in number of students, increased mobility of students, increased range of students' abilities and broadend backgrounds. Opinions as to what should be done often contradict each other, but there is a clear demand for action that will enhance the learning of the individual students, the effectiveness of schools and colleges and ultimately the quality of the nation's life.

Today we are seeing the beginning of another forward surge that may prove even greater. The electronic age is changing our traditional notion of education. Since last few decades innovations of all kinds are being experimented and the education has come more and more to understand that learning is an active process. The role of teacher, the role of the classroom, as well as the nature of the learning process itself must be re-examined in the light of new technology, for the sake of the nation's quality education.

The first step towards improving quality would be to free the teacher from much of his daily routine in order to give him time to serve as diagnostician and organiser or manager of functionally varied learning experiences. The second step would be to provide teachers with a large number of teaching techniques and specific curricular material. A third positive step would be the development of teaching material of a highly individualised nature in each subject. Each of these steps could be realised with the widespread use of electronic teaching aids that could take over much of the routine involvement in teaching and also provide better course materials. Classroom teacher then could give more individual attention to their students.

Lot of educators do believe that if technology is properly supported and wisely used, could help meet most of the pressing educational needs and many teaching problems can be solved partly or wholly by the proper use of the rich experiences that can be gained through certain media. In this technological age, therefore, today's teacher should take the full advantage of the existing technological resources for quality education.

EDUCATIONAL TECHNOLOGY

Any definition of Educational Technology must be subject to the concept held by the definer, and this involves consideration of at least two distinct concepts—the physical science or media concept, and the behavioural science concept. Here various definitions of Educational Technology are being given.

(i) The Educational Technology can be defined as the purposeful utilisation, in combination or separately of objectives, techniques, devices, events and relationships to increase the effectiveness of educational process. Educational Technology is fundamentally aimed at improving the efficiency of educational systems by increasing the rate, depth, precision and value of the learning which takes place.

(ii) Educational Technology concerns the systematic use of modern methods of technologies in teaching and learning. It involves teachers in a variety of roles, some of which are traditional and some still emerging. In this definition special consideration is given to the adaptive role of the teacher.

(iii) Educational Technology is a systematic way of designing, carrying out and evaluating the total process of learning and teaching in terms of specific objectives based on research in human learning, a combination of human and non-human resources to bring about more effective instruction.

Outside the limits of speech, man is dependent upon the tools of his age for his ability to educate or to learn from others. Twenty-first century man has acquired more tools of communication, more power to educate in last fifty years than he ever possessed in the hundreds of thousands of years of pre-recorded history. With the increasing rate of scientific advance and discovery the need has arisen for clarification of new methods of communication and their application. This is the core situatio1n with which educational technology has to deal. The greater the pace of change in the world, the more urgent it becomes for us to develop efficiency in the way our young people learn. This is true because education is a bridge between present and future, it is a bridge between what we are and what we may become—as individual, as a nation, as a world. But the test of the value of a new technique for education is not whether learning occurs. Learning is always occurring but we are to test whether the new technique improves the learning rate and depth of understanding as compared with the existing approach.

Educational Technology is still largely a classroom supplement. Teachers now have access to film projectors, slide projectors, tape-recorders. Video Cassette Recorders (VCRs), Video Cassette Players (VCPs) and computers etc. Teaching machines may ultimately prove more effective in a specific learning situation than text and printed material, since they offer greater control over the contingencies involving in learning.

The teacher normally supplements his verbal output with such materials as textbooks, blackboards, maps, posters, slides, overhead projectors, etc. Essentially these devices are limited to the presentation of immobile two-dimensional/orres.

In United States a Commission on Instructional Technology was established long back to determine whether the belief in technology's value for education is justified and whether it is justified to recommend actions to provide for the most effective possible application of technology to American Education. The Commission took 'Learning' as starting point instead of technology. The heart of education is the student learning and the value of any technology used in education must, therefore, be measured by its capacity to improve learning.

Technology will assist and support educational functions. Thus increasing the productivity of the teaching force and freeing them of the multitude of clerical record keeping chores and the elementary task of simply presenting information for students consumption. This can restore the personal touch to the educational process.

But there are many problems in adopting educational technology.

1. Well intentioned resistance to the introduction of technology – some people think that it will dehumanise a very human process.
2. Getting educational research applied – innovaters and leaders have problems in transitioning from research to application. Many successful researches are not carried out towards its application.
3. Scarcity of trained personnel to install/ maintain and supply new methods and equipment.

Few basic principles will affect the successful application of educational technology. The key to success is training and particularly in-service training. The real mass attack on training must take place at school and college level. In-service training needs to be developed on at least at two levels.

(a) At the elementary levels to ensure the elimination of fear and ignorance of the hardware and to show the productive potential in a curriculum situation.

(b) At the advanced level especially in its application to curriculum development.

If educational hardware is going to be used effectively during teaching situations the colleges and schools must be supported by an adequate technical assistance service. Every teacher should take this training in the first few years of his teaching career. Because of the size of turnover of staff in educational institutions, it is essential that in-service training in the handling of technical equipment be continuous until all have learned its use.

Next stage in training could be more advanced, concerned with the techniques of production. One can use this technique in the lecture room situation to take 'Off Air' programmes to enable large groups of students to see a detailed scientific demonstration clearly, or to use it in certain areas of the curriculum.

In order to use educational technology we should be familiar with the existing hard and softwares.

Hardwares (Technology in Education) : Hardwares include all sorts of teaching machines. Some common ones are listed below :

Projectors

(a) 16 mm film projector

(b) 8 mm/super 8 mm film projector (not being used now)

(c) 35 mm slide projector

(d) Opaque projector (Episcope)

(e) Overhead projector (OHP)

(f) Micro-projector

Tape-Recorders

(a) Spool tape-recorders (not much in use now in educational institutions)

(b) Cassette tape-recorder

Television

(a) Closed circuit TV / VCR, VCP

(b) TV telecast

Softwares (Technology of Education) : They include the hand-written or printed materials for effective teaching.

(a) Programmed instructional materials

(b) Self-learning modules

(c) Films, slides, OHP transparencies

(d) Audio-video tapes

(e) Multimedia packages

(f) Computer Discs (CDs)

Now let us discuss these Hardwares and Softwares of Educational Technology very briefly.

16 mm Film Projectors. A 16 mm teaching film though less flexible than verbal statement or description, is often far more effective. There is much to be learned which is incapable of demonstration. This can be done by controlling the speed of visual presentation, e.g., the flapping of a bird's wing, the unfolding of a petal, the clogging of an artery and the control of spacecraft etc., 16 mm films are available in India in every field of education. In Delhi there are some good resources for such films, like CIET of National Council of Educational Research and Training (NCERT), British Council and United States Information Service (USIS). Educational Institutions can ask for their catalogues and the films can be borrowed. Similar resources can be explored in each state or city. In addition to this some colleges, IASEs and University Departments have their own film libraries. These films are also available in the market for educational institutions to buy.

16 mm film projectors are now very common and most of the educational institutions have these projectors. These projectors make it possible to use 16 mm films (software of 16 mm film projectors)

which go along with the lesson. These films can be used as introduction, enrichment or follow-up of the lesson. These films are now being videotaped.

8 mm/Super 8 mm Projectors. 8 mm and super 8 mm educational films in different fields are also available in the market. They are lot less expensive than 16 mm films. They can also be produced very easily if the school or college is provided with 8 mm/super. 8 mm movie camera. These films shown with 8 mm/super 8 mm projector are an asset to classroom teaching. The teachers can give their own commentary or it can be audio taped before hand to be replayed whenever these films are used. But now these projectors are not being used in educational institutions.

35 mm Slide Projectors. 35 mm slides and film strips (software of 35 mm slide projectors) because of their characteristic similarities lead to joint treatment. Both are similar materials, both use the same basic principle of projection. Both can be adopted for sound accompaniment. But 35 mm film strips are not being used now. 35 mm slides on different subjects are easily available in the market, which are not very expensive. Such slides could also be made as desired if college or school has its own 35 mm camera. These cameras are getting common these days in India. 35 mm slides projectors project 35 mm slides. These projectors are available almost in every educational institution. Thus they could be used in coordination with classroom teaching. The teaching value of magnified projection has a dramatic impact and there is a further advantage that the class can examine the pictures etc., on the screen as long as desirable.

Overhead Projector. Overhead projector though very often being used in schools and colleges in western world, is not very common in India even now when we are entering twenty-first century. But now it is being manufactured by several firms in our country. Here the transparencies (software of overhead projector) black and white and coloured-photocopied or hand-made can be projected overhead. Thus the teacher can stand in front rather than at the rear of the classroom. These transparencies use transparent plastic material on which instructor writes or draws in the course of the lesson and this appears on the screen and a large class can see clearly what would be visible to only a small group if the chalkboards were used instead.

Micro-Projector. Microscopic slides can be projected by micro-projector and the entire class can see it at the same time. These projectors are either attachments for a microscopic or separate projectors with built-in micro-lenses. They are used much as slide projector but adjustment is more complex and the image is usually not so bright that is why the micro-projectors require complete dark rooms. Micro-projectors are also available for projecting microfilms.

Two types of recordings are in general use, those engraved on a disc and those magnetised on tape.

(i) The discs vary in the speed with which they rotate on the machines, because of these variations speed as well as size, the 'play back' machines the 'record-player' must be suited to the requirement of the records and vice versa. This is not being used now in educational institutions.

(ii) The second type of recording made on magnetic tape, involves a totally different sort of play back equipment. The magnetic play back or the 'tape records' can also be used for making recordings. These magnetic tapes could be in a spool or in the form of a cassette (software of cassette tape recorder); both of these involve different machines, the spool tape recorder and cassette tape-recorder respectively. But spool tape-recorders are not being used now in educational institutions.

Most of the colleges and schools have their own cassette tape-recorders or players. They can be used very effectively in classroom teaching by imaginative teachers. For example, instead of giving the same lecture to several classes a day or repeating the same lecture every year, a teacher would be able to devote days or even weeks to the preparation of one outstanding presentation to be audio taped and repeated, and up-dated as often as needed.

TV Telecast. Educational Television programme is another technique for effective teaching. The Educational TV project started in 1961 for Delhi schools. Since then it showed tremendous improvement. Due to the coordination with classroom teaching, this programme proved to be very useful for the students. Teachers knew before-hand what lessons at what date and time will be received on TV and what portions of the syllabus they were to cover in the classroom. Now such TV programmes are not being telecast.

Closed Circuit TV. Due to rapid technical advances, specially in the field of video tape recording the emphasis of closed TV (CCTV) has altered over the past several years and has become a powerful media. For this a TV camera, a Video Tape-Recorder and a TV Receiver are needed. The use of CCTV, rather than films etc., is justified by its facility to be immediate and the fact that it is easier to manage. Close-ups of demonstrations of scientific experiments can be shown very clearly to a big class and to several classes at the same time. Some of the good demonstrations or techniques can be video-taped and shown whenever desired.

But due to its high cost and lack of knowledge for its utility it is not very common in our schools, colleges and universities. Instead TV Educational Video Tapes-Video-Cassettes (software of VCRs and VCPs) are used in our schools with VCRs and VCPs. If will be nice if such equipment is used by us quite frequently.

Some Uses of Computers. Classroom uses of the computers generally fall into one of three categories. Computers are being used as a direct means of instruction in many developed countries. This use of the computer is often referred to as computer assisted instructions (CAI). Another widespread use of the computers in educational institutions is for calculating and analysing data. A third use of the computer is a device for computer simulated experiments. Other uses of computers in education are scoring of papers, filling up the grade sheets or mark sheets, time table preparation (scheduling), guidance, counselling and curriculum development. Now CDs and Internet are also in use.

Computer is a powerful and evolving tool for managing and sharing knowledge. Today clever software can turn a computer into a television, a canvas, or make it replay images and music, snap photographs, synthesise human speech, organise databases and libraries, and present a combination of animated drawings. Computers and communications are progressively becoming cheaper and faster.

Computers : Distance Medical and Surgical Facilities. Convergence of computers, communication, speech, text and images also presents an extraordinary opportunity in multimedia services and applications. These developments will change the way we live, learn, work, transact our business and communicate. For example, these techniques could allow doctors to examine patients in another continent and even monitor surgical operations at very far off places.

Computers : Future Attentive Assistants. Scientists are also working on image and pattern recognition techniques that can make computers ubiquitous. Speech recognition would replace the computer keyboard for most of the uses. There are attempts to develop computer systems for recognising faces, expressions and gestures. Such developments would enable us to create smart rooms which could see that people are in a meeting and shield them from interruptions. Such smart rooms would be networked and furnished with cameras and microphones. Thus these rooms could relay information from the room to other interested parties on the network. The computers could also assess what people in the room are saying or doing. Computers could compare the incoming information with models they have stored in memory, and arrive at decisions by tracking people's movement, identifying them and recognising their expressions. Therefore, in future computers will thus be playing the role of attentive assistants.

Internet

Present : The Internet is a large and global network of computers. Anybody can be a part of this network and share information with its users. The Internet provides access to essentially unlimited sources of information. Internet allows dialogue and exchange of ideas through Electronic Mail (E-Mail). Communication can be carried out at all hours and across large distances.

Future : Friendly ways of helping users to find what they want are already becoming available. In the course of time procedures for information quality control will also develop. The Internet will have all the essential features of a massive library system. It will of course take time before Internet possesses a large store of knowledge to rival the best of our libraries. The Internet and its successor technologies will have a profound effect on society.

What India is to do? We in India should develop a national information infrastructure, where using phone lines, cables, high speed data networks will allow open access for all to the electronic superhighway of information. All our universities and national laboratories should be connected to this information superhighway, so that researchers cannot only have access to important research journals and other library material but can also collaborate across large distances. The status of libraries in our universities is very unsatisfactory. Unless we do something about it, the research in universities will suffer greatly in quality. Low cost computers and internet connectively could provide a satisfactory solution to this problem. Today many of our higher educational and research institutions have working internet facilities, but many of them are operating at low bandwidth. In the area of software India has a lot of potential. We should now aim at high quality software development for automation, networking, design activities and telecommunications. As of now most of the internet software is imported. There is scope for us to design software for specific applications on the Internet appropriate to Indian needs. We should make every effort to see that India is not marginalized in this rapid race of information technology.

Can Computers recognise the owner? Have you ever wondered about the fact that while you can recognise your computer, your computer cannot recognise you? How would a computer go about recognising its owner?

It would recognise you by:

The way you speak : Most PCs today are equipped with a microphone. It would not be too hard to write programmes that can detect and identify voices to a limited extent.

The way you look : This is very difficult and involves having a video camera connected to the PC. The image from the camera would then be analysed to identify the person in front of the PC. This is an active area of research.

The way you type : Just as handwriting is unique, so is the way in which you press the key on a keyboard. A statistical analysis of patterns of key depressions (for how long, how hard and in what order you press keys while typing) can provide good clues to who the user might be.

The way you move the mouse : Hand-eye coordination is fairly unique in human beings. By analysing the way in which you move your mouse, a PC might be able to figure out who you are.

These are some of the ways in which a PC of the future might recognise its owner.

Programmed Learning Units. Programmed learning was first associated with teaching machines, and there appears to have been two schools of thought. One was represented by the Harvard Psychologist, Skinner who transferred his theories based on the clinical observation of animal behaviour to the field of learning in the classroom. His programmes were divided into different segments each called a frame. The learner reads the frame and because of its form prompted into making a reply, usually written one and is encouraged to go to the next frame and so on through a series of positive reinforcement. The careful shaping of these stimuli and responses was aimed at securing a carefully prescribed behaviour pattern at the end of the programme. The individual could go at his own pace and learning was secure and certain. The second view, seen at one time to be divergent and the learner should be offered alternative answers. This approach was associated with Crowder. The Skinner programmes were called "linear" and the Crowderian ones "branching."

A programmer, nowadays seeks to arrange an environment within which learning activities appropriate to the programme's objectives are provided. No such guidance is given with a text book.

Adjunct Programming another development can be the link between programmed instruction and a good textbook. It combines some of the progressive features of Programmed Instruction (PI) with the comprehensiveness of textbook. The goal of adjunct programming is to enable the student to learn as efficiently as possible from a good textbook.

What is generally considered an advantage of programmed instruction is the systematic, controlled, and sequential fashion in which content is presented to the learner. In programmed instruction provision can be made for differentiated instruction to accommodate individual differences.

Programmed Learning Units are self-learning programmes. Students tearn on their own with these programmes. Teacher is free to guide those students who really need his guidance.

Self-Learning Modules. Modularization of Instruction is another form of individualisation of instruction and self-learning; Modularization of Instruction is done by selecting, re-arranging or organising material and activities and breaking them into smaller sub-units in order to promote better understanding. The instructions are given in such a way that students know what specific objectives they are supposed to reach. Each sub-unit may have optional activities, from which students choose accordingly, all enabling them to reach the same objectives. Through such instruction the students can direct themselves through learning activities, with minimum assistance from the teacher; *i.e.* they can work at a particular rate that suits them.

Siddiqi developed a Self-learning Module "Man and Environment" and used it in her research study entitled "Development of Self-learning Material for Senior Secondary Biology and Analysis of Its Effectiveness". She found that students who used this module achieved statistically higher than those who did not use the module, and taught by the teacher in a conventional way.

Use of Self-learning Material. You can use programmed learning units and self-learning modules for effective science teaching.

Multimedia Package : Teaching ideas mainly through one medium, namely, the printed word, is no longer wise either pedagogically or technologically. Taking into account individual differences in the way students learn, it will be wise to use a variety of learning aids assembling them in an integrated form known a multimedia package consisting of (for example) programmed instruction booklets, self-learning modules/ books, slides, tapes (audio/ video), films, transparencies, experiments, CDs etc. The students who do not learn best through reading a text have, therefore, the chance of learning more or better by working with films, slides, tapes and CDs so forth. For the sake of differences in individuals, knowledge should be presented in different forms.

Such packages though so useful, effective, interesting and instructive are not being used in our country. It will be wise to develop some of such packages at least for try-out.

Example. A slide-tape programme is a Multimedia Package. On any topic you can make 35 mm coloured slides (35 mm slides on various topics are also available in the market) by your 35 mm camera. Load your camera with 35 mm coloured slide film. Take pictures. Give the film for developing. You will get a set of 35 mm coloured slides.

Write the commentary for each slide. Audiotape the commentary. Now your Slide-Tape Programme is ready. You can use it again and again in your classroom.

SCIENTIFIC APPROACH

The goals and expectations of science education change, and with them the curriculum. As the curriculum evolves so must the optimum-role of the science teacher. Today's science teacher is faced with numerous problems of how to teach what is given in his hands. Many science educators believe that the traditional teaching methods which are geared towards inculcating students mostly with factual knowledge, should be revised. Educational technology is here for our rescue. It is important that it should be used wisely as some of the earlier attempts to use teaching machines effectively failed because they were employed as alternatives to the presence of a teacher rather than as extension of his capabilities. It is upto us how best we can use the existing tools in science education. There are several tools as mentioned above which can be used in classroom for effective learning. But these materials are not being used in our educational institutions as effectively as could possibly be. Some of them are not available in the institutions due to their high cost or unfamiliarity of their utility. Some of us are against the use of technological tools with a plea that India's economy cannot afford the use of these expensive machines. But even those machines which are already available in the schools and colleges are also not being used fully. Science education is likely to expand substantially even explosively, over the next few decades and that can be achieved through the application of educational technology. It will be wise if the school and college science teachers should gather to learn the effective use of various technological tools and take with them the ideas which they think are wise and feasible for their classroom teaching.

A report commissioned by the US National Science Foundation speculates that by the end of twentieth century electronic information technology will have transformed western home, business, manufacturer, school, family and political life. The report suggests that one-way and two-way home information systems, called Teletext and Videotex, will penetrate deeply into daily life, with an effect on society as profound as those of the automobile and commercial television earlier in this century. This proved true. Now the, same is gomg to happen in developing countries like India in twenty-first century.

The study focused on the emerging Videotex industry, formed by the combination of two older technologies, communication and computing. It was estimated that 40 per cent of households in the US will have two-way Videotex by the end of the twentieth century, and this estimation came out true; Videotex system would enable individuals to create their own newspapers, design their own consumer guides. Furthermore this system will bring an increased flow of information and services into the home and at the same time, carry on stream of information out of the home about the preferences and behaviour of its occupants. All this hopefully is going to happen in the developing countries like India in twenty-first century.

INSAT-IA was up in space on September 4,1982 with capabilities for telecommunications, metereology and country-wide TV telecasts, but it was declared dead on September 6, 1982. Though it was possible to take this failure rather philosophically as a forerunner of future success, yet it was a serious setback to all our communicational developments. Then INSAT-IB was successfully launched by India on August 30,1983, though INSAT-IC launched on July 12,1988 could not be a success. Afterwards both INSAT-ID launched on June 12, 1990 and INSAT-2A launched on July 10, 1992 were a success. (For more satellites launched by India, see the Table 6.1) We enjoy many benefits of satellite technology. An all-India transmission of TV programmes has been possible through INSAT. The satellites bring to us live programmes in any part of the world. Satellite communication, weather monitoring, remote sensing, and collection of information about planets and outer space are some other applications of satellite technology.

It would be nice if we could produce enough software material for maximum utilisation of INSAT. The developing countries like India will have to use TV for reaching out the masses in the dark ghosts of illiteracy/ ignorance, disease, poverty and exploitation with a view to providing fundamental education. This is a tremendous task for all educators in general and educational technologists in particular.

Table : Launching of Indian Satellites

S.No.	Name of the satellite	Date of launching	Result
1.	Aryabhata	19 March 1975	Success
2.	Bhaskara-1	7 June 1979	Success
3.	Rohini	10 August 1979	Failure
4.	Rohini	18 July 1980	Success
5.	APPLE	19 June 1981	Success
6.	Bhaskara-2	20 November 1981	Success
7.	Rohini	31 May 1981	Failure
8.	INSAT-1A	4 September 1982	Failure
9.	Rohini	17 April 1983	Success
10.	INSAT-1B	30 August 1983	Success
11.	SROSS-1	24 March 1987	Failure
12.	IRS-1A	19 March 1988	Success
13.	INSAT-1C	12 July 1988	Failure
14.	SROSS-2	13 July 1988	Failure
15.	INSAT-1D	12 June 1990	Success
16.	IRS-1B	29 August 1991	Success
17.	SROSS-3	19 May 1992	Success
18.	INSAT-2A	10 July 1992	Success

It seems that the new media are still quite expensive and their penetration if relatively limited, but future developments hold a promise of considerably cost-reduction and competitive productionization. The cost of computer memory in the developed world for a bit of information was 100 cents in 1954, 1 cent in 1964, 0.5 cent ø 1974 and 0.004 cent in the year 1984. This cost will further decrease in the years to come. In India, the cost of a transistorised radio set has shown consistent reduction inspite of inconsistent price-rise. We do hope that the story would be repeated also a case of TV and Videotex. It is estimated that by 2000, more than six million households would own Videotex in the western world. The developing countries like India would have to chalk out their own plans and priorities in the field of educational technology. In order to do so, we would have to think globally and act locally.

In India, in several States and Union Territories, Educational Technology cells have been started functioning with 100 per cent financial support (for the first 5 years) from the Ministry of Education, under guidance of Central Institute of Educational Technology (CIET) of NCERT in New Delhi. The remaining States and Union Territories will also open similar cells gradually. Hopefully these cells will assist our teachers in effective science teaching using educational technology.

ON THE JOB TRAINING

NCERT organised the first ever interactive satellite based interactive teacher training programme to train primary school teachers on various topics of primary education using INSAT transponder with one-way video and two-way audio technology.

In the first phase the programme was launched in Karnataka on January 7-13, 1996 (7 days) covering about 850 teachers and 80 facilitators and course directors assembled in 20 different district centres (learning ends).

In the second phase, the programme was organised in Madhya Pradesh on August 2-8, 1996 (7 days) covering about 1400 teachers and 170 facilitators and course directors assembled in 45 district centres (learning ends).

The 7 days programmes each for Karnataka and MP had 14 Sessions, each of which were on various topics such as MLL, use of OB materials, multigrade teaching strategies, teaching of Maths, EVS (Science and Social Studies) and Language etc. Each of the sessions was about 3½ hours (2 hours of live interaction and 1½ hours of individual and group activities). Each session comprised of presentation, demonstration and discussion. Participating teachers interacted with panelists through telephone and fax, followed by group activities.

During the 7 days programme of Karnataka about 600 telephone calls and 240 fax sheets were received, and in case of MP about 700 telephone calls and 200 fax sheets were received, altogether about 7000 questions were asked through telephone and fax.

This experiment was highly appreciated by educationists, distance education experts, education administrators and teachers. Such programmes hopefully will be common in India in the years to come.

Another achievement of this Experiment is the successful networking of various national, state and district level agencies in the implementation of the project.

What is served to India, is what is cooking in Delhi. What you will get in education is now in included in Ninth Five Year Plan.

Educational Technology in the Ninth Plan is going to take a significant and massive turn. The focus in primary education during the Ninth Plan will have to be on quality because without enhanced, retention and performance of students, universalisation of education will remain elusive. The National Action Plan for continuing education of primary teachers envisages a series of change in the Ninth Plan. The main approach is to develop a training module using multi-channel learning which includes self-learning, action learning, face to face interactive learning and learning through interactive television. The entire multi-channel learning is a capsule model instructional design which is the core of educational technology. Self study materials, which are the basis of self-learning, are semi-structured learning modules. Action learning is conceptualised to be action experience and studies within the schools. Face-to-face interactive learning is proposed to build interactive and problem solving skills among the teachers to interact with the guidance of an expert tutor. The interactive television will bring in an opportunity for primary teachers to interact directly with the experts at the regional, state, and national level

The proposal is to set network in selected national, regional, state and district level institutes through satellite communication. The proposal also includes the setting up of block level resource centres with educational technology facilities for face to face interaction. With block and district level training centres, primary teachers would have access to more than 5500 centres in the country.

The proposed training network will have the capacity of training a few million people every year in the country. In view of both extended capacity of the training system and the need for training the supervisors and teacher educators who play critical role in teachers' performance will also be provided specially designed training modules once every 2 years.

This is for the primary teachers. It is likely that the training network will be extended for upper primary and secondary teachers as well. The universities are not far behind. IGNOU has proposed a network called OPENET interconnecting its study centres, state open universities and other distance education institutes and centres. The proposal is to use VSAT for delivery of courses.

From programmed learning, one way television and radio broadcast and educational technology equipments as teaching aids, India seems to be ready to graduate to satellite communication and computer communication. The new educational technology is likely to sweep the country very fast rather we, the teachers should get ready to receive and respond to this massive change which is being conceptualised.

Rationale. With the advancement of science and technology many new developments have taken place in the field of education. The conventional ideas about teaching are proving obsolete and inadequate. With the changing times the expectations from teachers have also increased. A teacher is not only a trainer or instructor in basic skills but he is also an organiser of worthwhile experiences for children. To meet these challenges, a teacher has no option but to adopt new technological aid. With the help of mass media, quality education can be provided to children and adults even in remote and inaccessible areas. The services of competent teachers and subject experts can be made available at any place, without their presence in actual classroom situation. Teacher is now expected to be part of an educational system where in machines, materials and media are important constituents of instructional process. The teacher has, therefore, to understand his roles in the new educational system, and it is for this reason that the present course has been included in the ETE curriculum.

THE AIMS

On completion of the course, the teacher trainee will be able to

- explain the concept and scope of educational technology and use of teaching-learning process develop skills to use and maintain hardwares.

- develop skills of preparing softwares and making their effective use.
- develop skills of effective use of blackboard, school TV programmes, educational radio broadcasts, educational video programmes develop skills to make use of waste material or low cost material available locally for developing teaching aids.
- develop skills for evaluating effectiveness of various technological aids, media and strategies.

Course Outline **External 40 marks Internal 10 marks**

Tune 45 hrs Unit 1 Introduction to Educational Technology 6 hrs

5 marks Meaning, need and scope of educational technology. Difference between 'Technology of education' and 'Technology in Education'.

Unit 2-Hardware and Software **12 hrs 10 marks**

Hardware

- Effective use of hardwares in teaching-learning process, their general maintenance and safety precautions.
- Television, VCR/VCP, Tape-recorder, Radio-cum-cassette player, overhead projector, slide projector.

Software

- Planning, preparation/development; effective use of charts, maps, flash cards;
- display materials for flannel board and bulletin board, transparencies, slides, audio programmes, slide-tape programme.

Unit 3 : Audio-Visual Aids and Mass Media **12 hrs. 10 marks**

- Meaning of A.V. aids and mass media, classification of A.V. aids
- Projected and non-projected aids
- Selection of appropriate teaching aids-Edgar Dale's Cone of Experiences

- Advantages and limitations of A.V. aids and mass media
- Effective use of Educational Television and Educational Radio, pre-telecast and post-telecast activities

Unit 4 : Innovative Trends in Educational Technology **15 hrs. 15 marks**

- Micro-teaching
- Simulated teaching
- Team teaching
- Programmed instruction Multi-media package
- Satellite TV transmission
- Computer aided learning

Practical Work : (for Internal Assessment) **07 hrs. 10 marks**

- Any two out of the following:
- Preparation of an audio programme
- Preparation of learning packages in one school subject
- Preparation of any low cost teaching aid

Questions

1. Write three steps which can improve science teaching in our schools. What will be the role of educational technology in achieving these steps?
2. What is educational technology? How can it help in science teaching?
3. State problems in adopting educational technology in teaching science. How could they be solved?
4. What are few basic principles of educational technology? How could they help in effective science teaching?
5. Name the hardwares and softwares of educational technology.
6. What is the role of the following for effective science teaching?

   (a) Projectors
   (b) Tape recorders
   (c) Television
   (d) Computers
   (e) Programmed learning systems
   (f) Multi-media packages.

7. What should be the role of a science teacher in the use of educational technology for better science teaching?
8. What is the future of educational technology?
   (a) in the developed world.
   (b) in India.
9. What is the difference between:
   (a) technology in education, and
   (b) technology of education?
10. Discuss the uses of computers in education.
11. What is the scope of self-learning programmes in today's science teaching? Discuss with examples.
12. What is the use of multi-media package in science teaching? Discuss with examples.
13. What is the future of educational technology in India? Discuss.
14. What is the use of Interactive Video Technology? Discuss with examples.
15. What is the picture of educational technology with Ninth Plan? Discuss.

17

TEAM TEACHING

Team teaching is comparatively a new idea in the field of education. It was a pattern which emerged in American education in 1954. It has assumed many dimensions and is now a big movement. Almost all the countries are now busy in making new expriments in this field. According to Shaplin, "A number of major universities are participating actively in the development of team teaching and there is a high level of professional interest, both pros and cons, expressed in meetings organised for the description and analysis of team-teaching.

This professional interest in team teaching is growing day by day. By and large, team teaching is becoming the subject of discussion and its literature is constantly growing.

THE CONCEPT

Team teaching is a comprehensive Item. It is a term with many faces. The sphere of team teaching is very wide. It is not limited to any one level of education. In the most general and most widely applied sense, it means giving two or more teachers joint responsibility for education of group of pupils larger than what is generally considered a normal size class.

Shaplin has defined team teaching in the following words : Team teaching is a type of instructional organisation, involving teaching personnel and the students assigned to them, in which two or more teachers are given responsibility, working together, for all or a significant part of the instruction of some group of students.

Team teaching may also be defined to include not only organisational, structure but also a highly complex philosophy of education.

According to M.B. Naik, In a team teaching method, two or more teachers make a plan of the subject or subjects co-operatively, carry it out, and always evaluate its effect on the students periodically.

This is actually a very simple version of team teaching. Team teaching is a technique of teaching the students in a collective form which makes teaching more effective and a joint venture

Professor Michael J. Apter has aptly remarked, "Team involves bringing together a number of classes whose teaching is then the joint responsibility of the teachers of these classes who now constitute a team."

In brief, team teaching refers to the following factors or components :

1. It involves more than one teacher *i.e.* there is a group of teachers.
2. Teaching becomes a joint responsibility. This includes instructional planning and other aspects of teaching. Team teaching is essentially co-operative teaching.
3. It is an organization of Instructional material or courses, of studies at all educational levels such as elementary, secondary or college levels.
4. The number of teachers depends upon nature and objectives of the course, the size of the class and the facilitates to be used.

MAIN INGREDIENTS

Team teaching refers to :

(a) Scheduling.

(b) Grouping of students.

(c) Assigning specific teaching responsibilities to the teachers.

(d) New building arrangements.

(e) Independent study time for pupils.

(f) Use of para professionals known as teacher aids or persons who assist the teachers and students.

(g) Replacement of the centralised library with resource centres.

This describes the team teaching.

The way the team operates is team.

THE HYPOTHESES

Risk has given the following hyptheses which underlie team teaching :

1. The best teachers in a school are shared by more students.
2. Teachers are provided with a schedule which allows time for better preparation and planning.
3. Teachers get more help from the non-teaching branches of the school such as test service, school office, guidance, audio-visual services, and the library.
4. Teachers should have, and can have, more exect knowledge of their students.
5. The best teachers in any system are entitled to recognition.
6. Teachers can grow and keep abreast of increasing knowledge.
7. Teachers do not plan and work in isolation. The team approach minimizes repetitious effort.
8. Teachers make better use of teaching technique, and technological devices.
9. Students develop better study habits.

10. Special student needs are more easily diagnosed, and remedial assistance easily planned.
11. Flexibility permits groupings and re-groupings of students.
12. The plan provides for flexible class size.
13. Resource people from outside the school are more easily used.

THE AIMS

The general aim of team teaching is improvement of instruction. It is essentially a new technique which makes use of all the resources available within a school or a college Team teaching aims at :

(i) Re-organization of teachers, students and schedules

(ii) Re-assignment of curriculum and class schedules.

(iii) Change the staffing patterns.

(iv) More extensive use of technological aids.

(v) Teaching every subject by a specialist, yet preserving the inter-relations of content and learning.

(vi) Making optimum use of all the skill and knowledge of every staff member of a school.

According to Shaplin: "Within the team, teachers see each other at work and join in the evaluation of instruction and learning under natural conditions where the objective is the improvement of instruction and judgement of their own worth. Teachers with greater technical expertness are responsible for influences the performance of their less expert colleagues. The team structure allow the school to identify those teachers who have greater knowledge and skill and to assign them greater responsibility and to reward then for successful performance."

GUIDING PRINCIPLES

Kenneth has described the following guiding principles in team teaching :

1. The size and composition of the group must be appropriate to its purpose.

2. The time allotted to any group must be appropriate to its purpose.
3. The learning environment must be appropriate to the activities of the group.
4. The nature and extent of the supervision of the group activities depends upon the purpose *of* the group.
5. The duties assigned to teachers must be appropriate to their special qualification and interests. This is very essential as some teacher, have a particular ability such as expounding their subject to large audience whereas the others for systematic attention to the individual pupils difficulties and so on. As a matter of fact every teacher should be given that role for which he is best fitted.
6. The level and style of instruction must be appropriate to each learner in the group.

FACTORS RESPONSIBLE FOR THE SUCCESS

The principles listed above call for specific criteria or factors which must be kept in mind as they are responsible for the success of team teaching. The criteria (factors) are :

1. Co-operation between team teachers.
2. Co-operation of the head. The success or failure of team teaching solely depends on the co-operation of the head who is the team leader.
3. Suitable material equipment including rooms and audio-visual aids. We must know and face the fact that there is no cheap, and easy way to educate human beings. We have to provide all the necessary equipment.
4. Teacher's willingness and faith in Team Teaching.
5. Proper Planning.

OUTLINE OF PLANNING PROCESS

Outline of Planning process as given by Joseph C. Graunis is given below :

1. Reading of general topic of the proposed unit by teachers.

2. Survey of the written materials and other resources.
3. Teachers individually and then together, consider scope of generalization relating to unit which is divided into phases.
4. Teachers together take out key lessons for collective planning.
5. Construction of team learning and evaluation exercises.
6. Periodic meetings for collective planning.
7. Daily planning on a contingency basis.
8. Co-ordination of team's daily plans.
9. Leaders help teachers set up conditions in class-rooms to facilitate planful behaviour of both teachers and pupils.

These steps go a long way in planning units in different subjects. With reference to the planning strategy the leader of each grade level must be inquiring continually about the team's opportunities and obligations, otherwise the strategy will fall apart.

ORGANIZATION AND ADMINISTRATION

The organization and administration of Team Teaching is a tough task. It involves a huge machinery and hence needs efficient personnel, mutual co-operation, proper planning and organisation.

In the light of the finding of a pilot project, it was suggested that understanding and the enthusiasm in of the teaching staff is the key to success for any venture of this kind. Further comments were, "Get the co-operation of all teachers and staff members, see that they develop a common philosophy and have access to common knowledge." Again, "Take time to get all parental understanding and consent." "Move slowly, evaluate every move."

Organisation and administration of team teaching is based on planning and preparation for team teaching. In the course of organisation we may encounter certain structural problems such as the size and the type of teams to be organised, the extent to which all teachers are likely to become involved and the ways the proposed structure will influence the professional behaviour and the morals of participants.

Again, Kenneth has suggested the following ways of organising teams in the process of team teaching :

1. At the secondary stage the simplest arrangement is for a number of specialist teachers to join forces in a single subject throughout the school.
2. Another arrangement is for the specialist teachers to join forces but to restrict their efforts to a particular age group.
3. An inter-disciplinary approach may be attempted *i.e.*, with subject specialists from different fields working together with a mixed age and ability group.

In this connection, it may be mentioned that the organisation of team teaching is a complex affair. It is therefore necessary to provide a congenial atmosphere of work, co-operation, team spirit and fellow feelings. Everyone has to be convinced that the purpose of team teaching is to bring qualitative improvement in instruction with zeal and missionary spirit. This will smoothen the problem of administration and organisation.

TEAM IN ACTION

The entire discussion on team teaching provides much enlightenment with regard to the operational aspects of team teaching. The practical implications of team-teaching are more or less confined to group arrangements for the purpose of instruction. It includes Large group-instruction, Class-size group instruction and Small-group and Independent Study.

In general, the team will be comprised of persons with different talents and therefore, with different responsibilities. It includes Team Leader, the Senior Teachers and the Team Teachers. As a human organisation, the team is subject to a great many stresses and strains.

TEAM LEADER

1. The success of team largely depends on the quality of the Team Leader. He has to create general climate and provide direction and stimulation to all the team members. Actually, the person with the most authority and responsibility is the team leader. "His job is to lead his team.
2. Better Planning. Team teaching overcomes repetition and allows every teacher to devote more time towards planning and preparation of his unit.

3. Effective use of Teaching Techniques. Team teaching leads to the integration of the curriculum. Teaching becomes more meaningful and effective. Teachers observe each other and thus improve their teaching techniques.
4. Better Follow-up Work. It ensures better follow up work as a number of specialists teach the same subjects to the same class.
5. Better Motivation. It provides better motivation for good teachers to become team leaders and better motivation for the students while they are being taught by a number of teachers. Teachers with greater technical skill influence the performance of their expert colleagues.
6. Very useful for gifted or intelligent students and slow learners. Team teaching is very useful for gifted or intelligent students, as well as for the slow learners.
7. Solves the problem of shortage of teachers. It also helps in solving the problem of shortage of subject teachers.
8. It ensures improvement of instruction and school atmosphere as a whole.

THE INDIAN CONTEXT

Team teaching is just a new innovation and is at the experimental stage in our country. Experience shows that Indian education is still traditional and stereotyped. It has not been possible to bring forth any reform. Various commissions have emphasised new experiments and given so many recommendations regarding teaching techniques and science of pedagogy. But no sincere and serious efforts have been made to implement them.

Indian education needs drastic change to give way to team-teaching

The trend is going towards hospitalization and team teaching can prove useful in some of the teaching subjects. We can give the benefit expert knowledge of different subject-experts to our students. It will be a sort of enterprise and a new movement will begin to make the leading process interesting and effective.

What is needed is comprehensive training and proper orientation the teaching personnel, administrators and the institutions.

A propetone should be established in the schools and possibly, the present structure, pattern of organisation, and scheme of studies in Education shall have to be changed.

Let us hope that the idea of team teaching will be accepted whole-heartedly by the teachers and others. The entire system of teacher-training and classroom teaching should be geared towards new innovations brought forth by Teaching Technology. Team teaching is certainly a valid technique and must be given a fair trial.

Questions

1. Define Team teaching. What are the main ingredients of Team teaching?
2. Describe the Hypotheses underlying team teaching.
3. What are the aims of team teaching?
4. What factors are responsible for the success of team teaching?
5. Give an outline of the planning process.
6. Describe the organisation and administration of team teaching.
7. Describe a team in action.
8. What is team teaching? What are its advantages? Can it be successful in our country?

18

MICRO-TEACHING

"Micro-teaching is a system of controlled practice that makes it possible to concentrate on specific teaching behaviour and to practise teaching under controlled conditions."

THE BACKGROUND

The quality of education we provide to our children depends, in a large measure, upon the quality of teachers we inject into the educational system. The quality of teachers, in its turn, depends on the quality of preparation they receive in our colleges of education (Teacher training institutions).

Considering the effectiveness of the present teacher training programme in general, there is almost unanimity amongst the professionals that our programmes are heavily weighted in favour of the theory course (Education Commission, 1966, N.C.E.R.T. 1978) By implication, practice teaching remains in alarmingly diluted form.

The teacher training seems to have no effect on what the future teacher does in the classroom, when he joins the teaching profession after completing the training rituals. There remains a big gap between theory and practice.

THE SHORTCOMINGS

In most of the training institutions, student teaching includes a few demonstration lessons by the method master (subject teachers), supervised block practice teaching, and a couple of criticism lessons. This is what is expected of the teacher training institutions. Thus even the minimum requirements are not fulfilled by the student-teachers during their training programme. Under the existing situations, it is well nigh impossible for them to acquire the desired level of teaching competence.

TEACHING, NOT COMPETENCY-BASED

Teaching is a complex activity. Even teachers with long standing face difficulties sometimes. The condition of the novice student teacher on the eve of completing his training remains very miserable. The sight of the student teachers with trembling legs and palpitating heart on the fateful day of the first teaching encounter, is not uncommon.

He is unprepared and finds himself in shallow waters. He is not confident whether he would swim or sink, whether he would be able to control the pupils, be able to communicate effectively and follow the sequence of activities. The poor fellow is almost bewildered especially when the supervisor assesses his teaching with a global overview.

In short, there are a numbr of serious handicaps for the student teachers in facing the actual teaching situations effectively. A few deficiencies in this respect are listed below:

1. Inadequate preparation of the student-teachers for the block student-teaching programme.
2. Sudden exposure to complex teaching situation, where
   - (i) Full class size comprising 30-40 pupils poses management and discipline problems to the beginner.
   - (ii) the duration of 30-40 minutes lesson is unduly long for a beginner.
   - (iii) the use of several component teacling skills in scale lesson prevents the beginner to focus on skills.

(iv) several concepts in a full scale lesson cannot be satisfactorily presented by the beginner;

(v) global supervisory comments rail to provide systematic and specific feed-back to the student teacher to make improvement in subsequent teaching.

NEW DEPARTURES

Teacher educators have frequently been questioned about the effectiveness of the teacher-education programme. There have been a few innovative alternatives for teacher educators to adopt, like micro teaching technique competency performance based teaching, role-playing, self-confrontation and others. Among them the most popular ones are micro teaching and competency,performence based teacher education programme. The conceptual rationale for the micro teaching technique is discussed below.

THE DEFINITION

Micro teaching is relatively new departure in teacher-training micro teaching was not dreamed of ever coffee on a rainy afternoon nor did it dvelop run blown as a delibrate solution to the problem of practice teaching. It evolved slowly as answer to a problem that is common in teacher education.

Micro-teaching is based on the assumption that there are certain patterns of behaviour, or perhaps more accurately strates which are crucial to effective class-room instruction. Micro-teaching provides an example of one of the most important developments in the field of teaching practice.

Micro-teaching is a teacher training technique. It is defined as a system of controlled practice that makes it possible to concentrate on specific teaching behaviour and to practise teaching under controlled conditions.

The complexity in a teaching encounter is reduced by practising teaching skill one at a time. This complexity is further reduced by having a small number of pupils, short duration of time and the content being reduced to a single, simple concept and one component skills practised at one time.

A MINIATURISED CLASS-ROOM TEACHING

Micro-teaching may be considered as a miniaturised class-room teaching or mini-teaching. It may be described as a 'scilled down' teaching encounter in class size and class time. (Allen and Ryan 1969)

In 1976, Clift described it in these words, Micro-teaching is a teaeher training procedure which reduced the teaching situation to a simpler and more controlled encounters achieved by limiting the practice teaching to a specific skill and reducing teaching time and the class size.

Micro-teaching technique was first developed in 1963 at Stanford University and was used for the training of Secondary School teachers. The concept has never been a static one. It continued to grow, change and develop both in focus and form. Some of the countries like U.S.A., U.K., Netherland, Scotland have set up micro-teaching laboratories. In India, a lot of work has been done in the centre of Advanced Study or Education, Baroda and N.C.E.R.T. The Technical Teachers' Training Institute, Chandigarh has its micro-teaching laboratory.

STEPS GENERALLY FOLLOWED

(Principles of Micro-Teaching)

The steps generally followed in a micro-teaching setting are :

1. A student teacher teaches a small class of 5 to 10 pupils (micro-class) for 5 to 10 minutes. There may be real pupils or peers acting as pupils.
2. The content of the lesson (micro-lesson) is generally a single concept. The whole lesson is built around a single teaching skill so as to maximise the use of the behavioural components involved in that skill during teaching.
3. A micro-lesson is carefully planned on the basis of a pre-decided model. The lesson should be observed either by a supervisor or peer supervisor using a specially developed evaluation performa for the skill. It can be recorded on a video tape for later evaluation. This session is known as teach session.
4. After this session, the trainee is given the feed back. This is known as view /assess/feed back/critique session.

5. During the next session, the trainee goes to another room where he re-plans or re-structures his lesson in the light of the feed back received. It is also known as re-plan session.

6. Next is the teach session where the trainee re-teaches to a different set of pupils the same unit which is re-structured.

7. After re-teach session there will be re-feed back regarding the lesson. This session is termed as re-viewfre-assessfre-feed back session.

All the sessions may be together called as one Micro-teaching cycle. It may be represented as shown diagrammatically below:

The basic principles of micro-teaching are very simple. A student teacher teaches a short lesson of about five minutes' duration to a small number of pupils. At the end of the lesson the pupils leave and the student teacher discusses the lesson with the supervisor. After a short practice the student teacher repeats the lesson with a different group of pupils making use of the feed back from the supervisor to improve his previous lesson. He thus gets re-feed back.

THE PROCEDURES

Different procedures have been used by different persons. A mention is made of the following procedure used by Mishra, Goswami and Kulshrestha (1979).

Teach-6 minutes

Feed back-6 minutes

Re-feed back by actual evaluation-4 minutes

Re-plan-4-7 minutes

Re-teach-6 minutes

Re-feed back-6 minutes

Total time-35 minutes.

There can be many variations within this broad outline; the size of the class may vary from 3 to 10 pupils; time may vary from 3 to 28 minutes; the pupils may, be either real or peers acting as pupils; the sources of feed back may be from one or many sources like self, pupils, acting as supervisors, teacher educators, audio-tape recording, video-tape recording and the like : the feed back can be immediate or delayed, prescriptive or descriptive, qualitative or quantitative; and variations in length of time devoted to any phase of the micro-teaching cycle.

MAIN PROPOSITIONS

Alleo and Ryan (1969) have mentioned the following as the main propositions of micro-teaching :

1. Micro-teaching is real teaching. Although the teaching situation is a constructed one, nevertheless bonafide teaching does take place.
2. Micro-teaching lessens the complexities of normal class-room teaching. Class size, scope of content, and time are all reduced.
3. Micro-teaching focuses on training for the accomplish-ment of specific tasks.
4. There is a provision for increased control of practice. A number of factors/variables can be manipulated. A high degree of control can be built into the training programme.
5. Micro-teaching greatly expands the normal knowlede of results or feed back dimension in teaching. Several sources of feedback are at his disposal. All this feed back can be immediately translated into practice when the trainee re-teaches shortly after the critique conference.
6. The main focus in micro-teaching is to train teacher trainees in specific teaching skills although learning on the part of the pupils is no less important.
7. Micro-teaching is also possible under simulated situations.

TEACHING SKILLS

Micro-teaching is based on the assumption that the process of teaching can be analysed into a number of skills called the teaching skills which can be defined, observed, measured and controlled.

The term 'teaching skill' is said to be a group of teaching acts behaviours intended to facilitate pupils learning directly or indirectly

NUMBER OF SKILLS

The exact number of skills involved is very difficult to decide. Different authors have drawn their list of skills. However, no list is final. It is also not necessary, perhaps never be, that a particular lesson will need all the skills with equal importance to teach it effectively. The Centre of Advanced Study in Education, Baroda (CASE) has identified twenty one teaching skills. They have studied thirteen of those in detail and prepared the Baroda General Teaching Competence Scale (RUTC) and measuring criteria for each of these skills. These skills are :

1. The skill of writing instructional objectives.
2. The skill of introducing a lesson.
3. The skill of fluency in questioning.
4. The skill of probing questions.
5. The skill of explaining.
6. The skill of illustrating with examples.
7. The skill of stimulus variation.
8. The skill of silence and non-verbal cues.
9. The skill of re-inforcement.
10. The skill of increasing pupil participation.
11. The skill of using black-board.
12. The skill of achieving closure.
13. The skill of recognising attending behaviour.

SOME ISSUES

The list of teaching skills raises several issues such as :

1. Is the list exhaustive?
2. Can these general teaching skills be applied to all teaching subjects?
3. Is it possible to provide training in all of the teaching skills in a limited course of an academic year?

Without referring to the controversial issues involved we can say ....view of the availability of insufficent time for training in all the teaching skill, priorities have to be fixed.

The basic skills like questioning, explaining, illustrating, reinforcement, stimulus variation, handling pupil responses, management of class may be accorded priority. They may be covered and others can be added cording to the availability of the time.

This problem can also be viewed from tbe organisational angles. Some of the student teachers are quite competent in some skills while they are deficient in others. So, the student teachers can be grouped according to skill competence-skill-deficiency.

Efforts should be made to cover as many skills as possible. They should be integrated ultimately. This will enable the student teacher to know where to use a particular skill; when to use and how much to use.

THE RATIONALE

The existing teacher-education ptogramme in India has a number of loop-holes. We find that-the practice teaching conducted these days is not so effective due to the defects in the supervisory system and certain points of disagreement and other apparent drawbacks. The important elements in the micro-teaching technique offer tentative solutions to some of the loop-holes.

The following points may be noted for justification for the technique to be implemented in India :

1. In micro-teaching the trainee concentrates on practising a specific well-defined teaching skill which includes a set of related teaching behaviour.
2. Micro-teaching provides for pin-pointed feed-back in behavioural terms.
3. It is not easy but safe for the student teachers to teach a small group. They will have less problems of class-room discipline.
4. There will be less administrative problems for teacher educators in arranging lessons for student teachers when the teaching sessions are arranged with peers as students.
5. Micro-teaching-provides an opportunity to undertake research studies with better control over conditions and situations.

6. The studies conducted in India indicate that micro teaching is an effective technique in the modification of teacher behaviour. It is certainly a better technique than that of the traditional approach.

THE REMARKS

Micro-teaching is a new departure in teacher training programme. Because of its merits it is a useful supplement in the present day teacher training programme. It is in no way a substitute to the existing pratice teaching programme Similarly, it is not a panacea for all the ill of teacher education. It has its own limitations and shortcommgs. It is a skill based technique. It is also a teacher-based and not stude technique.

In all we can say that with the available instructional materials. developed in Indian context supporting research studies, micro-teaching is definitely a solution to many other problems faced by teacher training programme in India. The technique needs fair trial in the colleges of education. Tutorial group period can be better utilised for this purpose.

A new technique known as *Mini-teaching* is in the offing. It is claimed that it is refinement and extension of micro-teaching and offers an improvement over micro-teaching.

THE COMPARISON

Conventional Student Teaching	*Micro-teaching based Student Teaching*
1. Objectives are not specified in behavioural terms.	1. Objectives are specified in be behavioural terms.
2. The class consists of 30 to 40 student-teachers.	2. Class is divided into small groups of 5 to 10.
3. Teaching becomes complex and threatening.	3. Teaching is relatively simple and non-threatening.
4. Feed back is not immediately provided.	4. Immediate feed back is provided.
5. The role of the Supervisor is vague and not helpful to improve teaching.	5. The role of the Supervisor is specific and well-defined to improve teaching.
6. Patterns of class-room inter-action cannot be objectively studied.	6. Patterns of class-room inter action can be objectively studied.
7. Student-teacher practises whole complex teaching behaviour.	7. Student-teacher practises only one skill selected for practice.
8. Time duration is 35 to 45-minutes.	8. Time duration is 5 to 10 minutes.

Questions

1. What it Micro-teaching? Discuss its chief characteristics.
2. Describe a Micro-teaching cycle. How will you organise a micro-lesson in the process of teaching practice ?
3. "Micro-teaching is myth." Comment.
4. Bring out the advantages of Micro-teaching based student teaching over the conventional student teaching.
5. Give a rationale of Micro-teaching to be followed in India.
6. Give a detailed description of Micro-teaching.
7. Describe a micro-teaching situation by planning a micro lesson.

19

TEACHING AIDS

We sense the world around us by our sense organs such as by touching seeing, smelling, hearing and testing. When these sensations have some meaning for us these can be termed as perceptions. These perceptions stand for facts and the facts later on are organized into concepts and generalizations. So for better learning we should perceive the thing clearly and in as many ways as possible. For the purpose of better perceptions and learning we employ some aids while we teach in the class. The devices that are used for observations only are called visual aids and those for listening purposes are audio or auditory aids. But the devices that can be used for seeing and listening simultaneously are known as audio-visual aids.

THE CLASSIFICATIONS

The teaching aids that we generally employ for teaching life sciences, effectively, can be classified as under :

Visual Aids: Black board or chalK board, charts, sketches, diagrams models, graphs, bulletin board final graph, motion pictures films and slides.

Auditory Aids : Radio, gramophone and tape recorder.

Audio-Visual Aids: Films and television.

Aids through Activity : Museum, aquarium, vivarium, garden, excursions, field trips, visits to places of biological importance and science clubs where activities like collection and preservation of organism are undertaken.

THE IMPORTANCE

The place of teaching aids in teaching of life sciences can be stated as follows :

1. When new things are shown to the students in the class-room these catch their attentien and students get motivated and, interested in teaching. Moving things catch the attention more readily and illustrations should be coloured to get more, response from the side of the students.
2. It has been found that amount of learning is more and retention is for a longer period of time when taught by using teaching aids.
3. Perceptions of the things are clear because these are sensed in various ways such as by seeing, hearing and feeling etc.
4. Learning become from concrete to abstract and students can conceptualize real things. False imagination and guessing is avoided.
5. Use of teaching aids gives vividity and activity is introduced in the classroom. Lecturing and passive hearing is minimized. Participation of the students in teaching learning process is more.
6. Inaccessible materials such as processes too slow, too fast things too small, too large, too complicated, far away and theoretical structures can be represented by the teaching aids.
7. Use of teaching aids involves students in the teaching learning process and helps develop scientific attitude and scientific method of working.

Teaching aids should be selected according to the topic in hand and considering the age, intelligence and social development of the students. In case of audio-aids language should be well structured, voice should be clear and as far as possible aid should be a substitute for reality. Visual aids should be clearly visible and the illustrations should be effective. So far as use of the aids is concerned, the teacher should very well know operating the aid. Students' participation in the use of aids should be sought and there should be no over use of the aids. The effectiveness of the aids, used in teaching should be evaluated from time to time.

There can be a long discussion about the types, their significance, working and preparation of teaching aids for teaching life sciences but here it will be limited to the description of some generally used aids.

CHALK BOARD

Generally a black board is used in the class room out there can be coloured boards and chalks also. Boards are usually fixed but there can be roller and hinged boards also. The class room boards are generally used for writing down certain statements drawing diagrams and sketches, making calculations etc. It is an economical and effective teaching aid. It helps in systematic teaching and sequential presentation of the subject matter. Working on the board catches attention of the students and its use etablishes a connection between lecturing and illustrations. While working on the black board the teacher should also pay attention to the class and the board work should not be long drawn.

CHARTS, DIAGRAMS AND PICTURES

These aids can be used, where the drawings are complicated and difficult to draw. Some phenomena can also be taught systematically by presenting the diagrams and pictures in sequence. These aids secure better attention and things can be presented in their ratio-proportions. During presentation the teacher should observe that the aids are clearly visible to the students and are serving the purpose for which tbese are integrated in the instruction. Some systems of organisms, anatomical details, some natural phenomena and different organisms can be very well shown by using these aids.

GRAPH AND BULLETIN BOARD

Flannel graph is a wooden frame on which a piece of flannel is tightly stretched, that gives the background on which some coloured cuttings of diagrams, apparatus and pictures of organisms etc. can be displayed with the help of pins. Bulletin board is a sort of notice board in the form of a frame or box which is covered with glass or thin wire gauze. News paper cuttings, articles for wall magazine, cuttings of science magazines etc. can be displayed on the bulletin board. The flannel graph can very well be used in class room teaching and the time consumed in making drawings and pictures on the boards or charts can be saved. The bulletin board material gives up to date knowledge to the students in concerned discipline if the material is regularly changed and students are encouraged to read that. Various activities such as those of clubs, excursions, seminars, projects etc. can be reported on the bulletin board.

SPECIMENS AND MODELS

Preserved specimens of living things and their models are good visual aids that can be employed in teaching life sciences. By seeing the actual things, students develop adequate concepts about them regarding size, shape, structure and colour etc. The teacher can undertake comparative studies of the organisms while using their representations. So museum material as well as prepared and purchased models should be used, as far as possible, while teaching in theory classes.

The teacher can deliver the topic along with dissections of animal and plant material. He can also set up some physiology experiments, to demonstrate some phenomena of making some quantitative study, while the lesson is in progress.

EPIDIASCOPE

When some figures, diagrams and sketches, which are on opaque surfaces, are to be projected, epidiascope is used. This device contains a source of light by which the object is brightly illuminated. There is a mirror, fixed at some angle to direct the light rays to the lens system The lens system magnifies the figure or diagram on the screen.

SLIDES AND FILM STRIPS

Slides and film strips are good visual aids and can be beneficially incorporated in classroom teaching. By arranging the slides and film strips in required sequence we can present the topic systematically. Certain, phenomena like growth in plants and animals, embryonic development, cell-division, seed germination, the process of fertilization etc. can be illustrated very well by arranging the slides or film strips in order.

For transparent material that is to be projected, we need some projectors. An overhead projector is generally used for classroom purposes. In the projector there is a source of light and the light is directed by a mirror fixed at the back of it. The light after passing through the-material *(slide or film strip)* falls on the lens system. The lens system now magnifies, the things to be shown, on the screen.

The teacher should be well versed in handling the projector. Adequate dark room arrangement are necessary for using the projected material.

RADIO AND TAPE-RECORDER

Both of these are audio-aids and can be made use of in teaching Radio brings us news and programmes of far distance. Some radio stations have regular science programme and talks on scientific discoveries and discuss certain science affairs. Some programmes can generally be listened on A.I.R. and B.B.C. The difficulty with using radio is that the programmes are generally not broadcasted during school time and also it is somewhat costly aid. Tape recorder is a convenient but costly device. Here the recorded programme, talks or discussions can be reproduced at any time and in suitable sequence considering the teaching. We can record and reproduce the-recorded material in the classroom such as singing of birds, radio programmes, speeches, discussions and the sounds produced by different animals.

FILMS AND TELEVISION

Films and television involve our senses of hearing and seeing simultaneously. Various films such as those on particular topics, classroom or school activities, historical events, life history of an individual, biological phenomena in which sequence of events have been shown can be, very well, integrated in the classroom instruction. Some other films such as industrial films, documentary films and news reels can also be projected from time to time for general information. The films can be shown wherever their use is considered effective as the teacher can explain some phenomena regarding its broad aspects and after it is shown in the film or the film is first projected and teacher gives some short explanation after that or it can be projected in parts, the way it suits in the process of instruction. After the film is shown the teacher should encourage questions and discussions in the class. Adequate dark room arrangements are necessary when the films are to be projected in the class.

Use of television in teaching is quite recent. Delhi has taken lead in the field of using television for classroom teaching. During television lessons a few minutes are allowed for introduction of the topic. The actual lessons on television are of 20 minutes' duration and these are followed by follow up work and explanation, the teacher regarding various difficult points and other aspects.

Use of films and television can do away with the actual operations on complicated phenomena and that involve some danger. Similarly the need for sets of costly apparatus and equipments, that cannot be arranged for every school, can be met. Phenomena shown by films and television gives an impression of being 'live' and learning and retention is quite satisfactory.

Use of films and television in teaching deprives the students of seeing the actual things and handling these personally. The teacher can also find difficulty in adjusting the teaching by these devices according to the abilities and interests of the students and according to the social and local environments. Teaching by these devices is effectively conditioned but interpersonal relations with the teachers and personal satisfaction of the students on what they have learnt counts a lot in our formal education. So for effective teaching use of these devices and teaching by the class teacher should be exploited to the maximum usefulness.

AQUARIUM

Aquarium is a good teaching aid and we can conduct several studies of biological importance on it. Some of the observations that can be made on aquarium are, inter-dependence of plants and animals, photo synthesis, reproduction in aquatic plants and animals, behaviour of animals, their development and feeding habits of animals. Studies on succession in populations can be undertaken on imbalanced aquarium. The students also come to know the role of oxygen, carbon dioxide, temperature and of light in the lives of organisms. Some plants and animals can also be cultured in the aquarium. An aquarium is a 'live' comer in the laboratory or classroom and it can supply certain materials for practical classes.

SCHOOL GARDEN

School garden is a good place to keep different plants growing and for rearing insects and other animals. The teacher can occasionally visit the garden to make certain studies. Students can undertake comparative studies on plants regarding their growth sizes flowers and habitats. Animals and insects can be studied in nature. School garden is a place where instruction can go along with activities and it provides us with various plant and animal material for experiments in the laboratory.

FIELD-TRIPS AND EXCURSIONS

Undertaking trips and excursions makes it possible for the students to study things in their natural settings. Students when on trips, can also undertake collection of plants an animals for museum and aquarium along with getting experience through activity. The material collected can be cultured and preserved by the students and in this way they also exercise certain laboratory skills.

VARIOUS PROBLEMS

In most of our schools teaching remains traditional that is teaching only by lecture method the teaching aids are either not suitable in the schools. When these are there, the teachers do not take pains to use these. The teachers are not will versed in the use of teaching aids as they are-not adequately trained.

Some Problems regarding use of teaching aids can be listed as below:

1. Our schools do not get enough financial aid and most of the time they are not in a position to purchase or prepare necessary teaching aids.

2. Schools are not well furnished even with other physical facilities, the arrangement for film libraries, museums, aquaria and other equipments is far to think of.
3. In rural schools electricity is not available and provision for projected material and use of television cannot the made.
4. Whenever a few teaching aids are available the teachers either adopt indifferent attitude towards their use or they are not properly trained in the methods of using those.
5. Wherever some materiel aids and films are available the teacher finds it difficult to integrate these in their lessons as these are not according to the topics or are not well prepared.
6. Sometimes misuse of the aids or use of damaged or not well prepared aids mars teaching instead of helping in clarifying, the concepts in students.

COMPARATIVE VALUE

Direct experiences with actual phenomena or plants and animals have highest learning value. Next to these come their representation by specimens, modules, films and other projected material, auditory aids, charts and slides and least are verbal symbols for them. So teaching in life sciences should be organised around some activity as-far-as possible and classroom teaching should be aided by films, slides, coloured charts, diagrams and demostrations. At lower levels more concrete things should be used but as the level of students influences we can go for abstract and complicated aids when ever these are unavoidable in teaching certain phenomena.

Questions

1. Discuss the importance of using teaching aids in teaching life sciences.
2. What teaching aids are commonly used in teaching life sciences? Discuss the difficulties that the use of these aids comes across.

3. What are the various audio visual aids utilized in life sciences teaching? Comment on the specific use of each aid for the enrichment of life sciences programme in the schools.

4. How can resources be utilized effectively for teaching life sciences to Secondary school children? Discuss with the help of two suitable examples.

5. Suggest the type of lessons that you would teach to illustration any two of the following teaching aids:

   (a) Model

   (b) Tape recorder

   (c) Micro-projector

   (d) T.V.

20

PHYSICAL FACILITIES

For teaching life sciences, effectively and efficiently, a laboratory with necessary equipment and material is essential. For developing application abilities, skills of experimentation, construction, improvisation and scientific attitude, interests and power of appreciation, laboratory work is essential. Laboratory work is also essential for achieving different aims and objectives of teaching life sciences.

THE LABORATORY

While constructing a laboratory for teaching life sciences, the following factors should be taken into consideration at the planning stage:

(a) The number of students working at one time.

(b) The minimum space required for each student for comfortable working.

(c) Number of life sciences teachers, available in the school.

(d) Space required for ancillary accomodation, storage and repairs.

(e) Trial should be made to design the class room and laboratory in such a way that it can be used for teaching life sciences to middle as well as high classes.

(f) Amount of money required for setting up the laboratory should also be considered.

The design and requirement of a life sciences laboratory for school purposes can be discussed as follows;

WORK SPACE

The essential requirements for a life sciences laboratory are few and these are spaces in which students are to work, a good source of light, a water supply and a flexible arrangement of tables and chairs. Other things can be electric supply, gas supply, but depending upon the location of the school, spirit ,lamps can be used in life sciences laboratory. For every student is required a suitable working area and a school laboratory can have a space in which 20 students can work, at one time. Size of the tables and chairs can be accorded according to the space available but tables of 6 ft. X 3 ft. X 30 inches are preferred. There should be a demonstration table with all supplies. The demonstration table should be larger and higher and there should also be a black-board at the back of it.

VARIOUS ASPECTS

Assuming the laboratory is on the ground floor for easy access to outdoor areas, consideration should be given to the amount of light reaching various areas. One long walt of the laboratory facing north gives suitable conditions for aquaria and working with the microscopes.

The opposite south facing wall is suitable for plant growth and selling up of a green house or Warden Screen (an extended wind own enclosed in glass on all sides, thus functioning as a green house). It is generally set up in cold places. In hot climates extended leaves are necessary to shade windows and in some areas having a blank wall is advised. Aspect of the life sciences laboratory depends upon geographical position and claimet of the school location.

ANCILLARY ACCOMODATION

Preparation room, ideally has access from both inside and outside of the laboratory. It should have a hot and a cold water supply and electric, gas supplies etc. There should also be means of heating and weighing. Preparation room can also serve the purpose of store for chemicals and glass wares.

An animal room, not communicating with the laboratory, is useful for keeping small mammals, insect breeding cages and cultures. There should also be a space for setting up of an aquarium. The walls inside can be kept projected in order to display some illustrative material and for keeping chemicals, reagents and stains which are generally used in the laboratory.

In cool climates a greenhouse or a Wardian case is essential for growing plants. In the tropics a verandah outside the laboratory with an easy access to water supply enables potted plants to be grown while protected from natural hazards.

MEASURES OF SAFETY

Certain precautions need to be taken to prevent accidents in the laboratory, *e.g.*

(a) At least one fire blanket and a chemical fire extinguisher should be provided in the laboratory and the students should know how to use them.

(b) Doors should open outwards. In case of explosion these can be opened easily and students can rush out. Laboratory should have more than one exits.

(c) Electric supplies to apparatus should be of low voltage. If power supply is fitted to the tables it should be away from the water source.

(d) Poisonous material should be clearly labelled and locked away when not in use.

(e) Highly inflammable liquids should be labelled and should not be used near a flame or electric appliances such as ovens and cent refuges.

(f) A first aid kit should be readily available.

(g) At places where alcohol is dutiable supplies should be locked away and consumption should be recorded.

FURNITURE AND FITTINGS

Modern laboratories have fixed working tables, fitted with gas and electric supplies and are provided with sinks at each working station. Movable chairs or stools etc. occupy rest of the room and can be used according to the need.

As some time is devoted on working with microscopes, the tables in life sciences laboratory are generally lower than those in other laboratories. However the main consideration is that the height of the tables and chairs, correspond so that there is a leg and knee room. A standard 3 feet high table and a bench or stool is preferable. Allow a inch space as a minimum between seat and table.

Individual work stations should have water, gas and electric supplies. There should be a sink with high swan neck tap, for working purposes.

Adequate-cupboards and display cases, some lockable, must be provided in laboratory and preparation rooms. Bulletin board should be fitted and shaded from direct light. A demonstration table is generally recommended in front of the room.

LIGHTING

The laboratory should be well lit as special lighting is needed for microscopes and growing of plants.

Microscopes : Standard microscope lamps with 40 watt bulbs are adequate for elementary work. In the tropics, day light is sufficient for most microscope work and it is less straining at the eyes in comparison to artificial sources.

Plants : Potted plants, alga cultures and photosynthesis experiments are aided by the provision of special light, if day light is not sufficient. Generally transmitted light or direct sunlight is available in enough amount in the tropics that can support plant growth in the laboratory.

BLACK-OUT

A good black-out arrangement is necessary if work is done with Projected materials. In hot climates an extractor or exahust fan will be needed as any form of black-out reduces ventilation in the laboratory.

WORKING SURFACES

Wood is the cheapest and best wearing surface-in most countries. It can be kept in good condition by regular application of linseed oil. Plastic surfaces are becoming more popular. The good quality of plastics resist acid and most of the organic solvents and can be used. Plywood surfaces can also be used but these are not long wearing.

FLOORING

Acid proof plastics either as tiles or self hardening liquid can be used. In warm climates cement or concrete is cheap and easy to maintain. Floor should properly be fitted with water supply, water disposal pipes or channels.

WASTES

The end products of dissections, micro organism cultures and other wastes become both unpleasant and health hazard and should be disposed off as soon as possible. Bacterial cultures must be sterilized before disposal. Sink waste disposal is good but other material that cannot be disposed off via sink should be buried in a pit which is regularly burnt out.

EQUIPMENTS AND MATERIAL

Nature of equipments and material required for life sciences laboratories depends on the level at which teaching is undertaken and amount of laboratory work meant for the students. At middle stage was hardly need sophisticated apparatus, and local environment can be made use of. At high and higher secondary levels we need some specialized material. But this also depends upon the status of the subject in school curriculum *i.e.* whether life sciences is taught as integrated in general science or it is an elective subject. In training institutions the nature of the material required is almost the same but some more material for demonstrations and illustrative purposes is required.

GENERAL REQUIREMENTS

While making a list of requirements for life science laboratory, the teacher should consider the following factors :

1. The types of apparatus needed for experiments and demonstrations.
2. The quality and quantity of the apparatus, considering the number of students working at a time.
3. The quantity of consumable material needed, taking into consideration the time devoted for laboratory work.
4. The money at the disposal of the teacher.

CLASSIFICATION OF VARIOUS EQUIPMENTS

Various equipments and material required in the laboratory for teaching life sciences can be classified into categories given ahead:

OBSERVATIONAL AIDS

Items of this type include things that are used for measurement of length, weight, mass, size, temperature, volume and time etc. These articles can be simple and compound microscopes, cameras-lucida and micrometer, burettes, pipettes, meter rods, thermometers, measuring cylinders, stop watches, potometers and auxanometers etc.

GLASSWARES

A large number of glasswares is required for life science laboratory and some of these can be petridishes, test tubes, beakers, glass jars, funnels, bell jars, watch-glasses, thistle funnels, conical flasks, round bottom flasks, retorts, staining jars and bottles.

ANCILLARY AIDS

There are several other things that are required for well working in the laboratory. The list of such items includes slides, cover slips, test tube clips, spirt lamps, dissecting boxes, dissecting trays, cavity slides, test tube stands, magnifying glasses, retort stands, tripod stands, wire gauzes, wooden stands, corks, cork borers, wash bottles, stain racks, water baths, large forces suction pumps, rubber corks, inset collecting nets, hair driers, inoculation needles, aquaria containers and aquarium accessories, filter papers, cotton, table lamps, first aid box, connecting rubber tubes, glass tubes, glass rods, table lamps, glass marking pencils, capillary tubes, microtomes, rozor sharpeners, bone cutters, slide boxes, centrifuges, droppers and soil testing kits etc.

CHEMICAL STAINS AND REAGENTS

Some commonly used chemicals, stains and reagents are potassium hydroxide, sodium chloride, sodium bicarbonate, ammonium hydroxide, sugar, glucose, dextrose, ethyl alcohol, methyl alcohol, butyl alcohol, hydrogen peroxide, formalin, methylene blue, eosine, hematoxylin, iodine solution, potassium iodide, fast green, light green crystal violet, carmine, Gram violet, safranin etc. Some other requirements can be ether, spirit, Canada balsam, vaseline, distilled water, glycerine, wax, starch, agar-agar, some acids generally rquired are carbolic acid, acetic acid, nitric acid, sulfuric acid, hydrochloric acid etc.

TEACHING AIDS

For effectively teaching life sciences we can have a large number of teaching aids. Some of these can be permanent slides of plant and animal tissues, micro organisms, cell structure and cell division, models of micro organisms and large organisms that cannot be put as such, various charts of structural details and some of natural cycles such as nitrogen, carbon and oxygen cycles, D.N.A. molecule, structure of cell, exposed visceral organs of animals and various plant parts. Some stuffed material and presented specimen skeleton and mounts of insects etc. can also be used.

SIGNIFICANT FACTORS

The quantity, types and quality of the equipments and material for teaching life sciences will depend on the following factors :

Finance : This is the most important factor that determines the quality and quantity of the equipments and material to be arranged at the laboratory. If the amount is less more important items should be purchased first.

Place of the Subject in Syllabus : The number of science subjects taught in the school also limits the quantity of equipment for each subject. If life science is one of the compulsory subjects the need for equipments and material will be moret-but if it is taught as core subject (integrated) in general science, lesser quantity will be required.

Scheme or Work or Method of Teaching : The equipment and material also depends on the method of teaching employed by the teacher. If demonstrations are given, these require lesser material in comparison to individual practical work. Requirements for teaching aids also depend-on the interest taken in utilization of these by the teacher.

Level of Students : As we cannot allow students of lower classes to handle complicate equipments, we just give demonstrations here. For the students of higher classes we can assign individual practicals. So quantity and quality of equipments and material will also depend on the level of students.

Total Number of Students in the Class : The quantity of material and number of equipments also depends on the size of the class *i.e.* the number of students in the class. Further if we group the students in practical groups of two or four lesser apparatus, in comparison to individual practical work, will be required.

Number of Hours Devoted to Teaching the Subject : The quantity of the material in the laboratory also depends upon the number of periods allotted to the subject for practical work. If more time is devoted to this subject more consumable material will be needed for practical work.

Location of the School : In rural schools we can collect a lot of biological material, from the surroundings or local environment, by organizing field trips and excursions. But in urban schools we have to purchase most of the things. In addition to this quantity of the material also depends on the storage capacity of the laboratory.

The Teacher : The number of equipments and quantity of the material is also influenced by the qualification, training in laboratory techniques, interests and attitude towards the use of those of the life sciences teacher. The teacher well trained in laboratory techniques and handling of apparatus, can very well manage the laboratory.

THE MUSEUM

A life sciences museum contains collected and preserved specimens, models, skeletons, herbaria etc., arranged in ordered and organized manner. Setting up of a museum can very well exploit the collection instinct of the students and the collections made, can be integrated in instruction.

Location of the museum depends upon the space available in the laboratory or it can be a separate corner attached to it.

Some Points that Can be Observed while Organizing a Museum

1. Space for the museum should be selected according to the volume of collection and location of it should be attached to the laboratory.
2. Models, specimens, material displayed in dissected form etc. could bear the names of organisms as well as those of different organs.
3. Specimens, models, stuffed animals, etc. should bear their common as well as biological names and if possible their classifications also.
4. Arrangement of the museum material should be in some order. Animals and plants in whatever form they are displayed, should be according to their classes and orders.
5. Every specimen should bear a card on which characteristics of its identification, place of collection, name of the supplier or collector and data of collection etc. are written.
6. Models and stuffed material can be displayed as such but the preserved specimens, deselected animals and mounts of insects etc. should be displayed in glass face cupboards.

The museum material can be arranged in various ways such as grouping models, preserved specimens, stuffed material, skeletons, herbaria and insect mounts, differently. This will be an 'artificial way of grouping the things, so preference should be given to the arrangement of museum material in biological orders and classes.

Museum Material: The life sciences museum may be stocked with various and numerous plants, animals and micro-organisms *(model etc.)*. In plant material we can have preserved specimen of algae, fungi, bryophytes, pteridophytes *(whole or parts)*, gymnosperms *(cones, leaves etc.)* and angiosperms *(different plant parts)*. In animals different preserved specimens may include members of porifera, coelentrates flat and round worms, molt uses *(snails)*, annelida *(earth worms, leeches),'* insects, fishes, amphibians *(frogs, toads)*, reptiles *(lizards and snakes)*, some birds and various lower mammals like squirrels, and rabbits etc.

In addition to the preserved specimens we can have models of organisms which are too small to be seen with naked eyes; which are too large to be put in the museum such as bacteria, viruses, some protozoans, and whale, elephant, tiger etc. Some stuffed material of snakes, crocodiles, rabbits, bats and birds can also be arranged. Life cycles of insects like, silk worm, mosquito, housefly and that of frog etc. and dissected specimens of animals with exposed visceral organs, insectivorous plants can also be kept. Herbaria, albums of roots. stems, leaves, flowers and fruits, plant and animal products of economic importance can also and place in the museum. Charts of various systems' *(digestive, circulatory, nervous)*, anatomical structures of plants, carbon and nitrogen cycle and of some other natural phenomena may be kept. Models of cell structure, cell division, embryonic development, tissues can also be displayed in the life sciences museum.

Sources of Material for the Museum : Material for setting up museum can be collected by organizing-field trips, excursions and tours or it can be purchased from some other agency.

Collections. A great variety of living things can be collected from our living world. Some of these can be butterflies, moths and other insects, frogs, toads, snakes, turtles, birds, nests cocoons, insect lanrae, leaves, stems, roots, fruits, flowers, grasses, barks, tubers, bulbs, corms, mushrooms, lichens, algal material, diseased plants, insectivorous and parasitic plants and different other animals and plants of various groups.

Public Museums : Life sciences teacher should be investigative and should determine whether any exhibits of specimens may be borrowed or purchased from commercial museum exhibits of raw material such as latex, flax, wool, silk, cotton, food stuffs etc. Material may be obtained at low cost.

Homes : The teacher should encourage students *to* bring things of illustrative importance from their homes and wherever they get these.

In this way the museum can be enriched. Collection or purchase of material can also be done from local stores and industries.

Butcher Shops and Slaughter Houses : These can also be contacted for anatomical material that is to be displayed in the museum.

Scientific Supply Houses : These are specialized in supplying specimens models and other objects to schools, can be contacted and required material may be purchased from them.

EDUCATIONAL VALUES

Students should be encouraged to study the museum material and things should be shown in the theory class. The educational values of life sciences museum are many, *e.g.*

1. Students can see the actual things or their models and develop adequate concepts about their size, colour, shape and structure.
2. Students see different new things concerning their lessons and they are motivated and get interested in studying living things.
3. Students make study of concrete things and then they draw generalizations about them, so learning is from concrete to abstract.
4. Students develop team work habits and they can undertake comparative studies on the organisms.
5. Working with museum material develops power of investigation in the students.
6. Making collections for museum, exploits the collection instinct of the students. They also come to know about the habitats and behaviour of different organisms when they are on excursions.

Questions

1. Discuss a laboratory, for teaching life-sciences at second stage, in which 20 students can work at one time
2. What equipments and material do you think are necessary for well working of a life-sciences laboratory?
3. Discuss the difficulties which our practical work in school of sciences laboratories face.

4. What are the values of museum in teaching life sciences. How will you organize a museum for teaching life sciences at school level?

5. Draw a plan of life-sciences laboratory for higher secondary level and give a list of essential requirments for the laboratory work in life sciences.

6. Discuss the utility of museum for life-science programme in schools. How can the teacher utilize the local resources for enriching the museum with the help of pupils?

7. Discuss the educational significance of

   (a) Museum (b) Laboratory Work.

8. Discuss the importance of practical work by students in teaching of life-sciences. Give the requirements of a High School life-sciences laboratory for 25 students.

21

LEARNING UNDER PROGRAMME

Progmmmed learning is a new innovation which is the result of the experimental study of the learning process in the psychological laboratory. In the words of an American psychologist, "It is the first application of laboratory technique utilized in the study of the learning process to the practical problems of education." That is why it is claimed that the origin of modern programmed instruction arises from the psychology of learning and not from technology. As a result of the extensive as well as intensive work undertaken in the area, programmed instruction has come to stay and is being increasingly used in most countries of the world.

ORIGIN AND BACKGROUND

The term programmed learning is new but the practice is not. The traces of programmed instructional work can be found in the work of Socrates "who developed a programme in Geometry"-It also owes something to psychologists like Freud who studied behaviour. But, more recently, programmed learning is claimed to have begun in America where the system is known as 'programmed instruction'. "The English term 'programmed learning' is nevertheless, probably more accurate, as this is a learner oriented system with emphasis on the method by which , material can be presented so as to be auto-instructional.

PRESSY'S WORK

The origin of programmed learning is often linked with Sydney L. Pressy, an American psychologist of Ohio State University. In the 1920s, Pressey devised practical machines which could tell the learner at once when he made a mistake. Pressey tried to market his device but failed. Being disappointed, he gave up work on his automatic teaching device in 1932.

SKINNER'S WORK

The next major break in this direction came as a result of experiments carried by Dr. B.F. Skinner, a Professor of Psychology of Harvard Dr.. Skinner presented his famous paper, entitled *'The Science of Learning and the Art of Teaching'*. Skinner gave an immediate reinforcing teaching device. He experimented with pigeons. He was convinced that once a desired behaviour is reinforced, it is more likely to re-occur. As the action is mastered, reinforcement is given with less frequency. 'Skinner gave it the name *operent conditioning* Skinner's device differed distinctly from other similar devices in one important way. Skinner programmed his material in an organised sequence. The increment of learning in each step of sequence is very small. The pupil, having solved one problem, finds little difficulty in solving subsequent ones. Thus he is reinforced frequently. He is led step by step through the material to be studied. There is minimum of error and maximum reinforcement.

WORK DONE AFTER SKINNER

Since Skinner's presentation, much work has been done on programmed instruction/learning. During the last few years, a flood of literature on automated teaching has been made available in whole America and Great Britain. Day after day, teachers, psychologists, publishers and commercial firms interested in teaching machines are moving ahead with making this device most sophisticated. No wonder, machines at present in use will probably appear crude in a short span of time and many new developments will take place in programming.

THE CONCEPT

Method of self-instruction : Programmed learning as popularly understood is a "method of self instruction or, whereby the learner proceeds through instructional material in short steps at its own pace, receiving immediate knowledge of the correctness of his answers.

Dr. Susan Mankle's View : Dr. Susan Mankle has defind programmed learning as a method of designing a reproducible sequence of instructional events to produce a measurable and consistent effect of behaviour of each and every acceptable student.

Michael J. Apter's View: In the words of Michael J. Apter, Programmed instruction is a method of instruction in which the information to be taught is broken down into small units which are to be presented to the student (usually in written form) in a carefully planned sequence. Each unit or frame contains not only information but is also terminated with a question.

Integrated Instructional System: Recent advances in programmed learning has widened its concept. It is now "an integrated instructional system which may employ programmed books, teaching machines, films in various forms, audio-visual devices, stimulators and actual apparatus. The instructor himself trained in formulating objectives and in diagnostic analysis of his teaching results, is an important part of this system." This system also implies a strategy in which various kinds of intellectual, emotional and motor experiences are provided to the learner in a controlled situation through the above mentioned devices, which ultimately result in behavioural modifications.

This new technology has four important components, which are :

1. Instructional goals – the system of objectives.
2. The entering behaviour-the system of input or assumptions of the programming.
3. The instructional procedure-the system of operation or sequence of content.

4. Performance assessment the system of terminal behaviour or output monitor.

Thus, programmed learning is a complex system of systems in which programmer, though physically absent, is as much a part of the whole precess as any medium of auto-instruction.

SALIENT FEATURES

The following are the salient features of programmed learning and programmed material:

1. Individualized system : Programmed learning is an individualized system; one person learns at a time.
2. Auto-instructional system : The learner learns through an auto-instructional device. The device teaches, correct and reinforces without the presence of-the teacher. However, the teacher is a part of the system, he is absently present.
3. Logical order of the material : The instructional material is nearly perfectly programmed. It is presented in a logical sequence. Each new step in the learning process follows naturally and logically each preceding step.
4. Material presented in minimal increments : The material is programmed in minimum increments. Each increment is only a small step in the learning process and thus reduces the possibility of error to the minimum.
5. Learner's own pace of progress : In a traditional classroom procedure, an average student sets the pace for the whole class. In programmed system, each learner learns at his individual pace-the average moving slowly, the brighter student learning quickly. The rate of accomplishment is established by each student's individual performance.
6. Instant check of the learner's answer : The student's answer is almost instantly checked against the correct answer which appears by the side of the next question or frame. If his answer is correct, he receives encouragement. The very fact that is correct, reinforces his learning. If his answer is incorrect, he is helped to locate the reason for

his incorrect answer. In the latter case, the learner may be sent to a further teaching item which will clarify any misunderstanding.

7. Intensive validation before the release of a programme : All reputable programmes are the subject of 'validation' before publication. This consists in testing the draft programme on a sample of student population of similar background and intelligence to that of the target population.

BASIC PRINCIPLES

Although the principles on which programmed learning was originally founded have undergone a number of modifications in view of factual researches, they basically consist of the following *six* fundamentals:

1. Principle of behavioural analysis
2. Principle of small steps.
3. Principle of continuous active responding
4. Principle of immediate confirmation
5. Principle of self pacing.
6. Principle of validation.

Below, the above principles have been explained in brief.

Principle of Behavioural Analysis. One of the most important aspects of programming is an exact behavioural or task anallysis. This consists of defining and breaking the task to be performed into separate components so that the programme objectives can be formulated. It has been well said that programmes are not written just for the sake of writing them. Programme must bring about learning which can be defined as a *'change of behaviour'* which is :

(a) observable, and (b) measurable.

Principle of Small Steps. Since programmd learning is a self-instructional device, step-size is very impartant. Instructional material must esentially be programmed through small steps. This will enable the learner master each step before proceeding to the next. Small steps have a number of advantages such as accuracy or response, minimnm errors, mastery of subject matter, easy evolution of programme sequence, etc.

Principle of Continuous Active Responding. Most programmed learning is based on the principle of continuous active-responding or, to use the technical term, on *overt responding*. By overt responding we mean that at very stage of learning, the student is prompted to give an active respoe, either by writing an answer or by carrying out the action. Mr. G. O. M. Lith of National Centre for Programmed Learning, University of Birmingham, has confirmed on the basis of considerable research that children learn and retain material when they are called upon to make a continuous active response (overt response).

Principle of Immediate Confirmation. Psychological experiments (of Thorndike in particular) have proved that learning becomes permanent when accompanied by success and satisfaction. Programmed learning makes use of this important finding in the psychological laboratory. In programmed learning the correct response is immediately confirmed. This becomes a sort of reinforcement for the learner to work further on the programme. However, care must be taken to reinforce only those parts of the behaviour which are compatible with the objectives of the programme.

Principle of Self-pacing. Programmed learning is an individualized process. This means each student-bright, average or dull-moves with the programme at his own individual pace. This is the principle of self-pacing.

Principle of Validation. Validation is a test procedure adopted by the programmer in order to make a definite statement on the terminal behaviour. *Terminal behaviour* is a statemnt of what the learner will be able to do on completion of the programme. For this purpose, it is essential to test the programme on as large as sample of target population as possible. This will enable the programmer to verify the claims made in favour of the programme. This will also enable the programmer to revise the programme and improve it.

These are, then, six important principles which can be regarded as the guidelines for programmed instructional materials.

STYLES OF PROGRAMMING

The following types/styles of programming are currently in vogue :

(a) Linear or Extrinsic Programming.

(b) Branching or Intrinsic Programming.

(c) The Mathetics.

Linear Programming : Linear Programming is based on programming ideas put forth by B. F. Skinnr. In a Linear programme, the subject matter is divided into quite small pieces of knowledge, known as frames. Each learner is taken through these frames, in small steps, and in the same sequence, along a single path or line. Student's response to the first frame is immediately confirmed before he goes to the second frame. The correct response to the previous frame appears alongside the forthcoming frame. The programme is so structured that the probability of correct responses become sufficiently high (nearly 95 per cent). Linear Programmes can be produced in book form for use on a linear teaching machine.

The following format for a Linear Programme makes the concept clear:

Format for a Linear Programme

Response 1. ....

Correct. 2. ....

Answer 1

Response 2. ....

Correct 3. ....

Answer 2

Response 3. ....

Correct 4. ....

Answer 3

Response 4. ....

Correct 5. ....

Answer 4

Response 5. ....

Skip Linear

Basically, the Skip linear type ot programming resembles Linear Programming. But, the former differs from the latter in this way. When the learner is going through the programme, at certain points he is given a test question or questions. If his response to the test question is correct, he is free to skip over a few frames and is advanced to a part ahead in the programme.

But if his response is (incorrect, he is made to go through the normal sequence in order to obtain further practice. In the given diagram, the learner is given a test item after the sixteenth frame. If his (response is correct, he is advanced to Frame 20, otherwise, he proceeds in the sequential order.

Test your Grasp of Linear Programme

1. The proponent of linear programming.
2. The linear programme is-(called, not called) a straight line programme.
3. The reinforcement-(decreases/ increases) the tendency to give a response.
4. The linear programme is also called – (intrinsic/ extrinsic) programming.
5. In a linear programme the learner learns by (making/ avoiding) the errors.
6. According to Garner the emphasis in a linear programme is on(stimulus/response).
7. In a linear programme discrimination – (is/is not) more important.
8. In a linear programme the learner – (can/cannot) skip over some frames.
9. In a linear programme the reinforcement – (is/is not) quick.
10. The printed linear programmes – (do not involve/ involve) logistic problems.
11. Towards the end, in a linear programme, the prompts are (provided/withdrawn) gradually.
12. Cheating is discouraged by – (revealing/not revealing) the answers
13. Basically Skip Linear – (is not/ is) the same as the model.

14. In Skip Linear the learner—(is given/not given) test at certain points.
15. The correct response in a Skip Linear (leads/does not lead) to other part of the programme.

(For answers see below)

Check your Answers

1. B. F. Skinner
2. called
3. increases
4. extrinsic
5. avoiding
6. response
7. is
8. can
9. is
10. involve
11. withdrawn
12. not revealing
13. is not
14. is given
15. leads

Example of Linear Programming

1. If we have Female *Bb* X Male BB (B stands for black and *b* for blue : B dominant over *b)*, their children will have eyes. (Black)
2. If we have Female BB x Male B, their children will have eyes: (Black) (Black, Blue)
3. If we have Female Bb x Male *Bb*. some have—eyes and someof the children will have—eyes and some will have —eyes.

BRANCHING PROGRAMMING

The branching or intrinsic approach to programming was devised by Norman A. Crowder of the Educational Science Division of U.S. Industries, Santa Barbara. He has defined branching Programming as a programme which adapts to the need of the students without the mediuim of an extrinsic device such as computor. The intrinsic approach to programming works like this.

The student is given the material to be learnt in logical units. The units are much larger than those used in linear programming. Each material unit is followed by multiple-choice answers, out of which the student is required to choose the answer which appears correct to him. According to the item which he has chosen. he is directed to different parts of the programm to check his answer. If his anwer is correct, the student is put on the main line or the programme the same way as it happens in a linear programme. If he fails to choose the correct answer, the preceding unit of information is reviewed, the nature and cause of his error explained and he is either returned to the original unit of information, or branched along a sub sequence which gives him additional information to correct himself. He is then put to a retest before he is made to return to the main line. A diagrammatic representation of branching approach appear on below.

Test your Grasp of Branching Programming

1. The branching method was originated by --.
2. In branching programming the frame size is much -- (smaller/larger) than that of linear programming.
3. In a scrambled text of branching programming the pages (follow/do not follow) in normal sequence.
4. In a branching programme the learner -- (can/cannot) skip over the frames.
5. In a branching programme (discrimination/generalization) is over important.
6. The branching programming is also caned -- (intrinsic/extrinsic) programming.
7. In a branching programme the assumption is that the learners learn by (making/avoiding) the errors.
8. The branching method-(can/cannot) provide infinite branching to take care of all individuals.

THE MATHETICS

What is Mathetics ? The credit for formulating the basic precepts of Mathetics goes to Thomas F. Gilbert. He gave these precepts in his article *Mathetics, the Technology of Education* which appeared in 'Journal of Mathematics' Vol. I, No. I (Now discontinued). The term itself has been derived from the Greek *mathlein* meaning 'to learn'. According to *K. P. Pandey*, "Mathetics is defined as the systematic application of reinforcement theory to the analysis and construction of complex repertoires which reprent mastery of subject-matter.' The whole system is rather technical. Although mathetical programming may be applied to any subject, the emphasis on task stimulation makes it a particularly suitable vehicle for teaching skills where 'transfer of training' forms an essential part of instruction.

The unit for a mathetical programme sequence is called 'exercise'. There are no restrictions on its size or extent. The main consideration in this case, however, is to have as big an exercise as the student can reasonably take at a moment.

RETROGRESSIVE CHAINING

The sequence of Mathetic model is retrogressive or backward chaining. This sequence can be explained like this. In a programme based on the mode of mathetic, the learner performs all the operations that will be required by him, learning by doing. Sequence or chains in which response sets up a unique stimulus state of affairs are taught backwards. It is because of this that the sequence in mathetics is often called "retrogressive chaining". The technique involved in retrogressive chaining is to start with the most motivating task or start with the mastery step. This step is the one that complete the task or procedure to be learned. Normally, not always, this is the final step in the sequence. All the steps involved in the process are displayed to the learner. The learner then completes the last task in the serial, the last but one and so on *regressing through the chain.* According to K. P.J'aNley, "The programmer continues in this manner, each time allowing the student to perfom one additional step until he has worked his way back to the first step in the procedure and can perform the entire task."

The steps involved in regressive chaining are:

(1) Demonstrate.

(2) Prompt.

(3) Release.

(a) The programmer demonstrates the introductory frame which is the mastery frame.

(b) Prompts are used in teaching frames to help the learner to give the desired response.

(c) The testing frame, the last in the sequence, is the release frame where no prompts are given.

22

LESSON PLAN

If any activity is well planned in advance comes out to be successful, so is the classroom teaching. If a teacher plans his lesson beforehand, he knows what he is going to teach, how he is going to teach, what teaching aids he is going to use, what questions he is going to ask, what questions students might ask, what objectives he is going to achieve and how he is going to evaluate that he has achieved his identified objectives. The answers of such questions make a lesson plan. For a beginning teacher it (lesson plan) may be a detailed script and for an experienced teacher it may be a small package of some teaching points in the written form or just in his mind. For a science teacher a lesson plan comes out to be very effective and economical.

It is advisable for a science teacher to select and organise in a logical sequence, the suitable material for classroom instruction. Where should he start today's lesson with respect to where he ended yesterday? If yesterday's lesson ended with the completion of a demonstration showing that certain solutions under given conditions conduct electricity, how should he develop his lesson today? Should the demonstration be repeated at the very beginning of the lesson? Should the students be asked to tell what they observed yesterday? Should the same apparatus for conductivity of solutions be placed on the demonstration table. Should the teacher state the conclusions drawn, yesterday? Should the basic generalisations be asked from the students?

When teaching a certain lesson, what questions should the teacher ask? Should the teacher answer all the questions raised by the students, or the students leave the classroom with some questions unanswered? When the teacher is lecturing or demonstrating, should the student note down all the information, applications or uses?

There are several possible answers to the above questions. The teacher should give serious thought to such questions when developing his lesson plan, in order to arrive at an efficient and economical approach to teaching. The format of the lesson plan and the actual written material in it are not of great importance. The significant factor is that the lesson plans provide the science teacher with the opportunity of checking which of the suggested teaching methods are potentially most effective for achieving the identified objectives of the lessons.

SIGNIFICANT ELEMENTS

The important features of what a lesson plan should contain are:

(i) Why should we teach this lesson (Objectives)?

(ii) What should we teach in this lesson (Content)?

(iii) How should we teach this lesson (Methods)?

(iv) How should we know that students have learned what we taught them (Evaluation)?

Objectives. In listing objectives for a particular lesson, careful thought should be given to such categories as understanding factual information and its application as well as developing : (a) problem solving skills, (b) scientific attitude, (c) critical thinking, (d) interest in science and (e) values. It is unlikely that objectives covering all categories be attempted in one lesson. Some of these objectives like developing scientific attitudes or problem solving skills may be attended over a long period of time after several lessons. Such objectives should be written as general objectives. When developing lesson plans, the teacher should write only those objectives (as specific objectives) for which he is quite sure, that he would be able to achieve at the end of that lesson. Sometimes some student-teachers write quite a number of objectives in their lesson plans, perhaps to impress their supervisors, while only few of them they probably achieve.

Content. The teacher should take up only that much content, which he feels he will be able to cover in the limited time. In introducing a lesson, especially when a new unit is being taught for the first time, the teacher should attempt to stimulate, motivate and generate student's interest in the topic. Student's past and present experiences can serve an effective approach to new units.

Other ways of launching content with the ultimate aim of motivating students to learn a particular topic may be : (a) giving special homework assignments that require research, (b) survey conferences, (c) investigations, (d) special readings, (e) experiments, and (f) observations. The teacher may also bring in or ask students to bring in new articles (from magazines, journals or newspapers) of contemporary importance and relate such reports with the content of the lesson as well as with the needs and interests of the students and the community. Students may also be encouraged to bring in various supplementary material pertaining to the topic of the lesson. In short the teacher should utilise all these means for the selection of content and should not limit himself only to the textbook.

Methods. There are several methods of teaching science. Now when the teacher has identified the objectives of the lesson and selected the content to be covered, this is the right time to select an appropriate method of teaching the lesson. He should choose the method/methods which best fits/fit in the lesson. The teaching method should be compatible to the cognitive level of students, identified objectives and existing classroom conditions (number of students, size of the classroom, duration of period, availability of apparatus for classroom demonstrations and experiments, and other audio-visual aids etc.). There are several audio-visual aids for teaching science. The teacher can select some appropriate audio-visual aids from those available and improvise or make some on his own which best fit in the lesson. It should be noted that only appropriate-audio-visual aids should be used in the lesson, and those too if they are actually needed. Sometimes mostly student-teachers use so many audio-visual aids in one lesson, which make the lesson more confusing instead of interesting and clarifying the difficult ideas. This should be avoided. The appropriate audiovisual aids may be used to introduce the lesson as well as during the entire lesson.

Evaluation. This part of the lesson plan helps the teacher to determine to what degree learning occurs during the lesson. Several key questions asked by the teacher (during the lesson or at the end of the lesson) and the kinds of responses obtained from the students will enable the teacher to evaluate the degree of learning. Students' questions will also give the teacher some insight into the nature of difficulties that some students might have. A summary which elicited from the students at strategic places during the lesson as well as at the end of the lesson will also provide the science teacher with an evaluation of the teaching-learning process.

LEARNING AND INQUIRY

The art of questioning is also critical when teaching a lesson of science. We should not underestimate the importance of questioning skills increasing or diminishing student participation. We ask questions for a variety of reasons.

(i) To obtain feedback about the level of understanding in the class.

(ii) To know what they already know.

(iii) To promote thinking.

(iv) To draw attention to something.

(v) To provide the student with an opportunity to verbalise his ideas in a coherent way.

(vi) To give opportunities to praise and encourage a student, and

(vii) To act as a measure of class control etc. etc.

To meet this variety of purposes requires many forms of questions, some of greater subtlety than those which have one simple, factual, and correct answer. To promote thinking requires more open ended questions, i.e., those having more than one acceptable answer.

In addition to questions and students' oral responses, evaluation in the course of a period may also be made by observing the students working at their seats or those who may be asked to come to the blackboard. When students are in the science laboratory careful observation of their work habits will also reveal the nature of their learning. A science teacher can observe a student's error at the board, at the desk or in the laboratory and correct the mistake promptly to prevent a block to learning the major and minor ideas of the lesson.

In addition to the four criteria suggested above for lesson planning, the science teacher should be conscious of some other important points when he is just about ready to teach. Why should these students desire to learn the solution to the problem or understand the scientific principle? Psychologists often refer to *motivation*. How does the teacher motivate the students to learn each lesson? The teacher can set the stage for learning by presenting an inspiring demonstration, a series of experiments, and questions or problems in which the students can become involved or in which they can identify themselves with specific situations.

Students interests, needs or experiences can serve as the springboard for introducing the lesson. Some teachers may begin with their own personalised experiences, the showing of a film or slides, or having a student or group of students bring in and discuss a science project. There are some typical ways in which the science teacher attempts to stimulate learning with the hope that the students will be motivated to learn. Here lies the need for flexibility in the lesson planning. Some students may actually assist in the planning of instruction if given the proper opportunity. Such students should be more strongly motivated to learn the basic ideas of the lesson under the guidance of the science teacher, so that they could assist their teacher in the classroom when teaching science to the entire class.

VARIOUS STAGES

There are many types of lesson plans. The Hebertian steps provide us with the best, basic lesson plan. Hebertian steps of a lesson plan are as follows:

1. Preparation
2. Aim

3. Introduction
4. Method (Presentation)
5. Application
6. Recapitulation (Revision and Conclusion).

Preparation. However knowledgeable you may be, and however certain you may be of what you wish to teach, you must plan how much and by what method you propose to teach for a successful lesson.

Time must be your first consideration. Very often the bell rings when the lesson is just half completed. Duration of period should be divided into three parts—time for teacher's activities, time for students activities, and time for recapitulation.

Secondly, you must plan your lessons in terms of the specific objectives for the lesson identified by you, *i.e.*, what you wish to achieve in a 30-40 minutes period at your disposal.

Thirdly, you must plan your lesson according to the cognitive level of your students, taking into consideration their age (maturity level) and aptitude.

Fourthly, you must well prepare yourself for the lesson asking yourself a few questions like these. Do you have the requisite knowledge and background for the lesson? Can you perform adequately the skills you propose to teach? Have you considered the way you will start and proceed for, your lesson?

Fifthly, you must prepare all the materials and teaching aids necessary for the lesson, asking yourself a question. Have you arranged these materials (specimens, charts, illustrations, maps, diagrams, models etc.) in a sensible manner so as to achieve sequence and unity in your lesson.

Sixthly, you must ensure that your students are prepared before the lesson starts with everything necessary for the lesson.

It has been seen infinitely that more lessons are ruined by neglect of these simple preparations. It would be advisable that a sound teacher should consider himself as a stage manager who must have all that is necessary in the way of effects, scenery and properties available at the precise moment that they are needed so that a smooth production is achieved.

There is, moreover, a vital psychological aspect to this question of careful preparation. Students react quickly to efficiency. If they are obliged to behold daily a fumbling an ill-prepared teacher they will speedily lose respect for such a person. On the other hand the daily spectacle of business-like preparation on the part of their teacher will earn their admiration, and incidently, their polite attention.

Remember

Prepare your lesson.

Prepare yourself.

Prepare your materials and teaching aids.

Prepare the material and aids for your students.

Aim. Following a successful preparation the teacher must state clearly the aim of the new lesson. (The aim may further be subdivided into some general and specific objectives which are going to be achieved during the lesson.) The students must know the purpose and objectives of the lesson. If they know clearly what they are supposed to achieve, then their thought processes will follow more easily the teacher's exposition, explanation and steps of the lesson.

Remember

A class of students without an aim is like a leaderless army.

The students must know where they are going.

The aim of the lesson must be stated clearly and emphatically.

Introduction. If the lesson has been sensibly prepared, the teacher will have taken pains to plan a suitable introduction. The introduction should not only set the atmosphere or mood for the lesson, but it should gather together the students and focus their concentration on to the subject in hand. To prevent initial in attention, attention should be paid to two aspects of the introduction stage of your lesson—social introduction and subject introduction.

Social Introduction. You should greet the students courteously and discuss with them the exciting things they have been doing. Be human and sociable with them for a minute or two and gradually calm them down by friendly conversation.

Subject Introduction. After this brief social introduction, you should introduce them to the nature of the present lesson. This is perhaps best achieved by reminding them (by questioning) of the ground covered in the previous lesson on the subject, or activity in hand. Educationally it is vital to proceed from the firm base of the 'known' before attempting to explore the territory of the 'unknown.' This can be achieved by putting the new knowledge which is linked up with their previous knowledge gained in the previous lesson or from everyday experiences. In order to develop curiosity for learning, the teacher should make the students realise that their knowledge is incomplete and a lot of new knowledge is still left to be acquired by them. Thus you may involve the following steps:

(i) testing their previous knowledge;

(ii) asking short reflective questions enabling students to realise their ignorance of numerous scientific facts and create interest therefore in learning the new subject matter;

(iii) using audio-visual aids; and

(iv) performing interesting demonstration relevant to the topic of the lesson.

Remember. Introduction is the bridge between the previous activity and the present activity.

Introduction creates the new mood for the new lesson. a Introduction is necessary to prepare the minds of the students for me new topic of activity. Introduction is the process of rallying the minds and bodies of children to face a new experience.

Method (Presentation). You have learned several methods of teaching science. You should practise all the methods in your practice teaching taking into consideration the : (a) objectives of lesson, (b) cognitive level of students, and (c) classroom conditions.

When teaching science it should be kept in mind that students' activities are predominant than the teacher's activities. Remember it is the student's lesson, and not your lesson. Restrict yourself to a brief introduction, statement of aim and a short, thought-provoking exposition and explanation and then employ to the full all the senses of the students (as for as possible) – the hands (learning by doing), the eyes (learning by seeing), the ears (learning by hearing), the mouth (learning by saying), the nose (learning by smelling), and the tongue (learning by tasting). Only at the end of the lesson you should use your voice emphatically to summarise the lesson. If your students find out things themselves and reach solutions by constructive reasoning there will be infinitely more satisfaction for them than if they are constantly 'told' by you.

Thus, after the students are prepared to receive the lesson, and the teacher has clearly stated the aim of the lesson, he should start the lesson, and the students should get the new ideas and knowledge. Here the teacher should draw out the maximum from the students by asking suitable questions. The lesson should proceed with the actual participation of both the students and the teacher. It can be made more interesting and concrete by the use of the suitable audio-visual aids and experimental demonstrations.

The new ideas and knowledge to be given to the students should be related as far as possible with their previous knowledge. This is a very important point to be kept in mind when introducmg new scientific principal and generalising some new scientific facts.

Finally the students are in a position to generalise what they have learned so far. Answers to some relevant questions now asked by the teacher, he will be able to draw out various scientific principles/ conclusions and formulae. Thus, the students receive the new knowledge and the teacher acts as a guide for them.

Remember. Your methods of teaching should a make the students think a make the students. Do a make the students. See a make the students. Say a make the students hear.

Application. In order to develop interest and satisfaction among students for the subject they should be made familiar with the use and application of various generalisations in daily life and conclusions drawn out. The new knowledge thus gained by the students becomes more meaningful and permanent for ever. In former'times application merely consisted of the students proving by stereotyped exercises that they had learned what teacher had taught them. The very words 'test' or 'exercise' explain this former conception. Without denying the value of this practice, we find that application has, to the progressive teacher, a much wider significance. As we have decided,, it is vital that the teacher employs an interesting, imaginative and lively method of presenting his subject matter, it is equally vital that such a presentation be matched by an interesting, imaginative and lively application.

Remember. Knowledge and skills must be applied and practised if they are to be lasting benefits to your students.

Minimum of presentation, maximum of application.

Match an interesting presentation by an interesting application.

Recapitulation (Revision and Conclusion). "Teach little, revise more" is an excellent slogan for a teacher. It is not correct to imagine that more than sixty per cent of anything you teach for the first time will be observed by the students. For this reason, you must reinforce what you have taught by causing the students 'to see, say and do' the things you have presented to them orally.

Revision is essential to any piece of teaching and without it the ablest presentation will only be partially successful. You must revise as you teach and you must revise as you have taught.

It is vital that no lesson should be concluded without an emphatic summary of what has been taught. At least five minutes must be allocated by the teacher in the lesson plan for this purpose of hammering home what has been taught, by a systematic review or recapitulation of what has been achieved.

Here the knowledge imparted to the students is tested by asking some relevant questions. This is a way of revising the lesson by question-answer technique. This also enables the teacher to find out whether the students have followed what he has taught them, and whether or not the method of teaching is effective.

This summary should be first drawn from the students by questioning and then repeated with vehemence by the teacher as he points to the main items summarised on the blackboard. Revision is thus oral, aural and visual. The teacher speaks and illustrates and the pupils hear and see.

Remember

Revision, Revision, Revision.

Now Summarise and Revise the Stages of Your Lesson Plan.

You have *prepared* your lesson thoroughly.

You have stated your *aim* clearly.

You have *introduced* it humanly.

You have employed an interesting *method.*

You have devised an imaginative *application.*

You have *revised* your lesson decisively.

THE MODELS

Some lesson plans are given in Appendix A as Sample. You can go through them before making your own lesson plan.

Planning a Unit is similar to lesson planning. A Unit may have several lessons. Therefore it may not be completed in one class period. It may take several class periods to complete a Unit. If Unit Plans are given in Teacher's Guides, they might be very useful for the science teachers specially the new teachers.

A new teacher feels difficulty in treating a topic in his class not because he does not know the subject matter, but because he does not know exactly how much subject matter in a certain topic suits the varying age-levels of the students. Again he faces the difficulty in selecting the teaching material. He also finds it difficult to decide what activities should be undertaken to cast a lasting impression on the minds of the students. Very often, the teachers specially the new ones do not have enough practice of how to evaluate how far the students have followed what they have been taught.

But for the many experienced science teachers it may be quite easy. Thus, a beginning teacher may take advantage of their experiences, but they are not always available to him. But if NCERT and SCERTs invite such experienced science teachers to develop Unit Plans on some selected science topics, it would be of great help not only to freshers, but to others too. Such a Unit Plan may also be termed as Teaching Unit.'

Steps of a Unit Plan. A Unit Plan may be written in the following steps :

1. Subject : (Physics, Chemistry, Biology or Science)
2. Topic : (Heading of the Unit)
3. Class : (To whom the Unit is to be taught)
4. Time : (No. of class periods)
5. Aids : (To be used during the entire unit)

6. Content : (Syllabus to be covered)
7. Sub-units : (No. and Name)
8. Objectives : (To be achieved after completing the Unit)

For Each Sub-Unit

9. Sub-unit No. and Name (Heading)
10. Time : (No. of class periods)
11. Teacher's Activities
12. Student's Activities
13. Joint Activities (Teacher's and student's)
14. Assignment
15. Follow-up Activities
16. Evaluation
17. References

Under these steps A Sample Unit Plan "Lifting of Heavy Bodies by Smaller Forces" for IX Physics is developed and is given here for guidance. Similar Unit Plans may also be developed in other science subjects – Chemistry or Biology and for any class level.

A Sample Unit Plan

Subject : Physics

Topic : Lifting of Heavy Bodies by Smaller Forces

Class:IX

Time : 11 periods, each of 30-40 minutes duration

Aids : Tool chest. Planks of wood, 16 mm film projector/VCR/VCP.

Introduction. Here a teacher is not to teach all that is given in the chapter on 'simple machines' found in any secondary physics textbook. What is important in the class level we are going to teach, *i.e;* the intellectual level of me learners.

1. Intricate mathematical calculations should be avoided.
2. Subject-matter not in keeping with the cognitive level of learners should be eliminated.
3. A teacher, however, may add something new that he deems necessary, even if it is not given in the textbook.

This Unit may be divided into the following sub-units:

1. Classification of different devices
2. Levers
3. Wheel and axle, and pulley
4. Inclined plane, and jack.

Objectives

1. To find out from children what devices they have used or seen being used for lifting heavy bodies.
2. To classify these devices into different categories.
3. To help the children understand how these devices are used in everyday living.
4. To help the children construct such devices or their models.
5. To enable the children to distinguish between the utility of the various devices in various situations.

Sub-Unit 1 : Classification of Different Devices

Time : 2 Class periods (60-80 minutes) *The Teacher's Activity* : To pose the following problems:

1. How can a child defeat a team of wrestlers in a tug of war?
2. How can a man have his truck lifted in order to remove a flat tyre?
3. How could a new born baby lift his father?
4. How can a man lift his scooter on a platform, which is about one metre above the road?

The Student's Activity : With the help of past experiences the students will:

1. try to solve these problems, and
2. suggest why certain devices are used and not others. (These devices will be listed on the blackboard).

Part Played by the Teacher : The teacher will give finishing touches to the list of the devices suggested by the students. He may ask the students to bring, either the actual devices or the models to the next class meeting. The teacher's own enthusiasm and initiative in this direction will be of supreme importance.

Joint-Activity (Teacher's and Student's) : The following day, the devices brought by the students the actual ones or in the form of models should, after demonstration and explanation, be classified into:

1. Lever
2. Wheel and axle
3. Pulley
4. Inclined plane
5. Jack

Questions

1. What is the need of lesson planning?
2. "Objectives, Content, Methods and Evaluation" are the four important features of what a lesson plan should contain? Discuss.
3. Why do we ask questions during teaching-learning process?
4. What is the role of motivation when teaching science? How can you motivate your students in your science classes?
5. What are the various steps of a lesson plan? Give a brief description of each step.

23

TECHNIQUES OF LABORATORY

Besides having necessary physical facilities for teaching life sciences the teacher should be well versed in the management of laboratory work and he should be well trained in some laboratory techniques for teaching the, subject efficiently and effectively. We can discuss some of the laboratory techniques as below :

USING THE MICROSCOPE

In case of compound microscope when eye-piece magnification is 10 times that is 10 X and objective lens magnification in45times that is 45 X the magnification of the microscope will be 450 X.

For the measurement of microscopic structures-we use occular micrometer and stage micrometer. The occular micrometer is standardized by using stage micrometer for particular lens system. Occular micrometer has equally spaced divisions; usually in one tenth of a millimeter, and we are to liberate the scale of occular-micrometer by stage micrometer, for the microscope we are using, stage micrometer has large divisions (01-mm) and each large division is further divided into ten small divisions. This means one millimeter is divided into 100 small divisions or one small division is equal to 0.01 mm. For calibration occular micrometer is fixed with eye piece and stage micrometer is fixed under the objective. If there are 50 divisions on the occular micrometer and these coincide with one large and six small divisions of the stage micrometer (16 small divisions) then 50 divisions of occular micrometer are equal to 0.16 mm. One division of occular micrometer will be

0.16/50 = 0.0032 mm.

We know 1 mm. = 1000 microns. So, one small division of occular micrometer is equal to 0.0032 X 1000=3.2 microns, for that microscope.

Now function of stage micrometer is over. If we are to measure length of a-cell we focus it under the objective. If the length of the cell coincides with 7 divisions of the occular micrometer the length of the cell will be 7x'32=22'4 microns. In order to draw the magnified things in their dimensions we use camera lucida.

PREPARATION OF TEMPORARY AND PERMANENT MOUNTS

Various preparations for microscopic studies can be discussed In the following way :

Cyclosis : Preparation for studying cyclosis (protoplasmic movements) are made temporarily. For this purpose we take Hydrilla leaves or cells of Elodea internodes and mount these simply in water. We can see chloroplasts moving (alongwith the protoplasm) in the plant material, when we see it under microscope. For mounting the material we can also use cavity slides.

Mitosis and Meiosis : A simple method generally used for temporary preparations for mitosis and meiosis is Iron Acetocarmine method. In this we take Allium cepa root-tips' formitosis and flower buds of this plant for meiosis. The material is warmed on a slide with a few drops of acetocarmine solution. The material is now crushed with iron needle. When the material turns quite soft a cover glass is put over it and the slide is sandwitched between two blotting papers. Now the slide is tapped to spread the material evenly. The cells get separated and we can easily locate the various stages of mitotic and meiotic cell divisions. If the slide is to be kept for some days it can be rinsed with, paraffin wax.

For permanent preparation the above preparation is dehydrated through 30%, 50%, 70%, 90% and absolute alcohol respectively by putting the slide for 2 minutes in each solution. The material is now cleared with clove oil, rinsed in xylene and mounted in Canada balsam.

Bacteria : (a) India Ink Preparation : Take a drop of India Ink on a slide and place some scrapping from the teeth (near the gum margins) in this drop. Spread the material on the slide and allow it to dry. Dehydrate it in absolute alcohol for one minute clear it by putting it in xylane for two minutes and mount it in a drop of Canada balsam for permanant preparation. Spiral forms of bacteria can be seen by proper light adjustments. (b) Gram's Stain Preparation : Clean a cover glass in ether. Put a small drop of water on it with some needle. Transfer some, bacteria culture to this drop. Spread the material and let it dry. Now fix the bacteria by passing the cover glass through flame for two to three times. Stain the material in Gram's aniline-gentian-violet solution. Rinse it in water ana put it in Lugol's Iodine solution (KI 2 gm. + 1 gm. iodine +300 mls. water) for one minute and again rinse it in water. Now stain material with safranin (1%) for one minute. Let it air dry and stain it in absolute alcohol. Mount it in Canada balsam. Gram-positive bacteria will stain blue and Gram-negative red (safranin).

Spores and Pollen Grains **:** Spores and pollen grains are mounted temporarily in glycerine and studied. Iodine solution can be used to stain the starch grains. For permanent preparation the spores and pollen grains are stained in haematoxylin (0'5%) solution for one hour. Now, the material is dehydrated progressively in 30%, 50%, 70%, 90% and absolute alcohol. The material is cleared with clove oil. rinsed in xylene and mounted in Canada balsam.

Maceration of Tissues **:** Maceration of the plant tissues is done for studying cell types as tracheids vosels cambial cells, sieve tubes, companion cells and parenchymatous cells, etc. In this procedure some wood portion of the plant is taken and cut into pieces, then it is heated with 2% nitric acid and spoken in order to separate the different cells. we can also use Jeffery's Maceration Solution (10% HN03+1O% chromic acid, 1 : 1) for this purpose. The material is now spread on a slide or in a watch glass and stained with safranin and light green solution for permanent preparation. Dehydration of the material is done by passing it through alcohol series. Before mounting the material in Canada balsam it is cleared with clove oil and rinsed with xylene.

Preparation for Hand Cut Sections : For anatomical studies, sections from roots, stems, leaves etc. can be prepared as permanent mounts. In this method we cut thin but complete sections from plant parts. Material is now washed in water and passe through 30% and 50% alcohol solutions. The material is now tained in safranin solution (safranin solution prepared in 50% alcohol) and further dehydrated in 70% alcohol. After this material is stained with light green or fast green solution (solution prepared in 70% alcohol). The material is further dehydrated in 90% and absolute alcohol, it is cleared with clove oil, rinsed in xylene and mounted in Canadrbalsam. Xylem elements lignified) will stain red and phloem elements (cellulose) will stain green. Generally for dehydration and staining, the material is kept for two minutes in each solution but the duration of time for particular plant materials can be experienced.

For getting sections of delicate and minute parts like embryo, embryo sac, ovary, seed and, seedlings we can embed the material in paraffin wax and sectioning can be done by microtome. Algal and fungal temperory mounts are prepared in methylene blue (cotton blue) and glycerine.

Protozoa : Large form like Paramaecium and Amoeba can be observed in a drop of culture medium covered with cover glass and light properly adjusted flagellates and ciliates can be stained with neutral red or methylene blue.

For permanent preparation transfer some concentrated culture on a slide which had been smeared with albumen fixative. Allow this to evaporate for some time and run the slide through stain (hematoxyline or eosin). Now dehydrate the material by passing it through alcohol series.

Rinse it in xylene. As xylene evaporates add Canada balsam over it and put the cover glass.

Sponges : Take small calcareous sponge as Scypha in a dish. Add to it some hot solution of NaOH or KOH to dissolve the organic matter. Examine the material while mounting in water. Spicules can be dried or fixed in balsam smeared on a slide. If small bits of bath sponge are dipped in cedar wood oil and cleaned with xylene and mounted in Canada balsam, we can see the brown saponin skeletal material.

Uncovered Mounts of Hard Animal Parts : Fish scales, skeletons of sponges, hard parts of insects such as mouth parts and exoskeletoa, hairs, feathers and compound eyes of insects are dried or dehydrated and cleared with cedar wood oil and xylene respectively. The material can be mounted in Canada balsam for permanent preparation.

Small insects like mites and ticks are dehydrated as such, by passing them through alcohol series. The material is cleared in clove oil', rinsed in xylene and can be mount in Canada balsam without cover glass.

Worms : Take the required parts or whole worms and remove the fixative by passing it through water. Stain the material in Delafield's Hematoxylin (100 mt. saturated solution of ammonia alum + 1 gm. Hematoxylin crystals dissolved in 5 mt. absolute alcohol +25 ml. methyl alcohol +25 mi. glycerine) or alum carmine (l gm. carmine crystals dissolved in 1:0 ml. 2'5% ammonia alum solution). Dehydrate the material in alcohol series, clear clove oil and then in xylene and mount in Canada balsam.

Skin Cells : For temporary mount take some sheet of skin (as that of frog), stain it with fountain pen ink, cover it with cover glass and examine Cilial movements can be seen in throat cells of frog taken alive and mounted in water. Skin sheet from human mouth scrapping can be put in,% formalin solution (to which 10% glycerine had been added) for some time and it can be stained with fountain pen ink, methylene blue or neutralred-and mounted in glycerine for temporary preparation. For permanent preparation usual dehydration and cleaning is done after staining. Material can be mounted in Canada balsam.

Blood Cells : For temporary preparation, take some blood smear on a slide still it with fountain pen ink and mount in glycerine. For permanent preparation blood smear is covered with Wright's stain for one minute. The stain is diluted by adding water. The slide is dried and mounted in Canada balsam.

Striated Muscles : Place a small piece of muscle in 1 % formalin solution for 24 hours. Take one fibre, stretch it on the slide and add to it pen ink and mount in glycerine. For permanent preparation stain with Delafield's Hematoxylin solution (for studying nuclei), dehydrate in alcohol series; clear the material in clove oil and xylene and mount in Canada balsam.

COLLECTION CULTURING AND PRESERVATION TECHNIQUES

A life sciences teacher should be well versed in laboratory skills and he should have the knowledge of

(a) the type of living material to be used in the laboratory

(b) the ecological situations (habitats) from where the, required material can be secured and

(c) methods of collection, culturing and preservation of such material.

Following are some suggestive methods for collection culturing and plant organisms.

ANIMAL ORGANISMS

Protozoa : Protozoans can conveniently be obtained from water surface scum, bottom of pools, ponds and ditches. Some members of protozoa like Amoeba and Paramaecium are generally used for laboratory studies.

Collection : Collection of the organisms can be done in bottles or jars with some water from the habitat.

Culturing : place a small quentity of grass or leaves etc. in a jar and add enough of water to cover it. Keep the jar at a place away from direct sunlight. Maximum population of the organisms will be got after 1-15 days.

Preservation : All protozoans can be preserved in 10% formalin solution. Formalia acetic acid alcohol (FAA) can also be used for preserving these organisms. FAA contains 50% alcohol 90 parts and formalin (formaldehyde 40%) 5 parts & glacial acetic acid 5 parts.. Bottles or jars should be waxed to prevent evaporation.

Sponges : All sponges are aquatic and mostly marine. Some forms like Scypha can be obtained from fresh water as in ponds, pools lakes and streams. These sponges are found in the form of soft white or brownish slimy blotches on sticks and submerged stones.

Collection : Sponges can be collected in any type of container such as jars and buckets but the material should be submerged in water, while in container.

Culturing : Culturing of fresh water form can be done in a balanced aquarium or fish pool.

Preservation : Sponges can be dried and mounted in boxes. These can also be preserved in 5%, formalin or 70% alcohol.

Worms : Planaria is found in fresh water, in pond, and streams attached in the undersurface of submerged objects. Parasitic forms like liver fluke tape worm (flat worm) and round worms etc. can be got from their hosts such as birds fishes, rats, dogs, cats and horses.

Collection : Planaria can be scrapped off from the submerged objects and the parasitic forms can be collected by opening the animals from expected infested organs. A hand lens can be used for this purpose.

Culturing : Planaria can be cultured in aquarium. Parasitic forms cannot be cultured but these can be kept alive for some days in 0'9% salt solution by adding 0'2% glucose to it.

Personation : Planaria can be sand witched between two slides and kept in 5% formalin solution. Parasitic worms are killed by beating them in water. Now the are put in 6 to 8% formalin solution to which some alcohol is added. After some time the material is taken out and preserved in 6% alcohol free formalin solution.

Annelida : Earth worms are generally found in moist soil with high humus content. Leeches can be collected from ponds.

Collection : A forecep can be used for collecting these organisms. Some mud in case of earth worms and some water in case of leeches from their habitat is put in the container which is used for the purpose of collection of these organisms.

Culturing : Earth worms can be kept in boxes full of mud with some humus content. Leeches can be kept in water in some container. Leeches have stored food and can be kept alive for several months without providing them food.

Preservation : Kin the organisms by heating in water and add some alcohol to it to get them relaxed. Take out the dead animals and preserve in 6% formalin solution.

Molluses : Snails and clams can be obtained from creeks and pounds. Oysters can be purchased.

Collection : The animals can be collected in jars alongwith some water and soil from the habitat.

Culturing : Snails and clams can be cultured in aquarium with some sand at the bottom of it.

Preservation : Kill the animals by beating in water and preserve in 6 to 8% formalin solution. Edges of the shells can be broken so that the preservative enters into the animal.

Arthropods : Insects are found in almost all habitats in air, soil, and water. The animals can be collected from ponds, lakes, fields, under stones, houses and from other plants and animals on which these are found as parasites.

Collection : Collection of insects is easy but there are certain equipments generally used for insect collection. These are cyanide-bottle carbon-tetrachloride-bottle, chloroform-bottle, nets and paper folds. In cyanide-bottle we have sodium cyanide covered with cork or saw dust and a layer of Plaster of Paris over it. Carbon-tetrachloride bottle contains some cotton saturated-with carbon-tetrachloride and in chloroform-bottle we have rubber pieces saturated with chloroform. Nets with circular wire frames are also used. Butterflies and dragonflies can be collected between paperfolds. When insects are collected for culturing use nets only.

Culturing : Many insects can be kept alive in captivity for a long time, others can be reared for complete life cycles. The procedure for culturing the insects may differ for particular insects, but in each case we have to provide necessary food and environmental conditions.

Preservation : The almost universal method-for preserving insects is by thrusting a pin through the body of the insect after it has been killed but before it has dried. When the insect dries it gets firmly fastened to the pin. Usually pinning is done through thorax. Very small insects which cannot be pinned, are usually mounted will glue on a heavy paper. The mounted as well as pinned insects can be kept in boxes. Crustacea water fleas etc. can be preserved in 6% formalin and spiders in 85% alcohol.

Fishes : Fishes can be got from rivers, ponds and lakes. Marine fishes can be purchased.

Collection : Fishes can be collected by angling or with the help of nets. When needed for culturing these should be captured by nets.

Culturing : Fresh water fishes can be cultured in aquaria or fish pool. Aquaria for marine fishes can also be arranged but these are more expensive.

Preservation : Fishes are best preserved in 6% formalin solution. If animal is bulky puncture it at places so that the preservative enter the animal body 15% Glycerine may be added to the preservative in order to prevent the animal body from becoming stiff.

Amphibians : Frogs and salamanders can be located near the rivers and ponds. Toads are found in gardens and fields generally in rainy season.

Collection : The animals can be captured individually by band or we can use nets and traps.

Culturing : Culturing of frogs can be done in aquaria with cages.

For salamanders sand and partially submerged stones can be kept in the aquarium.

Preservation : Amphibians can be preserved in 7% formalin solution with 15% glycerine added to it in order to keep the animal body soft for dissections. Puncture the body if the animal is bulky.

Reptiles : Turtles can be located in ponds and lakes, lizards are found in houses and snackes in fields or wasteland. Alligators and crocodiles are found in rivers and streams.

Collection : Reptiles can be located and captured individually. We can also utilize nets and traps. Snakes are best captured with the help of forked sticks.

Culturing : Most of the reptiles are carnivorous and feed upon small prey as worms, insets, small rodents and frogs etc. While culturing, the animals can be fed on fresh meat. The animals can be kept in cages by providing them which necessary food. Turtles can be kept in aquarium or pool.

Preservation : Snakes, crocodiles and alligators can be skinned off and stuffed. Any reptile can be preserved in formalin (6%) as other animals are preserved but a table spoon of sugar may be added to the preservative in order to preserve the colour of the animals.

Birds : Birds can be located in houses, gardens, near the ponds and in the areas of their nestling habits.

Collection : Collection of birds can be done by nets and traps. Some birds can be captured individually.

Culturing : Birds can be kept in cages by providing them with necessary food.

Preservation : Birds can be preserved in 7% formalin solution or they may be skinned off and stuffed.

Mammals : The study of mammals in nature depends on the location of the school. Suburban and rural school students may find mammals like rodents, hoofed and certain domestic animals in their surroundings.

Collection : Mammals can be hunted, trapped or individually captured. Method of collection may depend on the nature and habitat of the animal.

Culturing : It is not easy to keep wild animals in captivity. If kept alive, mammals require continuous and regular cleaning and sterilization of cages.

Personation : The animals can be skinned off and stuffed. If the whole of the animal is to be preserved, keep the animal in 6 to 8% formalin solution with body punctured, if bulky. There are some special methods to preserve. Mammals and other larger animals.

Texidermy : In this method skin of the animal is removed as a whole. The skin is cleaned and arsenic alum powder is rubbed on theraw surface. The skin is dried and stuffed. In stuffing the bones of head region are re-inserted and a trial is made to give the specimen its natural shape, using bones, wires and stuffing material like cotton.

Embalming : If the animal is large in size and we are to preserve it for dissections, we embalm that in this method the animal is anesthetized, by giving chloroform Embalming fluid is injected in aorta just above the heart. The following fluid preserves the animals and keeps muscles pliable :

Formalin 3%. 880 mi.+ Glycerine 100 ml. + carbolic acid (melted crystals) 20 ml.

Injecting : To study the circulatory system easily some substance is injected ill it. The substance solidities and gives a striking colour to the vessels. One such injection solution is formalin (4%) 100 mis. + Glycerine 100 mls. + Starch 450 gms.+water 950 mls. In this solution powdered carmine for red and lead chromate for yellow coloration is used.

PLANT ORGANISMS

Bacteria : Bacteria occur in every type of situations such as in soil air, water and can also be obtained from decaying plant and animal material.

Collection and Culturing : For this purpose a handful of decaying grass or weeds are placed in a container with some water. The container is placed at a warm and dark place. After 7 to 10 days we can find a vast number of bacteria motile non motile, rods (bacilli), spheres (cocci) and spirals (spirilli). Similarly a handful *of* dead flies can also be used for getting mixed culture of bacteria.

For pure culture of bacteria some nutrient or culture medium is employed. The culture medium is sterilized and inoculated with bacteria needed for culture. One such culture medium that can conveniently be-employed for this purpose is PDA (Potato dextrose agar) medium. PDA can be prepared by the following procedure. Pare and slice 100 gms. potatoes and add to it 250 mls. of water. In a separate flask put 9gms. of agar agar in 250 mls. of water. Cook the two solutions separately for one hour. Add distilled water to meet water loss due to evaporation. Strain off the liquid of the two solutions, mix in a separate flask, add to this solution 10 gms. of dextrose sugar and boil for half an hour. Filter the solution through cotton layer and put the medium in test tubes or petri-dishes. Now sterilize the medium and inoculate with required bacteria.

Preservation : Bacterial cultures can be kept for long times by providing new culture media. In case of nitrogen fixing bacteria, the nodules with bacteria can be preserved in 7% formalin solution.

Algae : Blue green algae and green algae can be obtained from fresh water ponds rivers, streams and ditches. Blue green algae like Rivularia and Gleotrichia are found free floating or attached to submerged plants. Nostoc. Anabaena, Aphanocepsa are found in gelatinous matrix as colonies. Oscillatoria is found floating in bits on the water surface. Green algae like Volvox, Chlamydomonas are found in pools in wet weather. Protococcus, Plemococus are found in shades in water. Hydrodictyon, Ulotbrix, Spirogyrd, Zygnema. Desmids, Diatoms, Cladophora. Pithophora. Ocdogonium. Chaya, Nitella etc. can be collected from fresh water but Vauchcheria is found on wet soil. Macrocystis and Sargasasam are marine.

Collection : Collection of the algae can be done in jars and bottles by picking up the colonies or filaments. Some cloth piece can be used to concentrate unicellular or colonial forms. Attached forms can be scrapped off from the substratum or material can be collected alongwith attached algae. For preservation unicellular forms can be concentrated by adding 100 mls. CuSO4 solution to 900 mls of habitat water.

Culturing : Most ofthe algae can be cultured in aquarium with adequate care for particular algae.

Preservation : Most of the algae can be satisfactorily preserved in Transea's Algal Preservative (6 parts water + 3 parts 95% Alcohol + 1 part formalin). We can also use formalin acetic acid alcohol FAA, 50% alcohol 90 parts + formalin 5 parts + acetic acid 5 parts. For colour fixation $CuSO_4$ can be added to the preservative and later on, material can be transfered to $CuSO_4$ free solution.

Fungi : Slime moulds like Fuligo, lycogala, Stemonitis etc. are found in swamp forests where wood is undergoing decay. Phycomycetes like Rhizopus and Mucor are found in-any situation but parasitic forms like Phytopthora, Peronospora, Pythium, Plasmodium, Albugo can be collected from their hosts. Saprolegnia is found parasitic on fishes. In Ascomycetes Exoacus, Uncinula, Microspora, Sclerotia, Cleviceps, Aspergillus, Pennicillium and Cladosporium are found as parasiric forms and can be had from infected plants. Among Deutromycetes also Actinomyces, Alteneria, Collectatrichum. Fusarium, Helmintbosporium are parasitic on plants. In Basidiomycetes have parasitic form like puccinia and Ustilago and can be collected from infected plants but saprophytic forms like lycoperdon (puffballs), Fomes (Bract fungus), Polyporous are found either on waste land or rotting wood particularly in rainy season.

Collection : Slime moulds are collected alongwith the substratum. In phycomycetes parasitic forms are collected along with the host material but saprophytic forms are collected in the form of aggregate mycelium. Similarly parasitic Ascomycetes, Deutromycetes and Ascomycetes are collected alongwith some highly infected plant organ Saprophytic forms among these are scrapped from the subsiratum or taking some part of the substratum alongwith the specimen. For collection purposes we can use jars, bottles or polythene bags

Culturing : Among slime moulds only Physarium polycepbalum can be cultured on raw rolled oats. Saprophytic Phycomycetes are cultured on P.D.A. but parasitic forms can be propagated by infecting the generations *of* host plants. It is difficult *to* culture parasitic Ascomycetes but some are cultured on PDA or peptone nutrient medium with special techniques for each fungus and similar is the case with Deutromycetes. Among parasitic Basidiomycetes we cannot culture any fungus artificially but the saprophyte forms can be cultured in wooden boxes providing garden soil with enough *of* humus or fungus can be kept alongwith the substratum in humid conditions.

Preservation : Most *of* the fungi can be preserved in F.A.A. solution bat 7% formalin solution is good for sexual stages. Parasitic forms that are collected alongwith infected plant organs can be kept as pressed specimens. For anatomical studies the specimens are kept in liquid preservative. Fungi that can be cultured artifically are kept in cultures for a long period *of* time by transferring them on new media.

Bryophytes : Marchantia is found growing about bogs and swamps, Coenoce phalum. Pellia, Riccia, Ricciocarpus and Anthoceros are found on mud banks and moist situations. Sphagnum occurs in very wet locations, often forms bogs. Funaria occurs in wet situations but Polytrichum occurs in wide range of situations such as bogs swamps and poor acid soils.

Collection : Collection of Liverworts and *Mosses* can be under taken in rainy season. We can employ polythene bags or jars for collecting these plants.

Culturing : Most of the liverworts can be grown in boxes containing moist soli in covered glass containers. The containers should be placed in-shade at cool place. Mosses can also be cultured by this method but Funaria grows well on wood ash. Protonema of Atrichum and Fuaaria can be cultured in Knop's solution.

Preservation : Liverworts-and Mosses can satisfactorily be preserved in F.A.A. with some copper sulphate added to it. It will preserve the colour of plants. Mosses can be dried and mounted in boxes.

Pteridophytes : Pteridophytes like Polypodium, Dryopteris, Asplenium, Pteris, Botrychium, Equisetum, Selaginella and Lycopodium are found in moist shady and rocky situations in hills. Azolla and Salvinia are food / floating on water surface in ponds and pools Marsilea grows on the banks of ponds generally partially submerged in shallow waters.

Collection : Required parts in case of larger plants can be collected. For culturing small plants with a ball of soil can be collected. Azolla and Salvinia can be collected as whole plants. We can use jars and polythene bags for the purpose of collection.

Culturing : Many ferns can be grown in pots providing them moist and shady conditions. Azolla and Salvinia can be grown in aquarium *or* fish pool.

Preservation : Leaves of certain Pteridophytes, alongwith sori, can be pressed and preserved. Parts of plants *or* whole plants can be preserved in F.A.A. with some copper sulphate added *to* it.

Gymnosperms: Gymnosperms like Cycas, Pinus, Picea, Ginkgo and Zamia grow in temperate regions like the Himalayas *or* at some hilly places.

Collection : Palts of plants like leaves' and cones (male and female) can be collected by cutting them off *from* the plants. For collection purposes we can use polythene bags *or* other larger container.

Culturing : Most of the Gymnosperms grow in plains successfully. The plants can be grown in botanical gardens at some protected places.

Preservation : Parts of plants can be pressed *or* dried and preserved. F.A.A. solution is good preservative for almost all Gymnosperms.

Angiosperms : Angiosperms are found in widely separated situations. According to their habitat these can be divided into hydrophytes, mesophytes and xerophytes. According *to* their mode of nutrition these are saprophytes, parasities and epiphytes.

Collection : Collection of the angiosperm plants or their parts depends upon the size of the plants and the material required. In case of trees and shrubs we can collect leaves, flowers, fruits and seeds etc. Small herbs can be collected as whole plants.

Culturing : Floating and submerged hydrophytes can be cultured in aquaria or pool. Mesophytes and xerophytes can be grown in school garden by providing them necessary conditions. Parasites can be kept on host plants and saprophytes, in garden soil with high humus content.

Preservation : Herbs can be pressed and preserved. Flowers of various plants can be pressed and kept in the form of albums. Fruits and seeds can be mounted in boxes. If we are to keep plant material for anatomical studies, we can preserve that in F.A.A. solution.

Questions

1. How will you measure the size of bacterial cell by using compound microscope ?
2. State the habitats of animals of different groups that are commonly used in life-sciences laboratory. Also discuss the methods of their collection, culturing and preservation.
3. Discuss the techniques used to preserve larger animals and especially mammals that are commonly put in life-sciences museum.
4. How will you culture bacteria and various fungi used in laboratory studies in life sciences?
5. Discuss the habitats, methods of collection, culturing and preservation of different algae, bryophytes, pteridophytes, gymnosperms and angiosperms, that are commonly used in life-sciences laboratories.

24

Kits in Use

To establish a link between laboratory and teaching it is desirable that students may use the experience gained in laboratory in their daily life also. For that purpose students can have science kits at their homes with some apparatus and chemicals.

Students can fix the knowledge gained in laboratory by doing experiments at home with small improvised apparatus in mini laboratories. Many great scientists made discoveries and invention without sophisticated apparatus. Knowledge and experience gained in this way is indispensable.

Mini Science kit may be a small portable box which can even bo carried away. It may be of wood iron or aluminium.

Gas jars may be replaced by test tubes, Woulfe's bottles can be replaced by other wide mouthed bottles, wires bent in various forms can be used as holders for funnels or test tubes. Small bottles obtained from doctors can be used for storing chemicals.

Apparatus should be packed in such a way that it does not strike with each other and break away.

Chemicals should be so placed that they do not spill away. In this way students can enjoy practicals outside school, and then do not reject the idea only for the reason that they could not afford costly apparatus.

Kits serve the purpose of mini labaratory. Science kit is a device of preparing folded *apparatus and material* and then to arrange them in a box which can serve as *demonstration table* also. In the *tool box* a cut Stencil is placed in such a manner that the different items of apparatus can be arranged in sequence or order according to the requirement. The science kit can be brought easily from one place to another. Science kits means organisation, planning and selection of the materials, and equipment into different sections in a small box along with stencils. They can be used for demonstration and experimentation purpose.

According to the recommendations of Kothari Commission (1964-65) and other committees, the disciplinary approach is now adopted at the middle stage in place of general science. With the introduction of improved curricula and advancement in science, technology and industry the different missions have developed improvised apparatus which is more effective than complicated technical devices. It has replaced the laboratories.

VARIOUS TYPES

Types of kits used at different levels are described below:

Primary level Science kits for demonstration and for students' work.

Middle stage for Demonstration-kits in Physics, Chemistry and Biology, (ii) Pupils' kits in Physics, Chemistry, Geology and Biology High School. (i) Demonstration kits. (ii) Pupils' working kits.

It is economical. Science kits are useful for demonstration, with set-up apparatus in less time. These can be used as mobile and mini laboratory, The teacher may use home-made apparatus and material for teaching-learning places and can maintain it in the small box carefully.

It provides a systematic knowledge and a basis for understanding the fundamentals of science. Through science kits real and stable knowledge of science can be provided to the students because it serves as a mobile laboratory. During demonstration teacher can draw very easily different diagrams with the help of stencil which lead the pupil for better understanding of the subject matter. This helps him work independently and then return the *nutcrial* in time. There is less scope of the breakage of material.

It develops methods of science such as observation, experimentation, problem solving and investigatory approach. When the students work with pupils' kits they get an opportunity to think, observe or reason and to arrive at a decision independently. Such an opportunely develops in them the quality of independent thinking, observation etc. Kits help in working on the *process of science* rather that the *product of science.*

It serves as a mini, mobile and improvised laboratory. Sometimes it is not possible for certain institutions to have separate laboratories for various science subjects. This particularly applies in the case of those schools imparting education upto middle or high school stage. For such school it can serve as a mini mobile laboratory because we can fold the apparatus and use it according to situation. There is no need of the working tables. A tool box containing apparatus and equipment of science can be arranged and used as demonstration or experimental table with all physical facilities so it serves as a means of mobile and improvised laboratory. Even the teacher can prepare improvised items with the help of kits in the class-room teaching. Different subjects or types of kits can be brought in the class for demonstration and set-up apparatus according to the requirements.

It develops the inherent scientific interest of the children. The kit help to unite the theoretical aspect with the practical field and also familiarize a student with the basic concepts and methods suiting the intellectual capacity of the students. They help in providing very conducive atmosphere for learning science because they are placed in the original situation where practical knowledge gained by them *travels from hand to head.*

It provides an opportunity for practical work. Here students get an opportunity to undertake practical work very easily and in a simplified manner. Through practical working, it is possible for them to acquire the knowledge of science in the real perspective. Hence they acquire new interest in learning the facts of science.

It develops mechanical, experimental and mental skills. When the children get an opportunity to handle various type of tools, equipment and material of science, they learn exprimental ana mental skills useful for solving the different problems of life.

Use of Science kits saves time resources as well as energy. In a small box all the required apparatus and instruments can be arranged in systematic manner and easily brought into the class-room, whereas in the laboratory, all the required thing, are to be placed at different places with the result that there is every likelihood of their being broken in the transit. Here there is no like likelihood of breakage and loss of time. Even the box containing apparatus can be folded to be used as a table for the set-up experiments. Therefore, we can say that the mini laboratory in the form of kits saves time, resources as well as energy. Science kits are portable and can be easily taken to different places as required by teaching after setting the apparatus in them.

Questions

1. What are Mini Laboratories or science kits? Describe the types of kits employed in Science at different levels.
2. What is the importance of use of kits in the teaching of life sciences?

25

SIGNIFICANCE OF UNITS

According to Preston, A unit is as large a block of related subject matter as can be over-viewed by the learner.

Behind this unit planning or the unitary concept of learning, the concept of learning that has been very much influenced by the rapidly growing acceptance of Gesalt Organismic field theories of learning. In this case we assume that effective learning takes place in which the Goals of learning are well known we know where we have to reach leads to complete attainment of a skill, and insight so that he can equip the skip or insight to othere various situations. This unitary concept has given birth to unit technique.

According to Bossing, "A unit consists of a comprehensive series of related and meaningful activities so as to achieve pupil's purposes, provide significant educational experiences and results in appropriate behavioural changes.

Heidgerken thinks that the most important aspect of the unit concept is the implication that what is learnt is larger and more involved than a few scattered facts.

Many years back Woodrow Wilson said there are elements in reaching learning Units, " The objective on which the unit is focussed, the subject matter which is selected as significantly pertinent to the objectives and activities or the things to do with the subject matter which are included to lead a student to attainment of objectives. Unit Planning came into exisence as a rebellion against treating learning of everyday as an isolated segment."

THE CHARACTERISTICS

1. The aims should be clear and well defined.
2. The aids to be used are very clear in a good unit as "A Multiplicity of materials," according to Hanson, is almost a neccessity for teaching process if the class is to realise the objectives.
3. In a good unit there is provision of evaluation and follow-up.
4. A good unit is always a complete integrated whole in its organisation.
5. A good unit provides activities for students. Students do not sit as mere passive recipients of knowledge.
6. According to Schorting a good unit leaves pupils free to work. They have chance to plan, organise and execute.
7. It provides correlation with the life and other subjects of children.
8. There is beginning as well as an end in a good unit.
9. A good unit is always comprehensible within the access of pupils.
10. It provides for individual differences.
11. It should permit some place for field trips, excursions, projects and demonstrations.

UNIT PLANNING

(i) It clears the aims-general as well as specific of teaching.

(ii) Teacher can cater to the needs, aptitudes and attitude of different students.

(iii) It works and develops in democratic atmosphere i.e. the students as well as the teacher work in a co-operative way.

(iv) It saves time and develops among students interest in learning as they actually know the value of contents learnt by them.

(v) It develops certain skills among the students and sharpens their insight.

(vi) The students can apply the knowledge gained in other life situation also.

(vii) As students learn independently it gives confidence, develops resourcefulness and reliance.

THE DEMERITS

(i) It requires efficient, hard working and trained teachers who are not all ways available.

(ii) Sometimes units are not systematically arranged, so they confuse and discourage students.

(iii) Evaluationis not possible at lower stage.

DEVELOPING A UNIT

Preparation : It is just to motivate the ,student for learning. This spirit should be maintained throughout and not only in the beginning.

Previous Knowledge Test : A unit should start from the ladder where the students are standing at present. The background of students should be questioned. The teacher should start with the pupils where they are.

Presentation : Subject matter is presented to students with the help of aids or direct or indirect experiences in order to add new experiences to the knowledge of students. Presentation leads to organisation of subject matter in which old experiences are intermingled with new ones and students assimilate these.

Summarization : At the end of the unit the whole content is summarized. Sectional summaries can also be provided.

Drill or recapitulation : This is done in order to revise the facts discussed so that students review the whole unit.

Evaluation : This is very essential part of unit. It only informs the teacher how much students have gained and what discrepencies are left in a unit and how to improve them. It can be done by questionaires, tests etc.

Proforma of a Unit

Subject

Name of unit

Major Objective of the unit.

S.No. (Topics)	*Concepts of lessons required*	*Number required*	*Time subject Content*	*Scope of*	*Method*	*Aids*

Unit Test

In order to produce a good test the teacher is to be very careful for its planning, and it is not a simple procedure.

Stages of Test Construction

Planning the Test : It includes the following aspects : Objectives and aims of science teaching should be clear. When particular portion is to be selected, aims of teaching science are to be kept in view. The contents chosen should be from syllabus and specified before hand. The purpose of test should be clear-whether it is for classifying of students or only memorisation of certain portion. Time, duration, choice and range of subject matter should be planned beforehand.

Preparing the Test : While preparing the test, a teacher should see that

1. Directions are very clear.
2. Questions are well phrased.
3. Individual differences should be provided but most of items should be of 50% difficulty.
4. To reduce guessing, items should be of matching type or multiple choice type.
5. Test should be of proper length, neither too lengthy nor too short.

6. More than one type of questions should be there e.g. short answer type, objective type etc, Objective type test should be before essay type.

Administration of Test

1. Seating arrangement, lighting etc. should be good.
2. Instructions should be clearly given i.e, division of marks, scoring procedure.

Scoring : It may be in the forms of grades.

A=Excellent B=Good C=Average

D=Below average E=Poor.

Evaluating the Test : After the scoring is done evaluation should be done by the teacher.

(i) Whether particular aim is achieved or not?

(ii) Whan type of test was it ?

Questions

1. What do you mean by Unit Planning? What steps should be followed while preparing a unit? What are the merits and demerits of unit planning?
2. Prepare lesson plans on anyone of the following units:
   (a) Living things.
   (b) Nutrition in animals and plants.
3. Name the major units in Life Sciences course for Primary, Middle and Higher secondary classes. Specify some experiments from any unit which can possibly be performed by a teacher or taken up by the students.
4. What is a Unit Test? Describe the stages of Unit Test construction.

26

CONTENT ORIENTATION

This unit, if properly dealt, would, to some extent, help to meet the shortcomings, that exist, in the training of pupil teachers at B.Ed. level, in the teaching of Life science.

Rapid explosion of scientific knowledge in all the basic sciences, and growing demand of the modern child in the advancing scientific world, not only make the teacher modify the subject matter but also necessitates for the would be teacher to possess up-to-date knowledge of these basic sciences.

WAYS OF ORIENTATION

In view of the above a teacher trainee needs:

(i) Up-to-date orientation in the Life sciences.

(ii) Exposition to the modern developments ill the Life sciences studied by him at University level. In addition to the orientation of the type mentioned above, he need acquisition of certain experimental skills, specially connected with the subject matter.

Unit : Living Thing **Sub-Unit : Photosynthesis**

Biological themes	*Concepts*	*Sub-concepts*
Development of modern concept of photosynthesisis a story of man's endeavour of search of the truth.	Concept of photosynthesis went on changing with the new evidence accrued fromed perimentation and observation carred on from time to time. Developments of concept of photosynthesis is the outcome of cumulative effort of the research workers.	(a) Earth manufactures the food which enters the plant through roots.(Aristotle) (b) Water is responsible for the living substances of the plant. (c) Atmospheric oxygen and its replenishment by green plants is an important factor in linking living and non living.(Priestley) (d) Sun-light is necessary for production of oxygen by green parts of plants.(Ingen Hauz) (e) Green plants absorb carbon dioxide from atmosphere under certain conditions. (Senchier) (f) Water is involved chemically in plant nutrition. (Experimental proof by de Senehier) (g) Water, carbon dioxide and light are key factors involved in photosynthesis. (Experimentals demonstration, 1772-1804)

Contd.

Biological themes	Concepts	Sub-concepts
		(h) Green plants convert sunligh [illegible] into chemical energy [illegible] manufactured.
		(i) Sugar is the principal energy containing compounds produced in plants green cells.
	Modern concept of photo-synthesis evolved through the use of scientific methods.	(a) Earlier attempts were also bassed on hypothesis (though not well formulated) framed to explain the process of food manufacture.
		(b) Earlier experiments reflected control of variable (though not fully) to test the hypotheses.
		(c) Conclusions drawn were based on the experimental observation.
Structure of photosyn-thetic organ leaf is well adapted to carry on the function of photosynthesis.	Different tissues and cells of leaf perform different functions in relation to the photosy-nthetic process.	(a) Veins of the leaf conduct water and nutrients from the soil through xylem tissues.
		(b) Phloem tissues of the veins transport the food prepared in the leaf to the stem and the roots.
		(c) Guard cells regulate the exchanges of gases.

Contd.

Biological themes	*Concepts*	*Sub-concepts*
		(d) Stomata help in transpiration of excess of water and conduct atmospheric carbon dioxide to the spongy tissue. (e) Vertical arrangement of pallisade cells just beneath the epidermal layer helps in reviving sunlight more directly for the chloroplasts. (f) Loose spongy layers which have chlo roplasts and a number of air spaces facili tate interchange of gases.
	Architecture of leaf is adapted to the demands of the changing environments (Maintenance of equilibrium in the face of change homeos-tasis) leading some times to changes in structure as well as function (Maintenance of over all organisation of the body in the face of change regulation).	(a) Opening and closing of stomata is regulated by the turpidity of guard cells. (b) Guard cells admit carnon dioxide where it can be used and keep the stomata closed till other conditions necessary for photosynthesis are available. (c) Number of stomata and their position a leaf varies from habitat to habitat de-pending upon the need for conservation of water for photosynthesis. (d) Structure of a leaf, its size and form change sometime to adjust to the environ ments (e.g. Reduction in size, thick cu ticle, sunken stomata in desert plant).

Contd.

Biological themes	Concepts	Sub-concepts
		(e) Function of leaf may change to maintain overall organisation of the whole body (e.g. complete loss of photosynthetic func tion in leaves of opuntia, Ruscus etc).
	Chloroplast is the functional unit of photo synthesis.	(a) Chlorophyll is the main pigment found in the chloroplasts and acts as agent of photosynthesis. (b) Chlorophyll traps the light-energy for photosynthesis. (c) Very little is known about the synthesis of chlorophyll.
Photosynthesis is a process of trapping solar energy which is the ultimate source of all life's energy	Cells and organisms require energy to do work for maintaining structure and function.	(a) Photosynthesis is the only process by energy is made available to animals. (b) All cells prepare their own A.T.P. and utilise energy from the chemical bondage of A.T.P.
	Autotrophs and hetero-trophs use different energy sources.	(a) Cells that are capable of transforming light energy into chemical bonds of A.T.P. are called autotrophs. (b) Most of autotrophic cells are green due to the presence of chlorophyll. (c) organisms that have certain autotophic cells within their bodies are also called autotophs like big trees.

Contd.

Biological themes	*Concepts*	*Sub-concepts*
		(d) Cells that use energy in the bonds of organic molecules manufactured by some other cells are called heteroptrophs.
	There ar different steps which are involved in photosynthetic process, process lead to the trapping of food manufacture by autotropohs.	(a) There are a number of processes in volved in photosynthesis, which are still not properly understood. (b) Photosynthesis may be envisaged as a two step process, the photolysis and car bon dioxide fixation. (c) photolysis involves splitting of water molecules into oxygen and hydrogen with the help of light energy trapped by chlo rophyll. (d) Carbon dioxide fixation involves syn thesis of carbon dioxide with hydrogen leading to the formation of a carbohydrate.
Chemistry of photo-synthesis can be better understood	Photosynthesis is a link between the living and non-living world. in terms of molecular nature of living process.	(a) Water used during the light transforming reaction is obtained from the soil. (b) Carbon dioxide from the atmosphere enters as a raw material and is used for synthesis in dark phase.

Contd.

Biological themes	*Concepts*	*Sub-concepts*
		(c) Both water and carbon dioxide com bine with the help of chlorophyll and in the presence of sunlight to form carbohy drates, the end product photosynthesis.
	Chloroplast carries the light transforming reac-action.	(a) Chlorophyll traps light energy to spit water molecule.
		(b) Light supplies the necessary energy required for splitting of water into hydro gen and oxygen.
		(c) Only chlorophyll can directly split up water.
		(d) Chlorophyll acts only as a catalytic agent.
	Light plays the prominent role in the first stage of photosynthesis (Photolysis).	(a) Light energy excites the chlorophyll molecules and energy realised is used in splitting of water and for changing of A.D.P. and T.P.N. in to T.P.N.H.
		(b) Only certain wave lengths of light are important for splitting of water molecules.
		(c) Chlorophyll molecules absorb much of red, orange, yellow blue and violet light waves and not the green wave at all.
		(d) Oxygen is evolved from splitting of water and not from that of carbon dioxide.

Contd.

Biological themes	***Concepts***	***Sub-concepts***
		(e) Splitting of water is a function of both chlorophyll and light. (f) A.T.P. is a high energy bond requiring considerable energy and releases consid erable energy when bond is broken. A.D.P. + Energy – A.T.P
	Fixation of carbon dioxide leads to the formation of carbohydrate in the second stage (Dark phase) involving synthesising reactions.	(a) Carbon dioxide fixation occurs through a cycle of many reaction some what like an endless belt of an assembly line in a factor. (b) T.P.N acts as hydrogen acceptor be coming T.P.N.H. (c) Half the hydrogen atoms split up from water combine with half their number of oxygen stoms (from Co_2) to form water again. (d) Half the hydrogen atoms combine with the rest of Co_2 molecules to construct glu cose molecules using the energy of A.T.P. (e) Glucose is converted to starch which is suitable for storing. (f) Glucose and not starch is the primary product of photosynthesis.

Contd.

Biological themes	***Concepts***	***Sub-concepts***
		(g) Water is the raw material as well as the by product of photosynthesis.
Synthetic production of carbohydraters is the only alternative solution to world's supply.	Very little amount of solar energy is utilised by land plants in photo-synthesis.	(a) Hardly 1/2000th of the total energy received on earth is captured by plants.
		(b) Unfavourable environmental conditions like the mountains, deserts etc. permit very little plant growth to utilise light energy.
		(c) Land plants carry only about 10% of the total photosynthesis taking place in nature.
		(d) About 90% of photosynthesis is taking place in seas, revers, lakes and ponds by microscopic aquatic algae.
	Through study of the complexity of photosynthetic process requires close call-aboration of scientists from different fields of speciali-sation	(a) Energy relationship of photosynthesis can be explained with the help of a physicist as only certain wave lengths of light are important in photosynthesis.
		(b) Molecular structure of various chlorophylls and their distribution in the chloropolasts can be better explained by a biochemist who can throw light on the complex process of energy transfer in many steps.

Contd.

Biological themes	*Concepts*	*Sub-concepts*
		(c) Detailed study of the structure of chlo roplast through electron microscope can only be done by a cytologist to explore the unsolved mysteries of the photosyn thetic process.

SUGGESTIONS

B.Ed. students are expected to orient themselves in the content as designed for Middle, High and Higher Secondary classes.

The students are advised to familiarize themselves with the entire course contents of X, XI, XII Class Life Science by at least any one of the books prescribed by the Deptt.

For each topic, the student teacher should be aware of the scope and depth *i.e.* concepts to be taught, the objectives of teaching those concepts, the study. It teacher activities the activities on the part of the pupil, the equipment and material needed and the technique of evaluation. Only then he can make his teaching meaningful and effective.

It may however, be mentioned that the would be teachers should enrich their knowledge of every topic by studying foreign books. Names of some very good books worth reading are given below:

1. Biological Science Curriculum Study; Biological Science-An Inquiry into Life. New York: Harcourt. Braco & World Inc. (Yellow Version)
2. Biological Science Curriculum Study; High School Biology. New York; Rand McNally Co. (Green Version)
3. Biology Teachers' Handbook-John Wiley and Sons. Inc.
4. Vance, B.B., Miller, D.F.; Biology for You. New York. J.B. Lippincott Co., Philadepma.

Questions

1. Why is orientation content is necessary? How can a teacher educator help his pupil teachers have orientation in the content ?
2. What books will you recommend for a B.Ed. student taking up teaching of Life Sciences in that they may have orientation to the content?

27

ORGANIZING THE SUBJECT CONTENT

At school level-the subject of life sciences has been taught in the form of botany and zoology as separate subjects. The content inclued was mainly concerned with classification of organisms, type studies, morphological and anatomical studies etc. Recently curriculum in life sciences has undergone a change almost all over the world. A balanced curriculum has been prepared for this subject and it includes topics on systematics, type studies, structure and function of organisms, heredity. evolution and environmental aspects. The subject in the text-books differ in its organization according to the approach followed in writing the books but the content has been divided into well defined units.

MAJOR UNITS

The units of secondary life sciences syllabus have been considered variously but the subject matter included under each forms a well defined part of the syllabus. The basic curriculum programme of B.S.C.S. consists of three biology text-books and related material for the use in tenth grade American high School. The major units of the subject considered in these books are given below :

AN INQUIRY INTO LIFE

Unit One : Unity, includes subject matter on what biology is about, life from basic structures and functions, living chemistry, the physiology and reproduction of cells, and the heredity material.

Unit Two : Diversity, is study of beginnings-viruses, bacteria, important small organisms, moulds, yeasts, and mushrooms the trend towards complexity, the land turns green, photosynthesis, stems and roots a study of complementarity of structure and function, reproduction and development in flowering plants, the world of animals, diversities among .animals, digestion, transportation, respiration, excretion, homeostasis, coordination, snpport, locomotion, reproduction, development in multicellular animals and the analysis of behaviour.

Unit Three : Continuity, includes topics like pattern of heredity, the chromosome theory of heredity, Darwinian evolution, the mechanism of evolution and the cultural evolution of men.

Unit Four : Interaction, includes study of animal balances in nature, ecosystems, mankind : a population out of balance, and a perspective of time and life.

HIGH SCHOOL BIOLOGY (GREEN VERSION)

This text book is divided into the following units or sections :

Section One : The world of Life; The Biosphere; includes study on the web of life, individual and population, communities and ecosystems.

Section Two : Diversity Among Living Things, includes matter on animals, plants and protists.

Section Three : Patterns in the Biosphere; examines patterns of life in the microscopic world, on land and in the water.

Section Four : Within the Individual Organism; explores the cell bioenergetics, the functioning of plants and animals and their behaviour.

Section Five : Continuity of the Biosphere; is a study of reproduction, heredity and evolution.

Section Six : Man and the Biosphere; considers the human animal and man in the web of life.

MOLECULES TO MAN (BLUE VERSION)

This text-book has been divided into the following units :

Unit One : Biology, the Interaction of Facts and Ideas; includes material on science as inquiry, the variety of living things, conflicting views on the means of evolution and the origin of living things.

Unit Two : Evolution of Life Process; is a study of fore-runners of life, chemical energy for life, light an energy for life and life with oxygen.

Unit Three : The Evolution of Cell; Presents master molecules the biological code and the cell theory.

Unit Four : Multicellular Origanums : New Individuals; considers the multicellular organisms, reproduction and development.

Unit Five : Multicellular Organisms : Genetic Continuity; includes pattern of heredity, genes and chromosomes and the origin of new species.

Unit Six : Multicellular Organisms : Energy Utilization; is a study of transport, respiratory, digestive, and excretory systems.

Unit Seven : Multicellular Organisms : Unifying Systems; treats the regulatory, nervous, skeletal, and muscular systems as well as organism behaviour.

Unit Eight : Higher Levels of Organisms; is a study of the human species, populations societies and communities.

Biology – A Text-Book for Higher Secondary Schools developed by N.C.E.R.T (India), 1966, consists of 58 chapters which are divided under seven sections. The content of secondary life sciences syllabus, according to this book, is as below.

Section 1 : Some Basic Facts About Life; includes nine chapters which deal with the aims of studying science, nature of biology, characteristics of life, cell structure; division and differentiation, an introduction of plants and animals and introductory knowledge about plant and animal major-groups.

Section II : The Diversity of Plant Life; deals with the structural details of different parts of flowering plants, fruit and seed dispersal, elementary knowledge about gymnosperms, microbes and viruses, algae, fungi, bryophyta and pteridophyta. This section includes fourteen chapters.

Section III : The Diversity of Animal Life; consists of fourteen chapters which deal with the study of fishes, amphibians, reptiles, birds, mammals, protozoa, porifera, coelenterata, platyhelminthes, mollusca, annelida, arthropoda and achinodermata. A trial has been made to discuss representative study of each group, Frog and man have been discussed in some what more detail.

Section IV : Plant and Animal Physiology; includes topics on composition of living matter; autotrophic and heterotrophic nutritious, transport and-circulation, respiration, excretion, water economy, growth and development, responsiveness and coordination. This section includes nine chapters.

Section V : Self Perpetuation and Reproduction; includes only two chapters-reproduction in plants and reproduction in animals.

Section VI : Evolution, Heredity and Adaptation; constitutes six chapters and these are concerned with the origin of life, evidences and mechanism of organic evolution, heredity and variation conditions affecting life and the different types of habitats.

Section VII : General; this section includes only four chapters and these are interdependence of plants and animals, span of life human disease, and biology in the service of man.

NEW SYLLABUS FOR VI-XII CLASSES

In India, recently a new syllabus has been developed for teaching life sciences from sixth standard to twelth standard. This has been done in order to implement the recommendations of Indian Education commission (1964-66). According to this new pattern life-sciences is taught as an integrated part of gemmule science upto tenth grade and student can specialize in this subject in eleventh and twelfth standard. The organization of subject matter in these books is being listed below.

Biology Part I, includes nine chapters, which deal with the plant life. Subject content includes importance of plants in nature cellular structure of plants, seed germination, absorption of nutrients transport of substances, preparation of organic substances, reproduction in plants and plant as a living organism.

Biology Part II, deals with the animal life, and includes matter on characteristics of various animal groups, types of animals included in those groups. Some representative studies of various animal groups have also been discussed. The text-book includes twelve chapters and these are, introduction to animal life, protozoa, coelenterata, worms arthropoda, molluscs, pisces, amphibians, reptiles, birds, mammal and classification of animals.

Biology Part III, is a study of anatomy and physiology of man. This book constitutes eleven topic. The subject matter deals with introduction to human physiology, general survey of human body, organs of movement, food and digestion, blood and blood circulation, respiration, metabolism, structure and functions of skin, nervous system and sense organs, human development and heredity, human body as an integrated whole.

Life Sciences for Classes IX and X, has been divided into the following seven major units.

Unit 1 : Introduction; deals with history and scope of life sciences, characteristics of plants and animals.

Unit 2 : Organization of Life; includes five chapters which deal with levels of organization, cell structure and functions, tissues in plants and animals, organs; organ systems; and organisms, individual ; population and community.

Unit 3 : Life Process; is a study of various systems. The unit includes nine topics and these deal with nutrition, photosynthesis, respiration, internal transport, excretion, movement and locomotion, reproduction, growth and development, control and coordination.

Unit 4 : Genetics and Evolution; constitutes three chapters and these are heredity and variation, basis of heredity and its mechanism, evolution of the life on earth.

Unit 5 : Agricultural Practices and animal Husbandry; has a discussion about crops and factors influencing crop production, various agricultural practices, improvement of crops, elements of animal husbandry. This unit includs only four topics.

Unit 6 : Human Biology, Health and Sutrition; has been divided into seven topics. These topics include subject matter on functional anatomy of human reproductive system, pregnancy and child birth, infancy; childhood and adolescence, trends in world population, population problm in India, communicabll; dissases of man, nutritional disorders of man,

Unit 7 : Man and his Environment; constitutes five chapters which deal with the knowledge of ecosystem, biosphere, ecological crisis, conservation of natural resources and conservation of nature, national and international efforts in this direction.

Biology : A Text-Book for Higher Secondary Schools (classes XI-XII) Part Volume I, deals with the anatomy and physiology of animals, this text book contains eleven chapters. The subject matter includes. microscopic structure of mammalian tissues digestive, respiratory, excretory, nervous, muscular, skeletal, endocrine reproductive systems and biological rhythms.

Biology : A Text Book for Higher Secondary schools (classes XI-XII) Part I Volume II ; includes topics on anatomy and physiology of plants and systematics. The subject matter deals with meristems water relations to plant cell, structure and functions of root, stem and leaf respiration, plant growth and development, plant movements, plant rhythms, systematics as a discipline and utility of systematics.

Broadly the above mentioned two volumes have been divided into two sections. First section deals with anatomy and physiology of animals and plants and includes 22 chapters. Section second deals with systematics and includes only two chapters.

Biology : A Text Book for Higher. Secondary Schools (classes XI-XII) Part II Volume I, has been divided into *two* major units.

Unit 1 : Cell Biology; constitutes fourteen chapters and these deal with the introduction and the cell theory tools and techniques. portrait of a cell cell wan and plasma membrane endoplasmic reticulum and ribosomes, golgi apparatus, microbodies energy, mitochondria, chloroplast centrioles and basal bodies, interphase nucleus enzymes and regulation hormones and regulation.

Unit 2 : Genetics has been divided into ten chapters. The matter content of this unit is physical and chemical basis of heredity, functions of nucleic acids cell division, principles of inheritance, linkage and crossing over, gene expression and interaction, mutation, quantitative inheritance human genetics, genetics and society.

Biology : A Text Book for Higher Secondary Schools (classes XI-XII) Part II Volume II, has been divided into three major units:

Unit 1 : Developmental Biology-Plants; first introduces the subject matter and includes reproduction and development in bacteria, Chlamydomonas, Spirogyra, Rhizopus, Funaria, Selaginella; Pious and other topics on seed, juvenility and heteroblastic development, flower, sexual reproduction, fruit, asexual reproduction, plant tissue and organ culture.

The unit contains fifteen chapters.

Unit 2 : Developmental Biology-Animals; is discussed in nine chapters. The subject matter is divided into developmental biology; definition ; scope and history forms of reproduction, basic features of embryonic development, development of frog, embryonic nutrition abnormalities during embryonic development cancer, regeneration and aging.

Unit 3 : Biology and Human Welfare; has been organised into fifteen chapters. The subject content includes domestication of plants by man, important cultivated crops, plant diseases, some important plant diseases of India, plant pests, forests in service of man, forest insects in service of man, livestock, poultry, fisheries, communicable diseases community health, non-communicable diseases, alcoholism and drug addiction, industrial microbiology.

The organization of subject matter in Indian books is not finally settled. There are going on changes and scrutiny of the syllabus, recommended for secondary schools. The original syllabus has now been condensed and further changes are expected.

EXPERIMENTS AND DEMONSTRATIONS

The B.S.C.S. Yellow Version programme has a laboratory manual, called "Laboratory Guide" that contains 89 "inquiries". Detailed procedures called "experimental designs" are given, students are asked to make and record observations, guided questions and statements are inserted to direct the students, guide questions and statements are inserted to direct the students' reasoning. The statements are made in introductory remarks and the inquiries are graded with respect to open-endedness. The inquiries are quite structured and the experimental procedures as well as specific questions to be answered are included. Most of the experiments are investigative rather than illustrative but are at a low level of openness. In the Green and Blue Versions there are no laboratory manuals. Instead, the investigation are inserted in the text books where they are related to the text book material. The investigations are similar to those described for Yellow Version in what is given and what is required of the students. Although it is convenient to have the laboratory exercises included in the text but this arrangement tends to place less responsibility on the students for hypothesizing predicting etc. since the information required in the experiments is at all times directly available to them in the text book. This arrangement has the advantage of making it necessary for the students to write up their reports rather than simply filling in the blanks (as is in many work books) : Many of the questions directed to the students ask for scientific reasoning i.e. "How do you account for your observations." How does the data support the original hypothesis?" Many of the exercises in these books can be presented by the teacher, using the techniques and procedures' described in the chapters. It is not always easy for the teacher to develop his own execises. The publisher laboratory programmes represent the thinking and experience of many leading scientists and educators and can help the teacher in well organizing his laboratory work.

The B.S.C.S. Laboratory Block Programme developed, provide students with the opportunity to carry out a series of investigations in depth in a particular area of biology. Each block is planned for six-week period of time. Not more than one block is generally used during one year of academic course because of time and equipment limitations. The block can be used at any time during the year or at the end of year or with any biology text book.

B.S.C.S. materials that can be used for laboratory purposes are

(a) Biology Teachers' Hand book,

(b) Laboratory Blocks,

(c) Laboratory Innovations,

(d) Biological Investigations

(e) B.S.C.S. Pamphlet Series,

(f) Patterns of life Series,

(g) Inquiry Slides,

(h) Single topics Inquiry Films etc.

A Laboratory Manual was prepared by N.C.E.R.T. for the use of A Text book for Higher Secondary Schools' meant for ninth, tenth and eleventh classes. Some illustrative demonstrations have been given in , the VI section and the can be arranged while teaching the subject. For the newly dveloped syllabus for 10+2 system of schooling, we need a work book or laboratory manual particularly for higher secondary classes (XI and XII).

Some experiments and demonstrations have been included in the texts meant for teaching from 6th standard to 10th standard.

Biology Part I, contains several experiments as on preparations for the ,microscope, composition of seeds, respiration in seeds, composition of soil, growth in roots, absorption of water by plants, photosynthesis, transpiration etc. Task given at the end of chapters requires students to undertake experimental work.

Biology Part II, contains a few activities included in the text and these are mostly about securing the organisms, studying their characteristics opening the organism and studying the internal organs. The tasks mentioned at the end of topics requires studying to secure different animals, studying their habitat, feeding habits, bebaviour their external features and internal organs and culturing and preservation of different animals.

Biology Part III, includes a very few experiments in the text but the task recommended for the students requires them study the structure of various organs and their functions, chemical composition of food material and action of digestive juices on food material. Some activities related to the functioning to the human body are also suggested.

Life Sciences for classes IX and X includes some experiments in the text. The procedure and directions for arranging the experiments are given and students are also required to note down the observation. Some experiments included in this book are related to study of internal organs of frog, evolution of oxygen and synthesis of starch during photosynthesis, aerobic and anaerobic respiration, up-take of water in plants etc.

Biology : A Text book for Higher Secondary Schools includes only a few demonstrations and these are about osomsis, root pressure and transpiration. There is an urgent need of having a separate laboratory manual for effective teaching of the subject at this stage.

Questions

1. Discuss the major units of life-sciences syllabus identified by Biology Sciences Curriculum Study (U.S.A.)
2. Under what major sections has the content been divided in life sciences books for schools, prepared by N.C.E.R.T. (India)?
3. In your view, what should be the place of experiments and demonstrations in life sciences syllabus at school level ? What is the position of these in books prepared by N.C.E.R.T.

28

DYNAMICS OF PROGRAMME PREPARATION

Papee Pipe has observed that foul general thoughts about preparation of programme must be given due consideration before setting down to work cut the details. These are:

(i) Preparation is just 100 per cent. 'technique'; art has very little to do with it. This technique needs 'hard work'.

(ii) Note that preparation accounts for at least 25 per cent of your total time. To give it less than it to deny it justics.

(iii) Do not bother about attained perfection in one step before you begin the next on. It is always fine to insert fine changes, but be sure that you write down any change you make.

(iv) Any discussion on programming, and for that reason the discussion that follows is of necessity, in general terms, do it the way that suits you-may emphasise one step more, another less.

With the above four ideas in mind, the following steps may be suggested in programme preparation:

Step I. Selection of a subject area or a unit to be programmed.

Step 2. Writing assumptions about the learners (the target population) for whom the programme is intended.

Step 3. Define instructional objectives in behavioural terms.

Step 4. Defining pre-requisite knowledge and skills in behavioural terms.

Step 5. Writing criterion test based on programme objectives.

Step 6. Deciding the order in which instructional matter is to be presented.

Step 7. Developing the content list including from writing.

VARIOUS STEPS

Step I. Selection of a Subject Area or a Unit.

The expert advice regarding the selection of a subject area or a unit to be programmed is that the programmer should begin with ,a small unit. He should not be ambitious to select a very wide and general topic This will avoid much afforestation and failure for a programmer. The unit selected must emerge directly from the programmer's own field of study. There should be 'ease' in the handling of the material. Moreover, the whole subject may not be brought on the wheel of programming. Certain subject units may be taught conventionally with profit. Notorious stumbling blocks to teamer, must be selected to be programmed. Logical order of material is an important criterion in matters of selection. And, above all, special students' needs must be given proper consideration.

Step 2. Writing Assumptions about Learners.

An important factor to be considered is the body of pupils for whom the programme is intended. The programmer must know fully well, as accurately as possible the major characteristics of the, learners-the target population. He must therefore, list basic assumptions about them-their age, sex, skills, interest, abilities, their background. etc. A pilot knowledge of these assumptions about the learners will matter much in deciding the scope of the programme and its actual writing.

Step 3. Defining Instructional Objectives

Preparing a statement of appropriate instructional objectives in terms of behavioural changes is an important aspect of programme preparation. According to B. Has. Bloom, by instructional objectives, we mean explicit formulations of the ways in which students are expected to be changed by the educative process, that is, the way in which they will change in their thinking, their feelings, and their actions.

Robert Mager has suggested how objectives of instruction can be rendered in specific behavioural terms.

A statement of instructional objectives is a collection of words on symbols describing one or more of your educational intents.

An objective will communicate your intent to the degree you have described what that learner will be doing when demonstrating his achievement and how you will know he is doing it.

Any statement on instructional objectives will take into consideration:

Terminal behaviour of the learner after he has completed programme.

Conditons under which the learner is to carry out the programme restrictions and limitations.

Tolerance or acceptable standard of performance, that is, error rate permitted etc.

Step 4. Defining pre-requisite Knowledge and Skills

Defining pre-requisite knowledge and skills in behavioural terms does not fundamentally differ from defining instructional objectives. This, in fact, is a statement on what should be in the repertoire of the pupil at the end of the programme. The list of pre-requisite knowledge and skills, a provisional, 'armchair' list, may be arrived at after giving an objective test to a sample of target population, by considering the errors committed by the students, a thorough list for pre-requisite skills to be covered by given programme may be developed.

Step 5. Writing a Criterion Test

Writing a criterion test based on programme objectives is to test the entire range of terminal behaviour or criterion behaviour, or instructional goals set by the programmer. This is meant to determine the success or failure of the entire programme. The results of the criterion test will help the programmer to modify his statements on instructional objectives and pre-requisite skills. A criterion test should preferably be made up of objective type test items. While constructing a criterion test, the correct choice of words, the clarity of language and the relevance of each test item should be maintained. A good criterion test is one which reflects representative elements of the universe of behaviour.

Step 6. Deciding the Order

Deciding the order in which instructional matter is to be presented can be compared to an essay plan where the writer first prepares a list of the points that he wishes to develop and then arranges them in the order which is likely to create the greater impact. After the programmer has determined the key concept which are to be presented to the learners, he arranges then in the most logical order, ensuring that they are interlinked within the sequence. Most Programme writers go on analysing, breaking down this concepts into sub-concepts until the skeleton of the programmes is clear.

Step 7. Developing the Content List

Developing the content list comes last. Here the programmer should were the complete information relating to each concept to be persented. He must mention all the relevant examples illustrations, diagrams, maps, charts etc. which would form an integral part of the content of a specific programme.

Questions

1. Describe the origin and background of programmed learning.
2. Explain in detail the meaning and concept of programmed learning. What are its salien features and basic principles?
3. Describe the types/styles of progrmming currently in vogue in a tabular form.
4. Explain the dynamics of programme preparation.

29

PROJECTS FOR STUDENTS

A project is a problematic act carried to completion in its natural setting." J.A. Stevenson.

A project includes a series of related problems and covers small portion of subject matter or an entire course. Project, as a method of teaching, builds a unit around an activity that is carried out in the school or outside it. This method is an effective method of teaching in every respect. It necessitates detailed planning, more foresight and more skill on the part of the teacher.

THE SIGNIFICANCE

Project as a method of teaching has several advantages towards learning sciences by the students. A project contributes to stimulating interest in science, satisfying scientific curiosity, developing scientific method of working and scientific attitude, giving practice in critical thining and increasing self confidence in the students. This method also involves the three main psychological laws of learning :

(a) Law of readiness (b) Law of exercise (c) Law of effect.

This means students get ready to learn as they are interested in aiming, they work on projects so their skills are exercised and success the project gives satisfaction to students, so retention is more. Work on projects also enhances democratic way of working and living subject can be taught in more correlated form and this also enhances resourcefulness and planning. Students recognize dignity of out and scientific principles have more meaning to them.

Teaching by project method is more useful in lower classes as it does help in specialization in a particular subject and teaching is not much organized. Projects should not aim at production but at developing skills, attitudes and method of working in the students. Projects prove more useful if planned according to age, intelligence interests and abilities of the students.

SIGNIFICANT STEPS

Providing Situation. Here the teacher should provide a situation which confronts students with some problem which the students feel responsible to solve. The interest of the students is aroused in solving that problem. Here the teacher can visualize the merits and demerits of the project he is aiming at.

Selection of the Project. The teacher should work as a latent force to channelize the interest of the students but after all students should have the feeling that the project is of their own choice and it is not imposed on them by the teacher. The teacher can tell the merits and educational values of the project and can induce discussion in the class about its feasibility. If the project chosen is not good, the teacher should not reject that but he should tell the demerits of that and students should be convinced to reject that.

Planning. This is an important step as success of the project is largely determined by planning. In this the students are assigned duties sources of material are listed, the procedure is visualised in detail and place, time and duration etc. are decided. The teacher should enhance discussion among the students and their feelings should not be suppressed. Duties should be allotted according to the abilities, interests and aptitudes of the students.

Execution. The project now comes in its process and practical form. The students work according to the duties allotted. The project is completed keeping in view the time and duration. The teacher acts as a guide and co-worker and sees that the project runs smoothly and is completed within the time.

Evaluation. Students review the project, find out mistakes committed and correct these wherever necessary. Self-criticism should not be avoided, if some phenomenon is set up, students can take down reading and where material products, they can evaluate the quantity and quality. The teacher here sees that the objectives of the project have been achieved.

Recording. Preferably, recording of the project should be simultaneous but wherever it is not possible it should be done just after the completion of the project. Data regarding choice of the project discussion held, planning and duties assigned, execution and entire procedure, material production or readings taken and mistakes reviewed, should be recorded in detail.

SETTING UP AN AQUARIUM

A well directed aquarium project may be used successfully at the beginning of the course, as a centre about which practically all the fundamental principles of life sciences arise spontaneously. The interest of the students can be maintained throughout the project and economy in learning is far greater since students make discoveries themselves and are not told of these by the teacher.

A project may be used to introduce the problems of an entire course or it can be used to review the whole course taught earlier (illustrative). Studying the inter-relationship of organisms in nature is of great value from learning point of view and an aquarium can also supply a lot of material for laboratory work.

Importance : In teaching life sciences an aquarium can be made to play an important role. Most of the fundamental principles of life sciences are found inherent in either a balanced or imbalanced aquarium. The dependance of animals directly or indirectly upon green plants for their oxygen and food supply is a striking phenomenon. The relation of CO2 and light to photosynthesis and resulting products, food synthesis, food storage, respiration, digestion, growth and reproduction in both plants and animals, the relation of bacteria to nitrogen phosphorus and sulphur cycles, parasitism and saprophytism can be studied on a balanced aquarium. The relation of one kind of animal to another, food cycles, sucession of one population by another, temperature effects, and water relations can be studied on balanced and imbalanced aquarium. An aquarium proves to be a live corner in the laboratory and students appreciate the co-existance of plants and animals. Different plants and animals, aquatic or amphibious can be cultured in the aquarium, with, some adjustments. A well stocked aquarium also supplies material for practical classes.

The procedure that can be followed when the class works out a project on an aquarium as a part or their learning activity:

Feeling of Choice : Depending upon where the project is used in the course, the approach to carry it out will vary. If the aquarium is used to furnish a source for most of the problems taken up in the study, the teacher may start some phases of its preparation in order to arouse curiosity in the students. If use of aquarium is sought after the students have learnt many biological phenomena, then the class may suggest making up of an aquarium. The teacher should tell the students the importance of the aquarium. In any case the students should feel that the work is of their own choice and not ordered.

Planning : The teacher should be well versed in the details of setting up of an aquarium. The preparation of it should furnish a series of problems which the class should discuss and decide upon. The problems involved are keys to fundamental biological principles which should be clearly understood by the students.

Suppose the class has decided to construct and study an aquarium the next step for the teacher would be to pool problems that the students suggest, could be solved when the aquarium becomes reality.

The teacher should also invite questions from the class which would be involved in setting up of the aquarium.

Some questions can be :

(a) What shall we use as tank?

(b) What kind of plants can we use?

(c) Where from can these plants be obtained?

(d) What kinds of animals will be required?

(e) What materials can be used for substratum ?

(f) What kind of water should be used?

(g) How often should the water be changed?

(h) What food should be given to the animals?

(i) Where should the aquarium be placed in the room?

The teacher can list the problems as above and allow the class to discuss and suggest the material and procedure for setting up the aquarium.

(a) What shall we use as tank ?

Growing of water plants and animals can successfully be undertaken in simple glass containers, yet many Schools go without an aquarium because, such tanks are not available. A large vessel almost of any kind can be used and small containers such as pans and jars are quite satisfactory for special problems. Let the class decide what it can provide.

If a glass container is available use it but why not let some wooden tub or other container and have two or more aquarium.

(b) What kind of plants can we use?

(c) Where from can these plants be obtained?

Students, after they have answered the second question and suggested some aquatic plants as Hydrilla, Vallisneria, Elodea and some algae etc., can be asked where from they will get these. Student may suggest buying of these plants, others, having them from fisheries, botanical gardens or from the surroundings like pools, ponds and streams. Getting of these plants from their natural habitats is educationally sound and economic.

(d) What kind of animals will be required ?

Fishes are most common and suitable animals that are used for aquaria. The quality and quantity may be studied and experienced.

Some other organisms like tadpoles, snails, some crustaceans and sponges can be introduced. About animals also we can have discussion in the class and their purchase or collection decided.

(e) What materials can be used for substratum?

Placing of shells, stones, sand and mud can be suggested, as sub stratum, by the students. This is a good question as the answer distinguishes between ornament and necessity. The quantity and quality of mud, stones and sand should be decided regarding their relative vallies and importance in the aquarium. Sand is necessary for burrowing animals. Mud is required for anchorage of submerged plants and mud and sand are sources of nutrients to the plants.

(f) What kind of water should be used ?

(g) How often should the water be changed ?

These questions can be discussed by asking about the contents of water from sources such as supply, ponds, pools and streams. The presence of micro-organisms in water can also be considered.

Chlorinated water is generally not recommended for the aquaria. Changing of later can be considered in relation to pollution and depletion of food material. Analysis of water can be undertaken from time to time.

(h) What food should be given to the animals?

Answer to this question requires some study of feeding habits of the animals placed in the aquarium. Requirements of food are directly related to pollution and change of water, presence of micro-organisms and the quantity of plants put in the aquarium. Whether the plants are of the value for animals regarding their food requirements, should be determined beforehand. This can be done experimentally by keeping animals in small jars with and without these plants.

(i) Where should be aquarium be placed in the room?

Here the temperature fluctuations mean and extreme, availability of light in the room are major considerations. Whether the aquarium is to be put near a heater or window or in direct sunlight should be decided. Putting of aquarium in direct sunlight is not recommended. If sufficient transmitted light is there in the room artificial light is not required. Effect of light on plants and animals can also be studied beforehand. Where temperature comes very low at nights, aquarium heaters can be used.

After requirements are decided, students are allotted duties according to their interests and abilities, as some can be asked to arrange for container some for plants and animals and others for the substratum. Time and duration for the project are fixed.

Execution : At this stage the project comes into its practical form. Students exploit their sources for material and the things are assembled. The teacher provides directions and acts as co-worker. He also sees to it that aquarium comes to reality.

Evaluation : After all the thing, are properly assembled it is observed that the aquarium functions properly. If the aquarium does not function mistakes are detected and reviewed. Here the teacher also sees that his objectives of teaching such as knowledge skills and training in planning have been achieved. After proper completion of the project students are encouraged to make observations on balanced and imbalanced aquarium.

Recording : A complete and detailed record of all material, procedure and events is to be maintained by the students. They should note down the importance of aquarium discussed, suggestions for container, plants, animals, water substratum and the resources extolled to get these things. They should also record duties performed by the students, time, duration, procedure and mistakes reviewed etc. They should also maintain the record of observations made on the aquarium.

Questions

1. What is the importance of Students' Projects in teaching life sciences. What steps will you follow in conducting a project with your class?
2. How will you conduct "setting up an aquarium" as a project with your class? Discuss in detail.
3. What is a project? Discuss a science project that may be undertaken by the tenth graders of a school. How should the project be planned and executed?
4. (a) Prepare an outline of an investigatory project for class IX or X students.

   (b) What guidance will you give as a teacher of biology to carry on the above investigation?
5. Discuss the significance and role of the following in teaching life sciences :

   (a) Teaching Aids

   (b) Students' Projects.

30

CURRICULUM IMPROVEMENT

In recent years curriculum reforms in life sciences have taken place all over the world. We can discuss it under the following headings.

WORK DONE IN INDIA

The work done in India towards improving life sciences programme, particularly after the inception of N.C.E.R.T, can be summarized under the following headings :

DEVELOPING A NEW CURRICULUM

The National Council of Educational Research and Training (N.C.E.R.T.) approached Professor P. Maheshwari to set up and guide a Biology Panel. The panel consisted of 16 representatives, professors, teachers, and research workers from several universities and research institutions. The panel drew up a revised curriculum and prepared a new text book "A Text-Book of Biology for Higher Secondary Schools". The chairman was in close contact with the new developments and practices of other countries while preparation of the text book was in process.

The members of the panel considered several ways of approaching the subject matter and discussed about their merits and demerits. Finally they decided to adopt a modernized traditional approach as it suited the prevailing standards and practices of teaching in Indian schools. The members agreed that students should be introduced to different kinds, of organisms, their activities, habits and their tissues and organs, as it is essential and basic to the understanding of concepts of evolution, ecology heredity and cell physiology. The approach combines the pedagogical advantage of proceeding from known to unknown and also prevents the students from getting lost in the intricacies of more advanced aspects of biology.

They discussed evolution separately into two chapters but an attempt was made to familiar is the student with this principle during his study of world of life. Biological phenomena common to plants and animals are discussed together as far as possible but have not been carried too far, as several aspects of plants and animals deserve independent treatment. Technical terms have been used only where they contribute to a easier communication and understanding. Important biological discoveries have been dealt in a historical manner, to give an idea to students, of how science progresses.

The book has been divided into seven sections. In the first section, the students are introduced to the subject matter of biology and the characteristics of living matter. An Introduction to the variety of plant and animal life prepares the students for more detailed study of these forms in second and third sections. The fourth section dales with main physiological processes in plants and animals. The fifth section is devoted to modes of reproduction in plants and animals. Heredity, evolution and ecology are included in the sixth section and the seventh section includes interdependence of plants and animals and the role of biology in human welfare. All the schools under Central Board of Secondary Education and schools in some states gave this book a fair trial. In the meantime the National Council has also produced some Indian adaptations of B.S.C.S. books. The Directorate of Extension Programmes for Secondary Education drafted a syllabus of General Science for class I to VIII with the help of specialists and teachers.

In implementing the recommendations of Indian Education Commission (1964-66), that general science be taught compulsorily upto 10th class, N.C.E.R.T. produced syllabi and text-books upto 10th class Biology Part I for sixth class deals with life of typical flowering plant and an introductions to major plant groups.

Biology Part II for seventh class deals with major animal groups with representative studies. Biology Part III includes topics on human anatomy and physiology. The book of Life Sciences for class IX, and X includes some major units like organization of life, life processes, genetics and evolution, agricultural practices and animal husbandry, Human biology, health and nutrition, man and his environment. Text books for + 2 stage have also been prepared.

LABORATORIES AND EQUIPMENT

The Government of India has been giving ,assistance to State Governments for the introduction of effective science courses in higher secondary schools. In two first five year plans aid was given for construction of' laboratories and purchase of apparatus. A panel was set up by Committee on Plan Projects of Planning Commission to draw up laboratory designs and lists of equipment for higher secondary schools.

IN-SERVICE PROGRAMMES

The Directorate of Extension Programmes for Secondary Education has been organizing a number of In-service Programmes for the benefit of secondary school science teachers. These programmes deal with methods of teaching, preparation and use of teaching aids, co-curricular activities in science, lesson plans, evaluation etc. These in service programmes have brought a keener awareness, among science teachers, about the new concepts and techniques of science teaching.

EXCHANGE OF TEACHERS

In 1958, forty science teachers were selected from training colleges and secondary schools from different states and were deputed to study modern methods of science teaching in U. K., U.S.A. and Canada by Govt. of India. On their return their opinions were pooled in a seminar ani a programme was drawn up for at levels. The suggestions were considered by All India Council for

Secondary Education and were incorporated in the programme of science – education for the third five year plan.

TELEVISION LESSONS

A programme of television lesson in physics, chemistry and biology for higher secondary classes was introduced in Delhi in 1961-62. Each lesson, when started, was of 20 minutes duration and preceded by an intrcdution by the subject teacher. The scheme was started in IX class and has been increased.

SCIENCE CLUBS

Science club activities in secondary schools were started during 1967-68 by All India Council for Secondary Eduction. In 1973 it covered about 1,114 school is given Rs. 1200 for the purchase of tools and apparatus. In addition to these there are eight basic schools with established science clubs with a grant of Rs. 3001 for each there are 60 central science clubs, established in training colleges, where extension services centres are located. These are given Rs. 2000 each per year. The programme aims at providing opportunities to young pupils to undertake activities of their interests and science teachers try to correlate the club-activities with classroom activities where-ever possible.

SCIENCE FAIRS

N.C.E.R.T. considered introduction of science fairs in order to improve science teaching. All India Council for Secondary Education in 1960 recommended a programme of All India Science Fairs to be organized on first December and these be followed by a science week. In the science week exhibitions, lectures and symposia etc. could be held. In 1961,54 extension services centres held science fairs with an aid of Rs. 500 given to each centre. Now the science fairs are held at three levels district, regional and state. In the year 1965-66, 264 district, 79 regional and 5 state science fairs were held.

NATIONAL SCIENCE TALENT SEARCH

Under the science education improvement programme, Govt. of India formulated a programme of Science Talent Search under which promising science students of-final year Sr. Sec. are selected and are given scholarships arid certificates of merit.

The main objectives of the scheme are :

(i) to identify students of marked scientific aptitude,

(ii) to stimulate scientific talent through competition,

(iii) to encourage schools to undertake scientific activities,

(iv) to expose talented students to challenges of science and,

(v) to build up a body of future scientists who will contribute to scientific advancement in pure and applied fields.

The scheme was started in 1963 and about 350 talented students are selected every year. In 1971, 359 students were selected and were given scholarships. The selection is based on an aptitude test, an essay competition a project report and an interview by a committee of specialists. The amount of scholarship is Rs. 100 p.m. and book allowance Rs. 100 p.a. at B.Sc. stage. At M.Sc. stage the scholar is paid Rs. 250 p.m. and a book allowance Rs. 250 p.a. At Ph.D. stage the scholar is paid Rs. 350 per month and Rs. 500 p.a. as book allowance. At schools and other institutes the students are offered accelerated programme of science instruction so that they can acquire enough knowledge and motivation to pursue a career of research in science.

SUMMER INSTITUTES

This is a programme of in-service training of-school teachers for a period of 4 to 6 weeks. This programme is jointly sponsored by the U.G.C and U.S.A.I.D. These institutes are designed to improve the school science teaching and inspire the teachers to continue learning in their fields. The teachers attending these institutes learn new ways of teaching science especially with methods that would enable the students to learn science by discovery rather than studying descriptive science. The programme had a small beginning in 1963 with only four institutes each in one subject (physics, chemistry, biology and mathematics) but the programme extended to 43 institutes and 8 of these were devoted to biology. In all 761 biology teachers had been benefited by this programme upto 1966.

PARTICIPATION OF FOREIGN ORGANIZATIONS

The U.S.A.I.D. India sought the cooperation of U.S. National Science Foundation to implement a large scale year round programme of academic support in modernizing curriculum, laboratories and teaching aids. Indo-American conference on Scientific and Technical Education was held in New Delhi in May 1968. Here it was resolved that N.S.F. A.I.D. will co-operate Govt. of India in the follow up activities to organize summer institutes, preparation of text-books, teacher guide curriculum material and strengthening of libraries and laboratories. U.N.E.S.C.O. Pilot Project has helped in curriculum renew C.F..D.O. and British Council also help Indian educational institutes.

WORK DONE IN OTHER COUNTRIES

In recall years, practically, every country in the world has revised or revolutionized the methods of teaching and content of science syllabi. All these courses have a common trend away from just learning of facts. An experimental approach to topics relevant to the life of the community is a feature of these courses.

There has been much intemation a co-operation in the development of new materials and this is being continued during re-writing of materials and their trials in schools. Several of the texts, noably the B.S.C.S books, Nuffield Biology and U.N.E.S.C.O. Pilot Project represent the foundations of which later courses have been built.

CURRICULUM STUDY

During 1957-58 educationists and biologists from schools, colleges and universities in the U.S.A. were given the task of devising a course of high school biology that was to have a sound scientific basis for future specialists and could suit the taste of general students. The B.S.C I. courses are intended for one year of high school (out of total four years).

The text books are therefore, more suitable for senior pupils in secondary schools and so background reading for teachers.

Three courses were developed, approaching the subject from different main concepts. The versions have come to be known as much by the colour of their bindings as by their titles. These are as follows :

Molecules to Man (Blue Version) : It is based on molecular biology. This is the most difficult version and covers much of the Advanced Level of General Certificate of Education and similar examinations.

High School Biology (Green Version) : It is an ecology based text and is of great use to the general reader. It can be used with advantage in sixth. It is well illustrated and interesting in content and can prove to be advantageous for non-science specializers.

Biological Science : An Inquiry into Life *(Yellow Version)* has an evolutionary emphasis. This version is suitable for countries having tropical fauna and flora. An adaptation of this was made at a workshop in India for students in Higher Secondary Schools.

The three versions, despite their special emphasis, all form a basic course of biology. No topic usually taught in school course is negelected. The excellent illustration and clear language make all the three courses especially suitable for background reading for senior pupils, whose mother tongue is not English but, who have, to study in this language.

A laboratory Manual and a Teacher's Guide for each version has also been produced.

B.S.C.S. group has developed many other materials and some of these are :

Biology Teacher's Hand book by J.J Schwab (1963) deals with using the B.S.C.S. materials, methods of assessment and preparation of laboratory reagents and gives background of physical sciences and statistics. Second edition (1970) by Evelin Klinckmann (supervisor) and third edition (1978) by W.V. Mayer (editor) contribute more to teacher preparations and use of B.S.E.S. materials.

Research Studies in Biology : Investigations for students is of interest to students who are to specialize in biology. This book suggests some research projects and problems that the student can undertake to solve.

Laboratory Blocks : These booklets, produced by committee on Innovation in Laboratory Instruction, provide a complete series of laboratory studies in specialized fields. The micro-biology block is especially useful.

Patterns and processes, a text and teacher's guide for slower pupils is a good example of the use of programmed learning.

Pamphlets on specialized topics are published frequently and these include results of latest research. These are means of keeping in touch with the latest developments for both teachers and senior pupils.

The B.S.C.S. materials, three main texts, laboratory manuals and teachers' guides have influenced teaching of Life Sciences in countries as diverse as Australia, India and East Africa.

NUFFIELD LEVEL BIOLOGY

Curriculum in United Kingdom started in 1962 and methods and materials were tried and tested. These were later incorporated in a scheme of work for Ordinary Level General Certificate of Education. The difference between "Nuffield" and 'Traditional' biology is that the former poses questions to which pupils are encouraged to find answers. There is a suitable background reading for every stage and basis is adequate for future specialization in biological sciences. A Teacher's Guide is also provided for each year which includes laboratory techniques and additional work for more able pupils. "Nuffield Biology" can be taught using minimum of equipment. An adaptation of this in India has been with the use of simple local apparatus in place of imported expensive items.

NUFFIELD COMBINED SCIENCE

The need of the study of a wide range of subjects during the first two years of a secondary school course does not always enable physics, chemistry and biology to be studied as separate disciplines. Therefore, Nuffield Foundation sponsored the predation of a junior science course with an approach similar to that of '0' level texts. "Nuffield Combined Science" came out in 1970. The course consists of ten topics from the sub-sections of which the teacher is able to select those most suitable for all classes. Two Teacher Guide Books and an Apparatus Guide have also been produced. Activity Packs for pupils are work books which give guidance for practical work, its recording and applications. Apart from its class room use, many topics can be studied in science clubs.

NUFFIELD SECONDARY SCIENCE

Sponsored by Nuffield Foundation. Secondary Science caters to the needs of average and below average upils of U.K. Certificate or Secondary Education. The course is arranged as themes, through which routes can be found to provide a sequence and content suited to the needs of classes in differing environments.

INTEGRATED SCIENCE

This has been developed for pupils of high ability who intend to specialize in art subjects but study science also. In the biology part of this course concentration is on aspects of convervation, world problems of food supply and population genetics and evolution with the elementary anatomy and morphology necessary to the understanding or fundamental principles.

CURRICULUM DEVELOPMENT IN DEVELOPING COUNTRIES

In recent years there has been an enormous expansion of educational facilities in developing countries of Africa and Asia. Accompanying the increase in institutions, teaching methods and content of the curriculum are being revolutionized.

The West African Examination Council initiated curriculum reform at Advanced Level by a total revision of the syllabus. The Biology Syllabus for Nigeria, Ghana, Sieria Leone and Zambia was completed during 1965-66. It has an ecological bias suited to the needs of biologists in countries where the economy is largely based on agriculture. Secondary Schools in some parts of West Africa have been using the Nuffield, Biology "0" Level courses for some years and advanced Teacher Training Colleges are meeting the supply of grammar school teachers by training non-graduates with modern approach to their work.

East Africa has a School Science Project at the trial stage. Physics, Chemistry and Biology courses are currently being tested in schools by East African Examination Council. Each course covers the four years of secondary school course equivalent to "0" Level G.C.E. Revision and rewriting of the courses is at an advanced stage. Three organizations have done much to sponsor curriculum renewal in developing countries. These are:

United Nations Development Programme (U.N.D.P.) : This organization through the U.N.E.S.C.O. has aided the establishment of Advanced colleges of Education, whose prime purpose is to train teachers for the first three or four years of secondary school curriculum. The Biology Pilot Project has been developed by U.N.D.P. personnel. This is a specific course for schools in Africa using local materials and facilities. It began in English speaking areas but is now being extended to French speaking areas. College, University and School teachers worked together in the production and making the course effective.

British Council : The British Council has established science offices in many countries. Assisting scientific development in general, they have also been responsible for introducing Nuffield Science Courses into countries diverse geographically and culturally such as India and Latin America. The council, together with U.K. Overseas Development Administration, sponsors in-service training in numerous countries. Their main contribution is the supply of tutors, equipment and books.

The Centre for Educational Development Overseas : C.E.D.O. was inaugurated in April, 1970. It communes the activities of pre-existing centre for Curriculum Renewal and Educational Development Overseas (C.R.E.D.O.), the Overseas Visual Aids Centre (O.V.A.C) and the centre for Education at Television Overseas (C.E.T.O.). C.E.D.O helps countries to realize their educational development on request. The activities undertaken by this organization are in-Service training, workshops conferences and work in examinations and testing. The centre is a clearing house for information in all aspects of educational development and has a library of text books, syllabi, curriculum material, films, filmstrips together with equipment from all over the world.

Questions

1. What has been done in India for improving life-sciences education at school level ? Discuss in detail.
2. What has been the role of D.S.C.S. and Nuffield Foundation in modernizing life-sciences curriculum all over the world?
3. What is the position of teaching life sciences at school level in developing countries? Discuss the agencies helping these countries for improving the standard of teaching this subject.

31

THE SYLLABUS

Education in India is a state subject and all the recommendations of committees and commissions regarding the improvement in education are not uniformly implemented. Previously there existed only High schools throughout India but after the recommendations of Secondary Education Commission (1952-53), Higher Secondary came up, as this commission recommended eleven years of secondary education. Central Board of Secondary Education implemented the recommendation and upgraded the schools to Higher Secondary Schools. Some states like Punjab implemented it partially and introduced pre-university class in the colleges. Some other states did not pay heed to the recommeadations and there existed only high schools followed by Intermediate college classes. Indian Education Commission (1964-66) recdmmended twelve years of secondary education and there have come up 10+2 Higher Secondary or Senior Secondary schools but the recommendations of this commission are still in their way of implementation. Now in India, their exist three types of schools regarding duration of education :

(i) High Schools

(ii) Higher Secondary Schools (11 year duration)

(iii) Higher Secondary Schools (10+2 year duration)

Similar has been the position of teaching of school subjects. There exists a diverse pattern in number of subjects and the content that is taught in the schools.

PRESENT STATUS

High Schools : In high schools there is no life sciences syllabus as such. It forms only a part of General Science Syllabus. The students learn-little beyond gaining some familiarity with a few plants and animals. They only get an elementry idea of digestion, respiration and photosynthesis. In most high schools there is either no laboratory work at all or it is limited to the description of just a few plants and animals' with the help of specimens, models, charts and slides.

Higher Secondary Schools : In Higher Secondary Schools of eleven year duration life sciences form only a part of general science syllabus upto middle or 8th class. In the books on general science from sixth to eighth class, topics included are reproduction in plants, germination of seeds and seed dispersal, adaptation of animals to their surroundings and migration of animals, vegetative propagation in plants, pollination-types and agencies, fertilization, structure of seeds, structures and functions in earth worm, fishes, frogs, birds and mammals, modes of respiration and intake of food in animals and some knowledge about the life of insects.

In Higher Secondary Schools, students taking science stream can take Biology as elective subject in ninth class and call continue this up to eleventh class. 'Biology' A Text Book for higher secondary schools published by N.C.E.R.T. is being taught in these schools. This book contains 58 chapters which are divided under seven sections. The sections of this book are as under.

Some Basic Facts About Life : Deals with historical aspects biology, characteristics of living things, their classification and an introduction to major plant and animal groups.

The Diversity of Plant Life : Deals with the life of typical flowering plant and an elementry knowledge of various plant groups.

The Diversity of Animal Life : This section contains topics on all major animal groups and typical study of each group but frog and man have been dealt in somewhat more detail.

Plant and Animal Physiology : Deals with the physiological functions in plant and animal systems.

Self Perpetuation and Reproduction : Deals with vegetative propagation in plants and sexual reproduction in plants and animals.

Evolution, Heredity and Adaptation : This section is devoted to evidences and mechanism of evolution, principles of heredity and and inheritance, different environments and adaptation of organisms to different environments.

General : This section contains some general topics like Biology in Human welfare, diseases and span of life etc.

Prior to the publication of this book by N.C.E.R.T., the Higher Secondary syllabus contained separate topics in Botany and Zoology and most of the emphasis was on structural descriptions of plants and animals and their classification.

Senior Secondary Schools : The new concept of 10+2 year schooling came up only after the recommendations of Indian Education Commission (1964-66). In this system classes from 1-4 were considered to be lower primary classes and 5-7 primary classes, from 8th to 10th were considered to be lower secondary classes and 11 th and 12th to be higher secondary classes. In this new system, science and mathematics are taught compulsorily upto 10th class as a part of general education and life sciences form a part of general education. Life sciences form a part of general science syllabus upto this stage. Students who choose science stream for their further studies can opt life science as elective subject in 11th and 12th standard. Syllabus and reading materials for different classes under the new system of schooling is still in the process of development. The drafting of syllabus and publication of books according to the guidelines of I.E.C. (1964-66) has been influenced by the frequent changes of governments at the centre and states. The books initially prepared by N.C.E.R.T are beings cretinized and condensed. The present status of the syllabus under this system can be discussed as follows:

Our primary schools are still of five year duration but the topics to be included at lower primary stage, as recommended by I.E.C. (1964-66) are :

(1) Biological environment
(2) Personal hygiene and sanitation
(3) Plants and animals in the surrounding
(4) Air, water and weather and their importance in life
(5) Care of the body
(6) Gardening.

Subject matter content of various books from sixth class to 10th pre pared by N.C.E.R.T. is, as follows:

The book Biology Part I meant for sixth class, contains topics on structure and functions in plant organisms, their importance in nature and in introductory knowledge about various plant groups.

The text book Biology Part II that is recommended for seventh class contains topics on major animal groups, representative study for each group and the way animals are classified-this is a general survey of animal kingdom.

Biology Part III, the book meant for eighth class is devoted to anatomy and physiology of human organism.

The book on life sciences that is being taught in ninth and tenth classes, contains topics on organization of life life processes, genetics and evolution. Agricultural Practices and animal husbandry, human biology, health and nutrition and man and his environment.

At Higher Secondary stage students can specialize in sciences and can take life sciences as one of the subjects. Here the syllabus includes Biology-A Text Book for Higher Secondary Schools which is divided into two parts. Part I is meant for eleventh class and Part II for twelfth class. Each part is further divided into two volumes. Part I volumed I of the book includes topics on anatomy and physiology of animals, structure of mammalian tissues, digestive, respiratory circulatory, excretory, nervous muscular, skeletal endocrine and reproductive systems and volume II on anatomy and physiology of plants-meristems, water relations, absorption and nutrition stem-transport leaf-photosynthesis, respiration growth and development movements and rhythms. Volume Part I of this book is devoted to cell biology and genetics and the Part II contains topics on developmental biology of plants, developmental biology of animals and biology in relation to human welfare.

ANALYTICAL STUDY

Following points should be observed while framing and analyzing any school life sciences syllabus:

(a) Contents chosen should be in relation to the aims and objective of teaching the subject.

(b) It should realize the needs of average intelligent and slower students.

(c) It should not be too much theoretical but should be based on activity and experience.

(d) The syllabus should be flexible, so that the teacher can find sequence of teaching regarding the local needs and can employ the local resource material in teaching the subject.

(e) It should help the students appreciate the work done by scientists and apply the knowledge in their daily life.

(f) The content should enhance scientific thinking in the students.

(g) Subject matter should be well organized regarding conceptual schemes and it should be in ascending order of difficulty.

(h) Provision should be made to include projects, excursions hobbies and club acitivities.

(i) Content of the subject should be related to the needs of individual and society.

In high schools there exists no life sciences curriculum but some topics in the form of fragments of knowledge have been included here and there in the general sciences books. Even after the schools were upgraded to Higher Secondary stage, the subject matter that was being taught had many defects. It was narrowly conceived so far as objectives of teaching life sciences are considered. Most of the teaching was theoretical and there was inadequate provision for practical work. Subject matter was unnecessarily overcrowded with technical terms. The subject matter was mostly concerned with structural and classificational aspects of the organisms. The syllabus content was least concerned with human body and the application of the knowledge of this subject in daily life.

N.C.E.R.T. SYLLABUS

(1) Introduction of specialization in this subject in ninth class was considered to be too early.

(2) The syllabus content was somewhat balanced as approach shifted from structural, classificational to functional and environmental aspects but it was less related to daily life activities of the students.

(3) Organization of the subject matter was still traditional as it was based on hierarchy of plant and animal groups and not on some set congratulate schemes and levels of biological organization.

(4) A trial was made to introduce the students about the functioning of their body but it was not enough.

(5) The syllabus content could not achieve its aim of teaching and learning based on totality of experience.

The newly prepared syllabus of life sciences for various stages under 10 +2 scheme of schooling is also not considered fool proof.

Some of the views regarding this syllabus :

(1) Postponement of specialization in particular subjects from 9th to 11th class is generally favoured;

(2) The subject matter particularly, at general education stage (upto 10th class) is organized, elating it to daily life and social needs.

(3) The content of general science syllabus is too much and puts much load on the students and it is favoured by adolescent psychology.

(4) Some people consider that the idea for this type of schooling is an imitation of the patterns followed in other countries particularly U.S.S.R. and indigenous requirements are not paid fun consideration.

(5) The subject matter according to new syllabus is of sophisticated nature and there are no laboratory facilities and adequately trained teachers to implement it properly.

(6) Although the new syllabus has been drafted and books are being written but there has not been provided the magnitude of practical work to be undertaken and sequence of teaching to be followed.

(7) Uniform syllabus for all communities and environments is considered to be of rigid nature.

The latest changes that are going on regarding the syllabus of general science is deletion and condensation of topics, in order to lighten the burden on students and to keep telepathy with the views of changed governments at the centre and states. Still the implementation of J.E.C. (1964-66) recommendations, all over India is incomplete and education policy undecided.

Some points, that First Asian Regional Conference on School Biology (1966), regarding school life sciences syllabus, considered are as follows :

1. It must inculcate the idea of science as inquiry.
2. It must consider the pertinent problems and needs of the community and emphasize the study of local fauna and flora.
3. It must be presented in logical and coherent manner based on the following themes :
   (i) The intellectual history of biological concepts.
   (ii) The change of living things through time.
   (iii) Diversity of type and unity of pattern in living things.
   (iv) The genetic continuity of life.
   (v) Inter-dependence of organisms and environment.
   (vi) Biological roots of behaviour.
   (vii) Correlation (complementarity) of structure and function.
   (viii) Regulation and preservation of life in the face of change.

4. The class time allotted to the subject shall ideally be not lesse than 180 full hours.
5. The content must correlate biology with other school subjects.
6. Consideration should be given to the best information available regarding students' learning process.

Questions

1. What points would you consider while framing a life-sciences syllabus for schools?
2. Discuss the present status of life-sciences syllabus in Higher Secondary and Senior Secondary (10+2) schools.
3. (a) What points would you bear in mind while framing a syllabus of life-sciences for secondary classes.

   (b) Critically comment upon existing syllabus of life-sciences for the Secondary classes in the light of your points.
4. Critically evaluate the syllabus of life-sciences provided by the Board of Secondary Education in your State. Give your suggestions for its improvement.
5. What are the criteria for evaluating life sciences syllabus? How accordance with far is the present High School syllabus of your state is in them?

32

EVALUATION AND MEASUREMENT

Evaluation is the overall assessment of educational outcomes brought about as a result of teaching learning process. So evaluation in life sciences will mean that it is the assessment of total learning outcomes brought about as a result of teaching this subject.

Evaluation include overall assesment, so tools (tests) and techniques employed for it are many. Testing is one of the means to evaluation and hence this term has a narrower application as compared to evaluation.

SOME SOURCES

Cumulative Records

(a) Intelligence tests.

(b) Aptitude tests.

(c) Achievement tests.

(d) Family background.

(e) Mental and physical health records.

(f) Records of behaviour.

Class Activities

(a) Performance on assigned responsibilities.

(b) Home work.

(c) Reports.

(d) Term papers.

(e) Laboratory work.

Some Other Activities

(a) Personal interviews and questionnaires.

(b) Record of observations made by the teacher.

(c) Performance on attitude scales or rating scales.

For overall assessment of the students we can have:

(1) Achievement Tests.

(2) Personality Tests.

(3) Intelligence Tests.

(4) Aptitude Tests.

(5) Interest inventories.

(6) Teacher's Observations.

(7) Interviews.

(8) Sociometry.

(9) Records.

(10) Pupils' products (their performance on questionnaires, check lists and rating scales.)

In this way we find that our achievement tests or class tests form a small part of the total evaluation process. We evaluate students regarding their learning in life sciences, in terms of the aims and objectives set for teaching this subject.

Our evaluation of the students regarding their achievement in life sciences includes their learning outcomes in the following fields:

(a) Knowledge of biological terms, facts, concepts, principles and formulae.

(b) Understanding of biological terms, facts, concepts, principles and processes.

(c) Application of knowledge of biology in new situations.

(d) Manipulative, dissectional, observational, drawing skills and techniques of collection, culturing, preservation and preparations for microscopic studies and their skills in locating biological information.

(e) Interests in plants, animals and their environments.

(f) Scientific attitudes towards biological phenomena.

(g) Appreciation of biological phenomena in nature and role of life sciences in our lives.

Our class tests generally measure the factual knowledge in life sciences and mostly recall-of it, understanding of certain phenomena or principles and application of the acquired knowledge in other situations or in solving some problems. Our class tests are achievement tests that measure how far we have achieved the objectives of teaching life sciences. We measure students achievement. For the purpose of measurement we should have some standard scale according to which we can say that students have achieved to some particular extent. As applied to education can there be any scale and if it is lot there how we can compare the students achievement?

According to Stevenson Measurement is the process of assigning numerals to objects and events according to rules.

We can assign numerals to objects and events in four forms or scales :

NOMINAL SCALE

Here we just label the objects or events as 1, 2, 3, 4 but these are without the concatenation of their quality. We cannot say whether 2 is better than 3 or vice versa.

ORDINAL SCALE

In this case we number the objects or events according to ascending or descending order of equally. We can say that 3 is better than 2 or 2 is better than 3 but here we are not sure of the magnitude of interval between the two consecutive numbers. We cannot say whether interval between 1 and 2 is equal to the interval between 2 and 3 and so on.

INTERVAL SCALE

When objects or events are ordered according to the ascending order of their characteristics and the interval between two adjacent numbers is equal, we call it numbering according to interval scale. Degree marks on a thermometer is an example of this scale. For calculations we can utilize the operations of arithmatic but not the X and-7-. In this scale we do not have absolute zero on the scale. In case of thermometer we cannot say 20°C is double the hot 10°C. For such calculations we are to convert these readings into absolute zero scale by adding 273°C to each and then 2x(273°+100) =1= 270°+20°.

RATIO SCALE

It is an interval scale, with numbering according to ascending or descending order-of quality with equal intervals and with absolute zero. The scales which measure length, weight and temperature. : (with absolute zero) are examples of ratio scales. Here we can utilize all mathematical operations such as +,-, x, ÷etc.

Scales by which we measure educational achievements are not ratio scales because in case of achievement we cannot have absolute zero when we are testing living orains. Generally students' scores are operated upon utilizing all arithmetical operations which is not correct approach.

We do not even measure the educational achievement according to interval scale. For example we give a test of 30 marks containing 30 items to a class. Student A in the class achieves 24-marks and student B achieves 8 marks on it. In such cases we generally say that A is three times better than B. But if we add 8 more items (easy, that, both of them can do) in the test. Now the score of A will be 32 and that of B will be 16. Here it appears that A is twice better than B. In the first case if A wants to improve his score by 4 and B also wants to improve his score by 4. This means A and B want to attain 28 and 12 marks respectively. Will they work equally hard for it ? No

So we can employ interval and ratio scales for calculating our results regarding the students' achievements on the class tests. Nominal and ordinal scales are of no use in marking the progress and comparing the results of students on achievement tests secondly, we cannot apply arithmetical operations on these scales. The only alternative left is that we measure the achievement of a particular student in comparison to the achievement of the total population of students being tested. For this purpose we can have grading of the students' scores. Grading should not be applied to small populations being tested because there the total group may be higher or lower achiever and the grades will not be able to show the total quantitative achievement of a particular student on that particular test.

GRADING

In grading we change the raw scores (marks 00 the test) into standard score (value in relation to score of the population'. A score on a test is simply a numerical description of an individual's performance on test. In the process of grading raw scores of the population tested are taken and mean and standard deviation for these are calculated. Now score of the individual is taken and grade for that is assigned after converting it into standard scorer.

Standard score (Z)=X-M/6

where X=raw score of the student

M = mean of the total scores

6 = standard deviation

Example:

X scores 75 and Y scores 50 on a test of which mean of the total scores is 55 and standard deviation is 10.

Then

Z for X= 75-55/10 = 2

Z for Y=50-55/10 = 0.5

Now normal distribution curve is drawn and it is divided into parts according to the points of scale we are using for assigning grades. We generally use five or seven point scales. If we use five point scale and consider the spread of the curve up to + 3.5 S.D. Units then :

What is Testing? Testing means subjecting to conditions that purport to show the relation of theoretical assumptions with statistical standard.

Types of Tests : As stated above the process of evaluation involves a number of tests. Here we will limit our discussion to:

(a) Essay type tests (Unit tests) and

(b) Objective type tests (New type tests).

Characteristics of a Good Test : Whatever may be the test used in the process of evaluation as an efficient tool for this purpose, it should have the following characteristics :

Validity : Validity of a test is defined as the extent to which it measures what it is supposed to measure. A test in life sciences for eighth class will be invalid if we give it to tenth class students because it will not measure what we want to measure at this stage in this subject.

Further a test which includes only some questions from a small part or the syllabus will be invalid when we want to measure the achievement of students out of the whole syllabus.

Reliability : When a test measures what it measures, all the times, it is called reliable. When a test is given to the class from time to time and scores on this test do not differ with the administration of the test, it will be a reliable test. A test may not be valid as eighth class test for tenth class, but the scores may not differ from time to time when it is administered to tenth class.

Objectivity : When the scores on the test do not differ when it is marked by different examiners, it is called objective test. As it is in the case of objective type tests when a question requires only one answer to it the scoring on it will not differ from examiner to examiner. The objective type tests can also be scored by machines.

Practicability : A test should be of the nature that it can be given in school conditions. It should not be too stretched or too short and can be finished within the time allotted. Generally duration for the test is allotted as the period of time in which 75% of the students finish the test. The test should also be practicable from the point of view of administration.

ESSAY TYPE TESTS

In tests of this type we include questions that require longer explanations. Students can deal the topic in depth, they can express their own views and can apply their knowledge for explaining the solution of some problem or they can explain some phenomenon or procedure to its intricate details. By employing such tests we can measure the power of expression, comprehension, thinking and reasoning, writing skills, judgements and their power of application of the acquired knowledge in new situations.

In spite of the positive characteristics tests of this type suffer from some serious defects mentioned below :

1. Essay type tests are not valid because here we require longer explanations and questions from some selected parts of the syllabus are included in the test. If we try to include representative question of the whole syllabus, the test turns to be impracticable. Sometimes the questions are so structured that students are not able to understand to which extent they are to deal the subject matter.

2. Scores on the essay type tests are not constant when these are administered from time to time to the same subjects. This means that such tests are not reliable. These tests enhance the tendency of learning by rote in the students and the subject matter is forgotten after the test is over. When the test is again admistered the answers of the students to same questions differ to a large extent.

3. Essay type tests are not objective in the sense that scoring on such tests greatly differs from examiner to examiner. The marks on the tests are influenced by personal bias, attitude, different views about the adequacy of answers to the questions by different examiners.

4. Sometimes these tests require longer explanations and the time allotted is tentative as we do not experience it by administration of the test beforehand and students are not able to complete the test within the allotted time. These tests also involve fatigue and this way students performance is influenced.

5. The questions on such tests are not arranged in ascending order of difficulty.

NEW TYPE TESTS OR OBJECTIVE TESTS

These tests have a recent origin and due to their positive characteristics have become very popular. In tests of this type we include items or questions that require short answers.

Objective Type Tests are of more value due to their following characteristics :

1. In objective tests we can include a large number of items or questions because answers to these are short. So we can include questions representative of the whole syllabus and hence these tests are more valid in comparison to essay type tests.
2. Reliability of these tests is also high as scores on these tests do not vary much when these are administered from time to time. The questions require particular answers and students are to supply those every time, they take the test.
3. These tests are more objective as scoring on these tests does not fluctuate from examiner to examiner. The questions require particular answers and students' performance is either wrong or right and attainments are to score according to the answers. No personal feelings or bias is involved. So subjectivity is reduced to minimum. Tests can be scored even by machines.
4. The tests are more practicable as time for these is decided by experimental administration and these also involve least administrative difficulties.
5. The tests can be well graded as the difficulty values of different items can be calculated by pre-tests and items on the test can be arranged according to the ascending order of their difficulty value.

The objective tests are also not fool proof because by employing these we cannot measure the power of expression, comprehension, depth of knowledge, ability to apply the aquired knowledge and writing and drawing skills of the students. These tests also enhance guess work and copying.

Types of test items for objective type tests:

There can be several types of test items for objective type tests.

Some of these can be illustrated as below:

Completion Type : Here a statement is furnished with some gap either in between or at the end of it. The statement gives correct meaning when we fill the gap e.g.

(i) There are .... chambers in mammalian heart. (four)

(ii) Hair on the body are found only in .... (mammals)

Alternate Choice Type : In this case statement is made and it is marked true/false, right/wrong, correct/incorrect etc., students are to choose one as answer to the item.

Multiple Choice Type : In items of this type a statement is given or a question is drafted and there are given four or five choices one of which functions correctly with the statement or it forms answer to the question. e.g.

(i) In angiosperms conduction of water takes place through

(a) Xylem.

(b) Phloem.

(c) Pith.

(d) Epidermis

(e) Cortex.

(ii) What is the function of xylem tissue in plant ?

(a) Photosynthesis.

(b) Transportation.

(c) Reproduction.

(d) Absorption.

(e) Transpiration.

(f) Matching type.

Items of this type have words or statements in two groups but not in correct order of one to one match. For scoring correctly studens are to sort out correct words or statements from the second group, that match correctly with words or statements in the first group, e.g.

1. Robert Brown	A. Described the cell.
2. Crick and Watson	B. Formulated principles of inheritance.
3. Morgan	C. Described the cell nucleus.
4. Mendel	D. Formulated the D.N.A. Model.
5. Robert Hooke	E. First to map the chromosomes
	F. First to induce mutations with X-rays.

Short Answer Type : Here questions which require short answers are given or some in complete sentence is formulated which on completion gives correct meaning. e.g.

(i) What three kinds of ecological relationships exist in a biotic community?

(ii) In symbiosis.............. Using Objective

Type Tests : Following steps are generally followed when we make use of objective tests in the process of evaluation:

Planning : The objectives of teaching the subject are stated in the form of behavioural changes that we aim at bring about as a result of teaching learning process. The length of the test and types of items to be included in the test are decided. The items should be representative of the whole syllabus and time, age, intelligence and testing conditions are kept in view.

Construction of the Test: The types of items are constructed according to the decided number for each type. Items should be well structured, correctly worded and in case of multiple choice type of items the choices should function equally well with the stein. After editing the items, the test is administered to the class for the purpose of finding out difficulty value and discrimination index for each item. In the final form of the test items with high discriminating index are selected and these are arranged according to the ascending order of their difficulty.

If an item of the test is correctly answered by 20 students out of total 35 students the difficulty value of the item will be 20x100/35 =57%.

Generally items with difficulty value ranging from 20% to 80% are selected. For calculating discrimination the papers are ranked in ascending order of scores. Now the papers are split into two groups-higher and lower. The higher group constitutes 27% of the papers having highest scores and lower group constitutes 27% of the papers with lowest scores. The item for which we want to calculate the discrimination value, is taken and the correct responses to it in the higher and the lower group are tabulated. If correct responses in the higher group are 12 and correct responses in the lower group are 5 and the papers used for item analysis are 24 then discrimination power of the item 12-5/½x24 =.58 or 58%, if calculated in percentage. Generally items with horimination value above 0.2 are selected. If the test is to be standardized its validity and reliability are also determined and norms are set for it.

Administration : Administration of the test includes arrangement for seating, light, other physical comforts and a strict supervision to avoid copying etc. Difficulties regarding administration of the test are visualized beforehand and removed.

Scoring : Scoring of the objective tests is done with the help of keys or machines and marking the correct and incorrect responses in different ways.

Scoring fornadoe far different attune are as follows : (a) For items with two alternatives

Score=Correct responses – Wrong responses

(b) For multiple choice items

Wrong responses

Score – Correct responses

EVALUATION OF THE PRACTICAL WORK

In practical examinations we generally aim at testing the

(a) knowledge of experimental persecutes.

(b) skills in manipulating apparatus and dissections.

(c) ability to carry out simple measurements or qualitative potations,

(d) power of identification-of things and chemical-analysis or substances,

(e) ability to convey clear statement of observed facts.

(f) ability to tabulate calculate and make generalizations on the basis of observed facts.

DEFECTS OF PRACTICAL EXAMINATIONS

Our practical examinations suffer from a number of defuse and the aim of all laboratory work is paralyzed by the approach we follow in organizing class practicals and their examination. Some of the draw back can be summarized as follows :

1. We do not have any clear objectives, stated for our practical and hence we do not have the clear idea of what we are testing in practical examinations.
2. Practical experiments are listed and performed in traditional way and this hardly finds any place for problem solving and these are of illustrative nature.
3. The practical work rails to develop scientific skins and scientific method of working in the students and these are not representative of the whole syllabus.
4. Laboratory practicals find low place in comparison to theoretical teaching.
5. Viva-voce and practical records are superficially examined. Sessional work finds little consideration.
6. Examiners are most of the time biased or influenced by personal matters, while evaluating practical work.

Examination in practical work should involve evaluation of knowledge, skills abilities that are involved in laboratory work Sessional work and records should find better place and so far as possible testing should be objective. Statements of the experiment should be structured properly and these should be of investigatory nature.

PRACTICAL EXAMINATION

For evaluating the performance of students in the laboratory, check lists can be used. These lists contain certain actions which are arranged in the order they occur in examination. Use of check lists provides a reliable technique for evaluating laboratory procedures and it makes the examiner aware of the operations involved in a particular procedure. Students performance, tabulation of data, calculations and deductions should be well examined.

NOTE BOOKS AND RECORDS

Since laboratory work is performed by students working together in groups, so their note-books are also group products and it will be difficult to grade these. The amount of time required for reading the practical note-books is too much, so note-books in the class should be evaluated by "at the spot checking". Students' Individual reports about the practicals can be asked by the teacher and evaluated. Viva voce examination should be relevant and should evaluate the deep understanding of the subject matter. Objectivity in practical examinations should also be paid need to.

Where practical examinations are external the examiner should consider sampling of scientific skills and content of the syllabus before giving the practical. The practicals should be able to distinguish poor and bright students and these should be of graded difficulty value. Attempt should be made to test all students under standard condition. Only these practicals or parts of practicals should be given for which equipments and material are abundantly available.

Questions

1. What evaluation techniques can be employed in the over-all assessment of students progress at school?
2. What scales of measurement can be appropriately employed in evaluation of students achievement in life-sciences? Why should we use grading system? Discuss with examples.
3. What should be the characteristics of a good test? Discuss these in relation to essay type tests and objective tests.
4. Write short notes on:
   (a) construction of objective tests
   (b) evaluation of practical work in life-sciences.

5. What are the criteria of a good test? Give practical suggestions to support your answer.
6. You have taught a unit on 'Ecological Crisis' to class IX students or on 'Breathing' to class VIII students. If objectives were knowledge, application of knowledge and inculcation of attitudes, what behaviour changes would you look for in your students as an evidence of achieving these objective.
7. (a) What is the importance of objectives in life-sciences?
   (b) You have taught "Blood circulation" to class IX students. Develop six test items (4 multiple choice and two matching type) to test knowledge and application (3 for knowledge and 3 for application).
8. There is inter-relationship between objectives, learning experiences and evaluation. Discuss with the help of two eximples.
9. What is objective based evaluation in life-sciences? Describe the procedure for cons truction of unit test in life-sciences.

33

NEW TRENDS

From the point of view of teaching life sciences at school stage the new developments in this field can be discussed under three headings :

(a) Modern developments in various branches of life sciences.

(b) The impact of new developments on school life sciences curriculum and

(c) Structuring the subject matter keeping in view the learning behaviour of the students.

MODERN DEVELOPMENTS

The nineteenth century biologists concerned themselves mainly with the morphology and anatomy of plants and animals. The subject has undergone much changes in its content and character in the twentieth century. It has been made possible largely by the availability of new techniques of physics, chemistry and other disciplines. Electron microscopy, ultracentrifugation, spectroscopy and more reliable methods of chemical analysis have contributed a lot in the studies of life sciences.

The rediscovery of Mendel's laws of heredity created interest in the field of genetics, the chemical basis of heredity has been established, artificial means of inducing mutations in plants and animals have been discovered and we are now able to synthesize D.N.A. the master molecule in heredity. By the application of new knowledge of genetics we have produced high yielding, disease, frost lodging and draught resistant varieties of several crop plants. Improvements have also been done in domestic animals. poultry and milk yielding animals. Genetics is also being studied in relation to increasing radio-activity on the earth surface and people are in search of devising some means to protect the human population from radio-active hazards.

Intricate details of cell structure, transportation within the cell, synthesis of proteins, energy utilization at cellular level and the process of photosynthesis are now better understood. Now we better understand the role of hormones, vitamins and antibiotics in the living system. The functioning in different plant and animal systems like transportation and nerve action have been studied in detail. Chemical analysis of various plant and animal product have been undertaken and their nature is better understood.

So far as medicine is concerned, we are now in a better position to cure all types of diseases such as infectous, degenerative and allergies. Today we have several antibiotics, sulpha drugs, antiseptic surgery, cornea and heart transplantations, radiation techniques transfusions injections and vaccines to combat all these diseases. Researches of last 40 years have added more recent disciplines like virology, radiation and space biology. Attempts are now being made to have cure for cancers heart diseases and finally to synthesize life itself. Reproductive and developmental physiology of organisms is now well understood. The implications of all these developments are centred around the better survival and welfare of human race.

It will difficult, here to enumerate all the new developments of life sciences but we definitely see a change of trend in the study of this subject. We now find that emphasis largely shifted from systematics, morphology and anatomy to functional aspects of living systems. Recently the work is more inclined to study life in different environments. Some other people like psychologists and lociologists also take interest in studying life from different angles.

IMPACT OF MODERN DEVELOPMENTS

The new developments in the field of life sciences have influenced the teaching of this subject at school level, in many ways. There is now a change in the form of teaching this subject, the subject content and the ways and means adopted for teaching.

Trend towards Teaching Botany and Zoology as Combined Subject : In the nineteenth century, there was a tendency towards compartmentalization of the subjects. The knowedge of common phenomena involved in all life processes shows that these Compartments merge into each other. The work of last fifty years in cell physiology, biochemistry, bio-physics shows a lot of commonnes in plants and animals. In the; field genetics, cytology, evolution, physiology, emblyology we find that a lot of common principles are involved in plants and animals. Keeping this in view most of the English and American schools have composite biology course and at places it has been extended upto B.Sc. level. In India also similar attempts have been made recently. When botany and zoology were taught as separate subjects, emphasis was mostly on classification and structural description of plants and animals. When biology was recommended to be taught as composite subject the emphasis shifted to functional, evolutionary and hereditary aspects. The most recent trend in this the subject as life sciences which includes all aspects such as classification, anatomical and histological studies functioning of the living system, behaviour, evolution, genetics and life in relation to the environment.

Change in subject matter content : The previous courses were dull and descriptive. Nowadays tendency is to retain essentials of morphological and anatomical details and inclusion of more chapters on physiology, ecology, genetics, evolution, interdependence of plants and animals and role of life sciences in our life. In the traditional curriculum we do not find any place for recent knowledge. In the curricula developed in India and abroad we find that the text books include subject matter proportionately to the importance of different disciplines and according to learning behaviour of the students. For every stage of teaching this subject, instructional objectives are predetermined. Recent studies on younger students show that they can easily conceptualize the principles from physiology. genetics and ecology in comparison to morphological descriptions. Upto recently biology was nothing more than cutting up of frogs, collection of hay or insects, and naming plants and animals in an unfamiliar language. Now the recommendations are that a student need not spend too much time on learning the variations in the organization of flowers and vertebrae but a balance should be maintained between depth and breadth, of various disciplines of Life Sciences. In India syllabus at higher secondary level required students to study roots, stems and the smallest bones of frog in detail but they remained ignorant of their own body. But the new curriculum evolved by N.C.E.R.T. includes topics on all broad aspects of life sciences.

Changed Ways and Means : In India, the curriculum has been modernized in the sense that the content is balanced. Text books have been published for different stages of schooling by N.C.E.R. T., but the methods of teaching are still traditional and equipments and material are not sufficient to meet the demands or teaching this subject. Approach in teaching, wherever material is sufficient, is illustrative, not investigatory. Research and financial aids are not enough to modernize the teaching facilities. Researches and experiments bave been undertaken in U.K. and U.S.A. in order to improve school biology teaching. Work done in America (B.S.C.S.) is of more importance in this direction. The overall programme includes text books with new and balanced contents and approaches, better printing and illustrations. Directions for laboratory work have beea developed. Laboratories have been modernized. Teaching is in coordination with the learning behaviour of the students. The B.S.C.S. text books & help books have influenced the teaching of biology all over the world. Some of the countries using B.S.C.S. materials are Australia, Brazil, Canada, Columbia, Taiwan, India, Israel, Italy, Japan, Korea, New Zealand, Philippines, Thailand, Turkey, Countries of Tropican' America, English speaking countries in Africa, Denmark, Sweden and Mexico etc..

More stress today is on use of better teaching aids, sequencing the teaching, keeping in view the conceptual maturation of the students, better laboratory facilities, investigatory approach in teaching, utilizing demonstrations, projects and problem solving methods. Programmed instruction, use of films and guided learning have been experimented. Curriculum needs continual renewal as there have been no developments in life sciences during the last twenty years. Some recent studies in organism behaviour, population growth, genetics, diseases, environmental conditions etc. need due emphasis on teaching these at school level.

STRUCTURING THE SUBJECT CONTENT

Nowadays we find a general tendency to organize the knowledge of a discipline into definite fundamental concepts. These concepts are later structured into major concepts, the number of major concepts and their organization form the curriculum at a particular stage of teaching the subject. The inclusion of the subject content is also determined keeping in view the learning behaviour of the students.

DEFINITION OF A CONCEPT

A concept is an abstraction to classify objects, ideas and events. We can also say that a concept is a summary of essential characteristics of a group of ideas or facts that epitomize the common features or factors from a large number of ideas. There can be several definitions of a concept as an abstraction that organizes a large number of ideas in a logical relationship, the resultant of generalizing mental process, a generalization relating the particular to general, a mental construct, a theoretical construct and the simplest pattern that helps us to order the world around us.

ATTRIBUTES OF A CONCEPT

Concepts are characterized by the following attributes :

1. Concepts are ideas possessed by individuals or growth in symbolic form.
2. Concept of an object, phenomena or process is in continuation from simple to complex.
3. Concepts emerge with experience and these are resultant of abstract thinking.
4. Concepts are neither true or false but these are either adequately or inadequately developed.
5. Concepts have relations to people, things, other concepts, conceptual systems and processes.
6. Nature of a concept may be determined by the procedure that led to its formation. Concepts can be rendered

inadequate as a result of new knowledge and so should be constantly revised.

Three Categories of Concepts in Life: Most of the concepts in life sciences can be divided under three categories :

Classificatian: The system of concepts that facilitate description of a phenomena as :

(i) Mammals have four chambered heart and hair on the body.

(ii) puring the process of respiration food is oxidised and energy is released.

(iii) Spenilatophte plants form seeds.

Correlational: The system of concepts that facilitates prediction as :

(i) When we enter a warm room we perspire.

(ii) Starch may be changed into sugar by the activity of amylase coenzyme.

The process of photosynthesis increases with the intensity of light, if other factors are kept constant.

Theortical: The system of concepts that facilitates explanation or phenomena made up of theories as:

(i) An atom is made up of electrons, protons and neutrons.

(ii) The images of objects, that we see are reverted in our mind

(iii) Migration or birds is controlled by their body hormones.

Concepts have various dimensions and these move along these dimensions in their development. The development of concepts may be from simple to abstract, from vague to clear and from exact to precise concepts change along other dimensions also and develop relations with other become part or other systems of ideas outside the original limits of classification. A concept has intensive and extensive aspects. In intensive meaning a concept may stand for a particular thing as nucleus for the central body in acidic for biologist and central part of an atom for a physicist-but in its extensive meaning nucleus may also stand for the central body in an administration central part of a city or central part of a ball or any other object.

In order to avoid a semantic discussion about th differences among "couuncept" , "gereralization" and "principle" we can include all these under a single category and can be called fundamental concepts in a particular discipline.

The basic things that concept learning involves are sensations and perceptions. We get sensations of objects by our sense organs and the process of interpretation or giving meaning to sensations results into perceptions-The concepts emerge from a group or pattern of percepts. The concepts extend through the process of integration or synthesis. The learner discovers qualities of a concept as he extends the use of concept in new relationships.

In relation to mental operations concept learning is thought to involve thought about semantic material. Learning of concepts mostly requires learners to think in a cognitive or perhaps convergently productive way about semantic aspects of classes and relations. Evaluative thinking may also be involved where ambiguous objects (those involving interference) are conceptualized about classes, relations and system.

Concepts and generalizations in life sciences, should not be given to the students but we should facilitate their development by anaching meaning to new words, used in building the concepts, using the concepts in a variety of situations, repeating the concepts in a variety of contexts, introducing the concept at understandable level of the students and presenting the concepts so that their characteristics are emphasized.

Concepts may be helped to develop, in the students, by indoctrinisation, induction, deduction, extrapolation, interpretation, analysis, synthesis and by some other means. But with reference to the development of concepts in life sciences the following things should be considered :

1. Level of intellectual development of students in relation to learning-classificational, correlational and theoretical concepts.
2. The intensity and extensiveness of facts given to students from which they are to build concepts.
3. The representativeness of stimuli of the total class, sequence of presenting stimuli and remoteness of the

stimuli from reality should be included, regarding experimental maturation of the students.

4. To what extent cultural background has its role and at what level students are able to conceptualize abstract concepts.
5. How lecturing, demonstrations, laboratory work and activities contribute to conceptual learning.
6. The role of language development the relationship of transfer with concept learning and to what extent students should be allowed to have their own concepts etc.

Concept learning is achieved when the students are able to recognize the example of concept, relate concepts to each other in formulation and use of generalizations, apply a concept in new situations, develop analogies of the concept, explain the observations, in his environment and solve problems using the concept.

There are two controversial positions on sequencing curriculum. For Gagne, the highest level of learning is problem solving and this is achieved by learning of facts, concepts and principles at lower level. In this type of learning one begins with simple things and learns complicated things in a pyramid fashion. But for Bruner one should start learning with problem solving and then will learn the fundamentals because these are needed for the purpose of solving problems. According to Gagne we should sequence the curriculum from simple to complex but, according to Bruner we can start with complex things and give a plant to make students learn simple components when they are working with complex things.

In the present life science curricula we find that students are first introduced with the individual organisms, various types, their habitats and morphological characteristics. Later on they study the structure and functioning of the organism body. Further the students are introduced with the subject matter on genetics, evolution, embryology, regulation, ecology and interdependance of plants and animals : Stratification of organisation populations, communities and eco systems are also taught. Some knowledge about role of life sciences in our lives is also given in the text books in order to make the students able to apply the knowledge of this discipline in their daily life activities.

Broadly speaking we study the life from organization point of view in a vertical hierarchy which constitutes various levels such as molecular, cellular, tissue-organ, organism, population, communities and world biome. We also find that each level in the vertical hierarchy is stretched horizontally by the application of concepts of evolution, genetics, ecology, behaviour, regulation and of structure and function of organism body. The knowledge of the discipline is also structured keeping in view the learning behaviours of the students. The learning behaviours also include various levels in a hierarchy from simple to complex. These levels are knowledge, comprehension, application, analysis, synthesis and evaluation.

Threading the curriculum, keeping in view the objectives of teaching a subject, the structure of knowledge of the discipline and learning behaviour of the students, is a difficult job and requires contineous research and follow-up studies.

Questions

1. Discuss the modern developments in the field of life sciences and their impact on school life sciences curriculum.
2. What is the role of concepts in teaching and learning of life sciences? Discuss with examples.
3. What are the modern trends in structuring the school life sciences curriculum ?
4. Discuss the value of concepts in learning of life sciences. How can the teacher help the pupils in acquiring clear concepts in the various areas of life-sciences? Illustrate your answer with specific examples.
5. Discuss the basic considerations underlying curriculum construction in life sciences at higher secondary stage. Point out the impact of modern developments in life sciences on the curriculum of this subject in the schools.
6. Discuss the need for reorientation in the various aspects of life sciences education in our schools". How can the teacher equip himself to contribute effectively in this respect?